WONDER WOMAN

THE JUST WAR

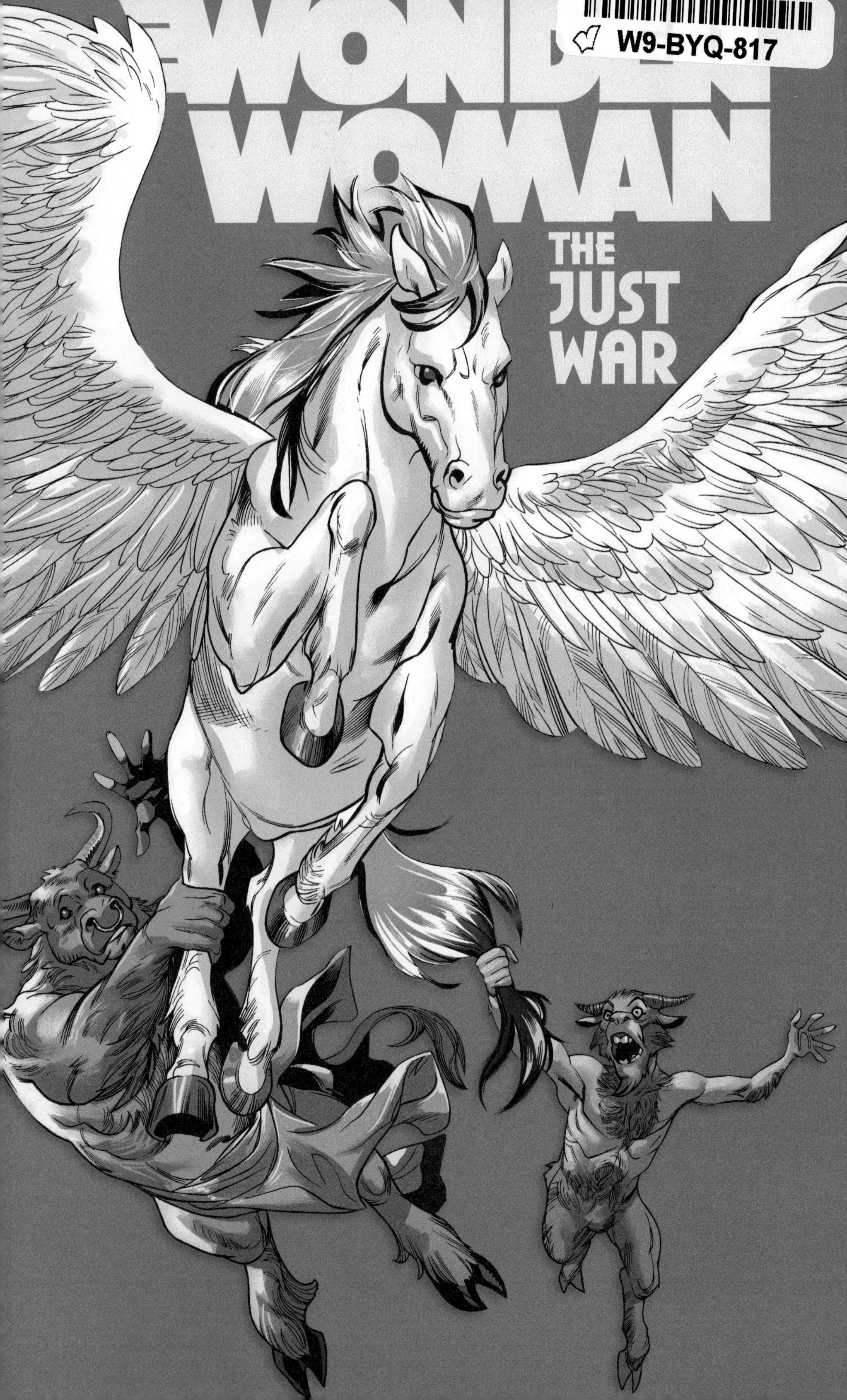

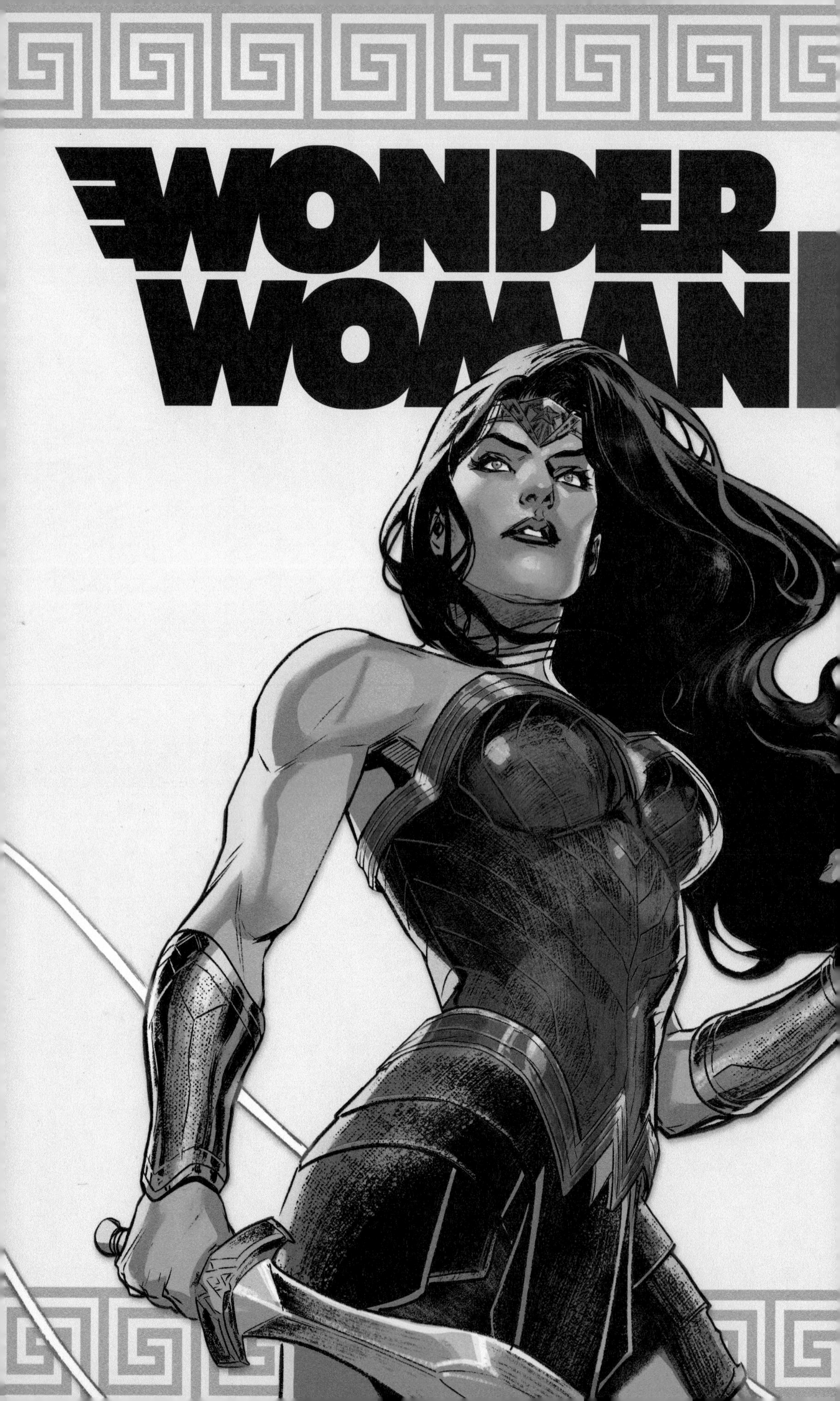
WONDER
WOMAN

THE JUST WAR

G. WILLOW WILSON
WRITER

CARY NORD
XERMANICO
JESUS MERINO
EMANUELA LUPACCHINO
PENCILLERS

MICK GRAY
XERMANICO
ANDY OWENS
RAY McCARTHY
INKERS

ROMULO FAJARDO JR.
COLORIST

PAT BROSSEAU
LETTERER

TERRY DODSON & RACHEL DODSON
COLLECTION COVER ARTISTS

WONDER WOMAN CREATED BY WILLIAM MOULTON MARSTON

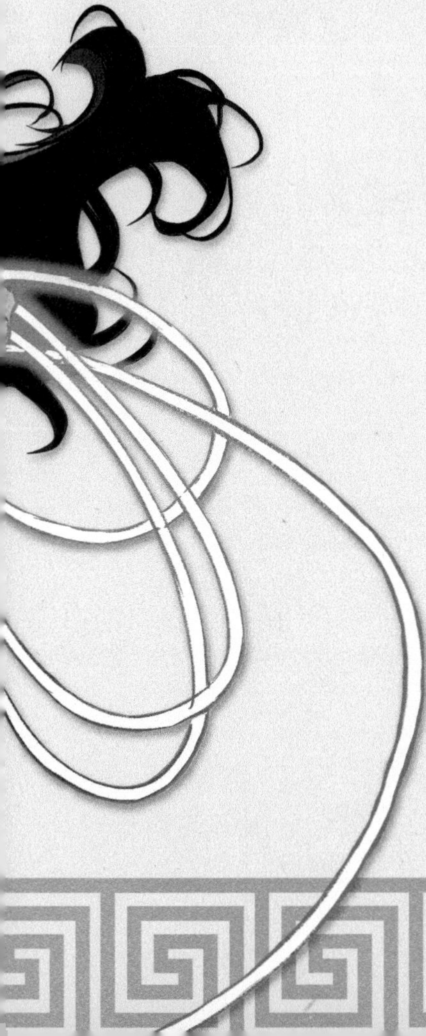

CHRIS CONROY
Editor – Original Series

DAVE WIELGOSZ
Assistant Editor – Original Series

JEB WOODARD
Group Editor – Collected Editions

ROBIN WILDMAN
Editor – Collected Edition

STEVE COOK
Design Director – Books

MEGAN BELLERSEN
Publication Design

DANIELLE DIGRADO
Publication Production

BOB HARRAS
Senior VP – Editor-in-Chief, DC Comics

PAT McCALLUM
Executive Editor, DC Comics

DAN DiDIO
Publisher

JIM LEE
Publisher & Chief Creative Officer

BOBBIE CHASE
VP – New Publishing Initiatives & Talent Development

DON FALLETTI
VP – Manufacturing Operations & Workflow Management

LAWRENCE GANEM
VP – Talent Services

ALISON GILL
Senior VP – Manufacturing & Operations

HANK KANALZ
Senior VP – Publishing Strategy & Support Services

DAN MIRON
VP – Publishing Operations

NICK J. NAPOLITANO
VP – Manufacturing Administration & Design

NANCY SPEARS
VP – Sales

MICHELE R. WELLS
VP & Executive Editor, Young Reader

WONDER WOMAN VOL. 1: THE JUST WAR

Published by DC Comics. Compilation and all new material Copyright © 2020 DC Comics. All Rights Reserved. Originally published in single magazine form in WONDER WOMAN 58-65. Copyright © 2019 DC Comics. All Rights Reserved. All characters, their distinctive likenesses and related elements featured in this publication are trademarks of DC Comics. The stories, characters and incidents featured in this publication are entirely fictional. DC Comics does not read or accept unsolicited submissions of ideas, stories or artwork. DC – a WarnerMedia Company.

DC Comics, 2900 West Alameda Ave., Burbank, CA 91505
Printed by LSC Communications, Owensville, MO, USA. 4/24/20. First Printing
ISBN: 978-1-77950-345-9

Library of Congress Cataloging-in-Publication Data is available.

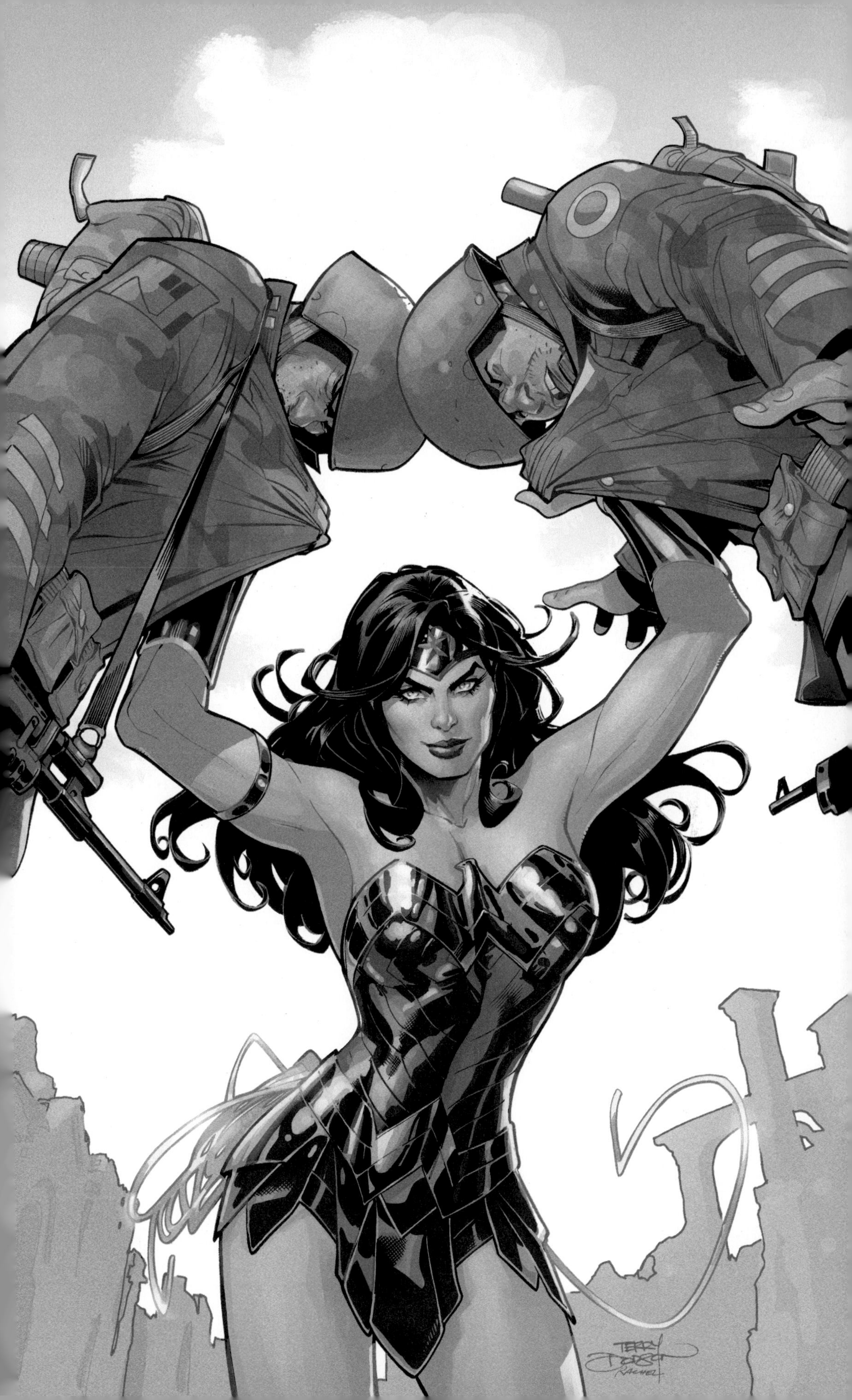
TERRY DODSON
RACHEL

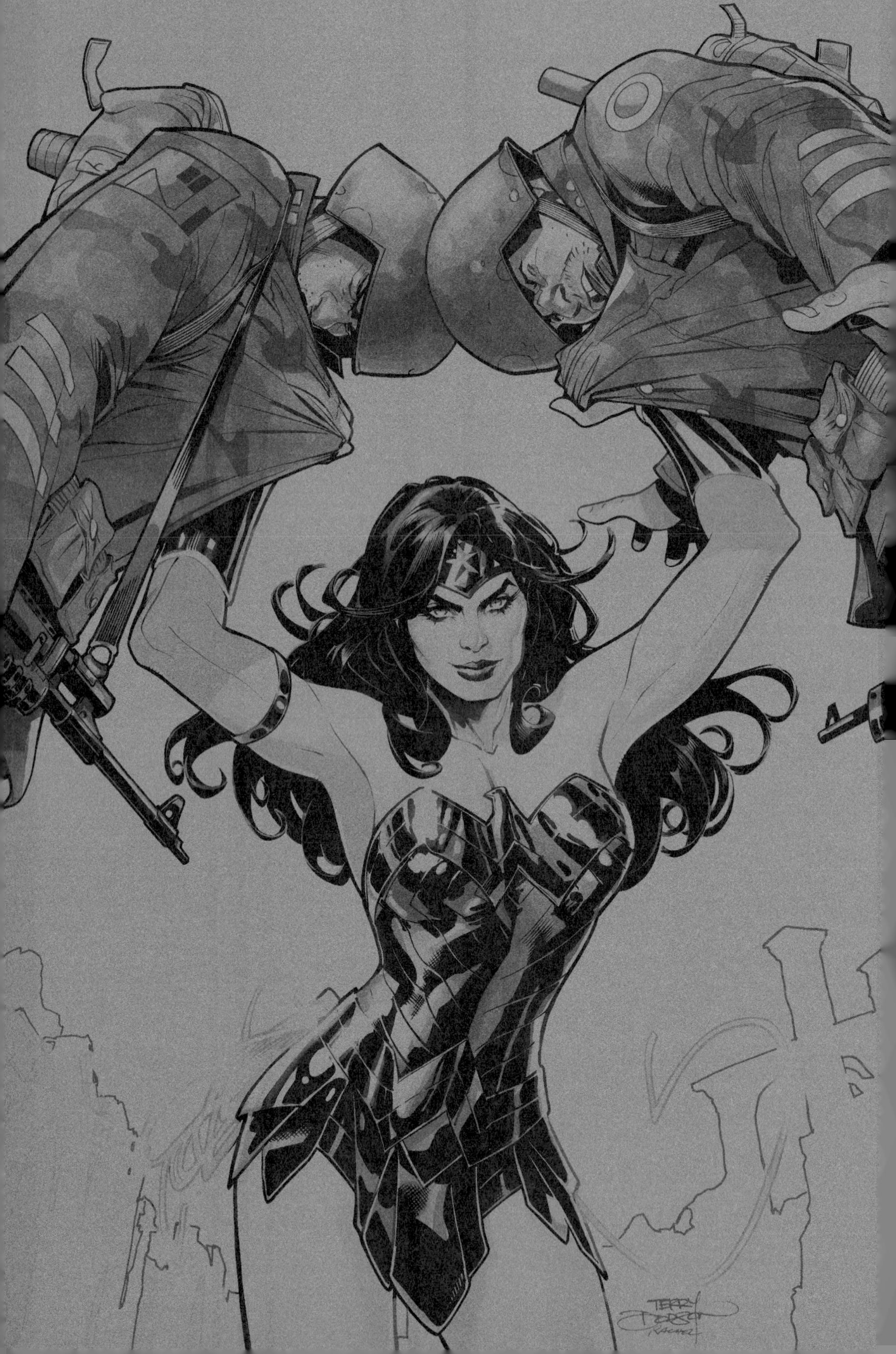

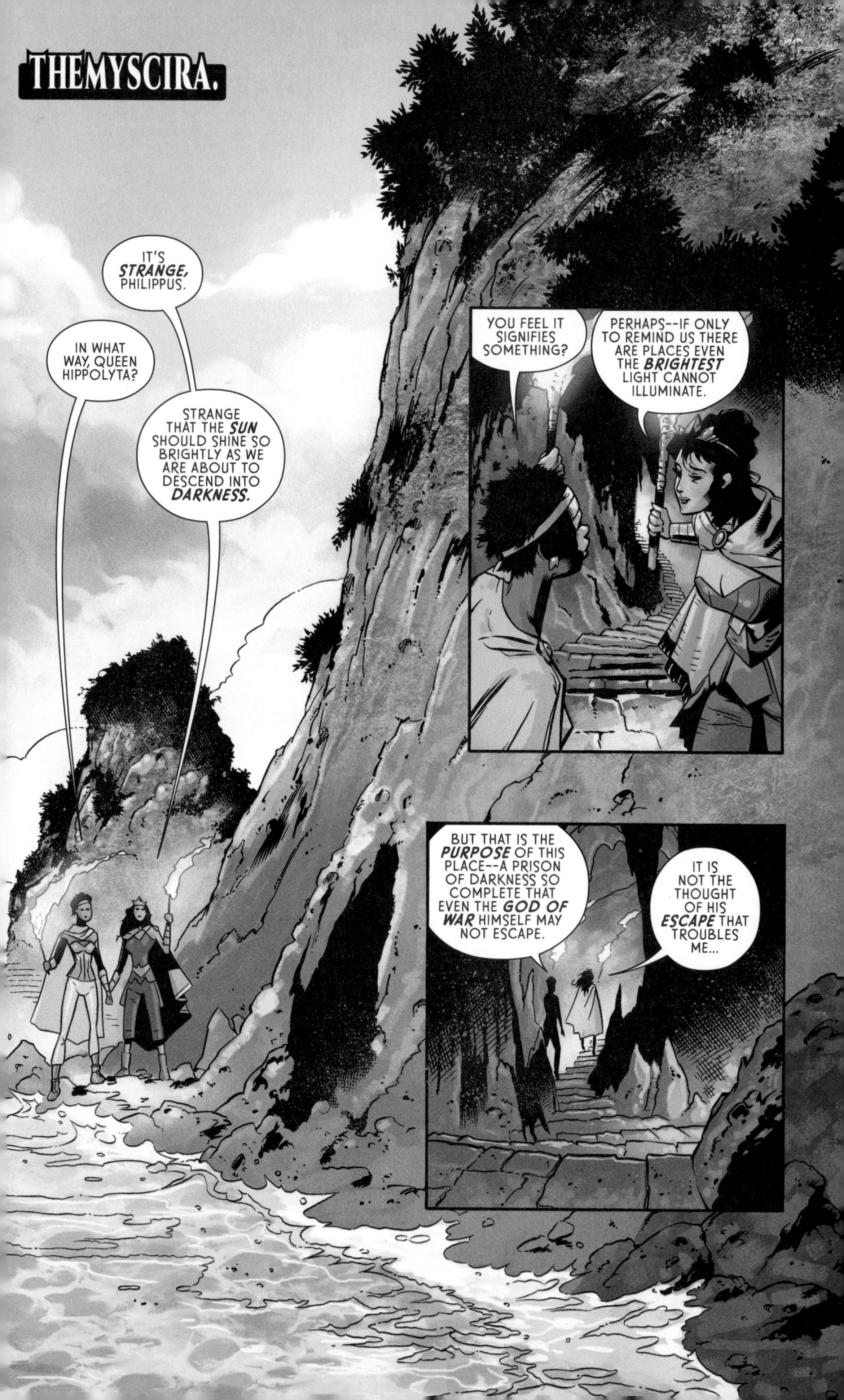

THEMYSCIRA.
IT'S STRANGE, PHILIPPUS.
IN WHAT WAY, QUEEN HIPPOLYTA?
STRANGE THAT THE SUN SHOULD SHINE SO BRIGHTLY AS WE ARE ABOUT TO DESCEND INTO DARKNESS.
YOU FEEL IT SIGNIFIES SOMETHING?
PERHAPS--IF ONLY TO REMIND US THERE ARE PLACES EVEN THE BRIGHTEST LIGHT CANNOT ILLUMINATE.
BUT THAT IS THE PURPOSE OF THIS PLACE--A PRISON OF DARKNESS SO COMPLETE THAT EVEN THE GOD OF WAR HIMSELF MAY NOT ESCAPE.
IT IS NOT THE THOUGHT OF HIS ESCAPE THAT TROUBLES ME...

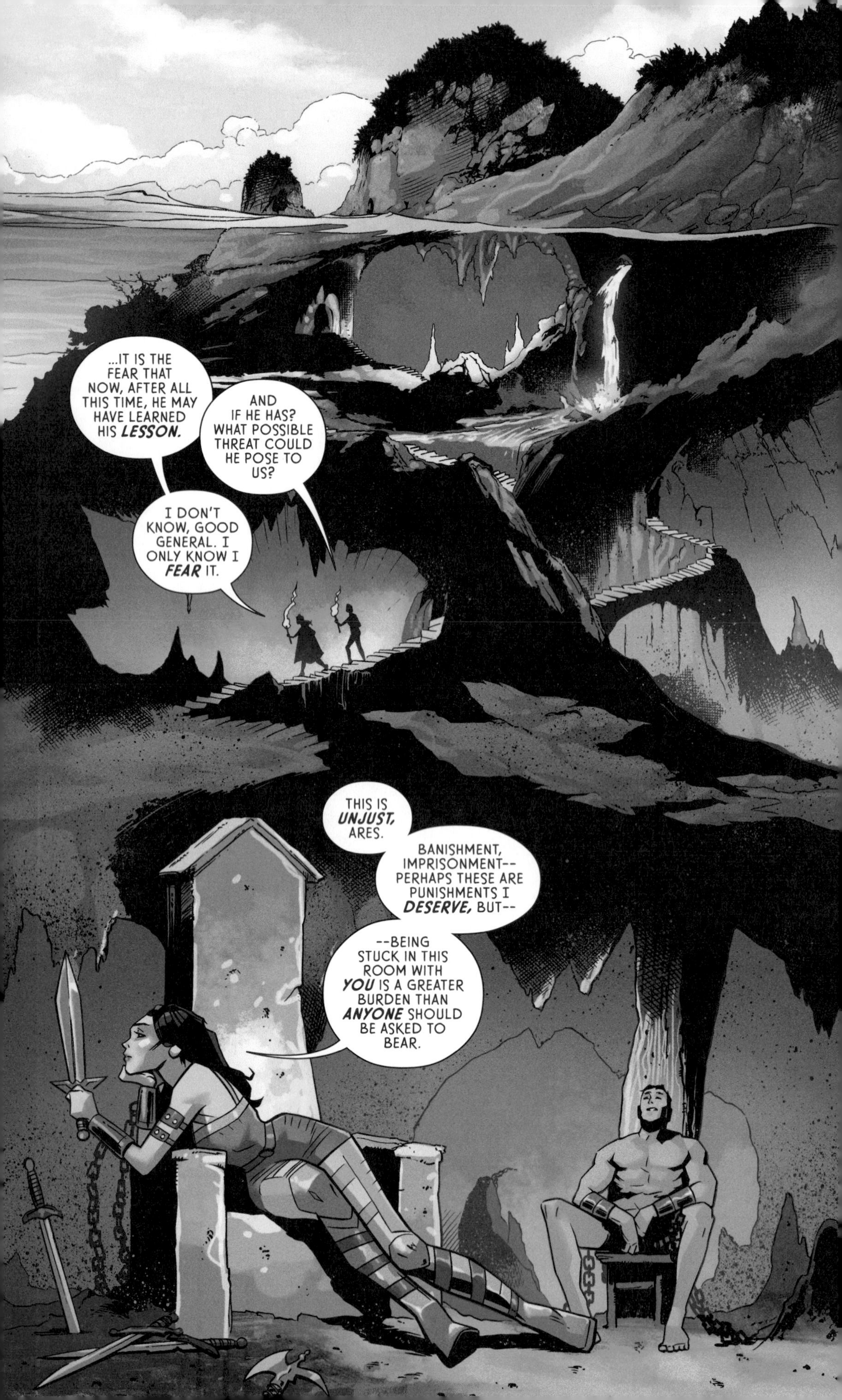
...IT IS THE FEAR THAT NOW, AFTER ALL THIS TIME, HE MAY HAVE LEARNED HIS *LESSON.*
AND IF HE HAS? WHAT POSSIBLE THREAT COULD HE POSE TO US?
I DON'T KNOW, GOOD GENERAL. I ONLY KNOW I *FEAR* IT.
THIS IS *UNJUST,* ARES.
BANISHMENT, IMPRISONMENT--PERHAPS THESE ARE PUNISHMENTS I *DESERVE,* BUT--
--BEING STUCK IN THIS ROOM WITH *YOU* IS A GREATER BURDEN THAN *ANYONE* SHOULD BE ASKED TO BEAR.

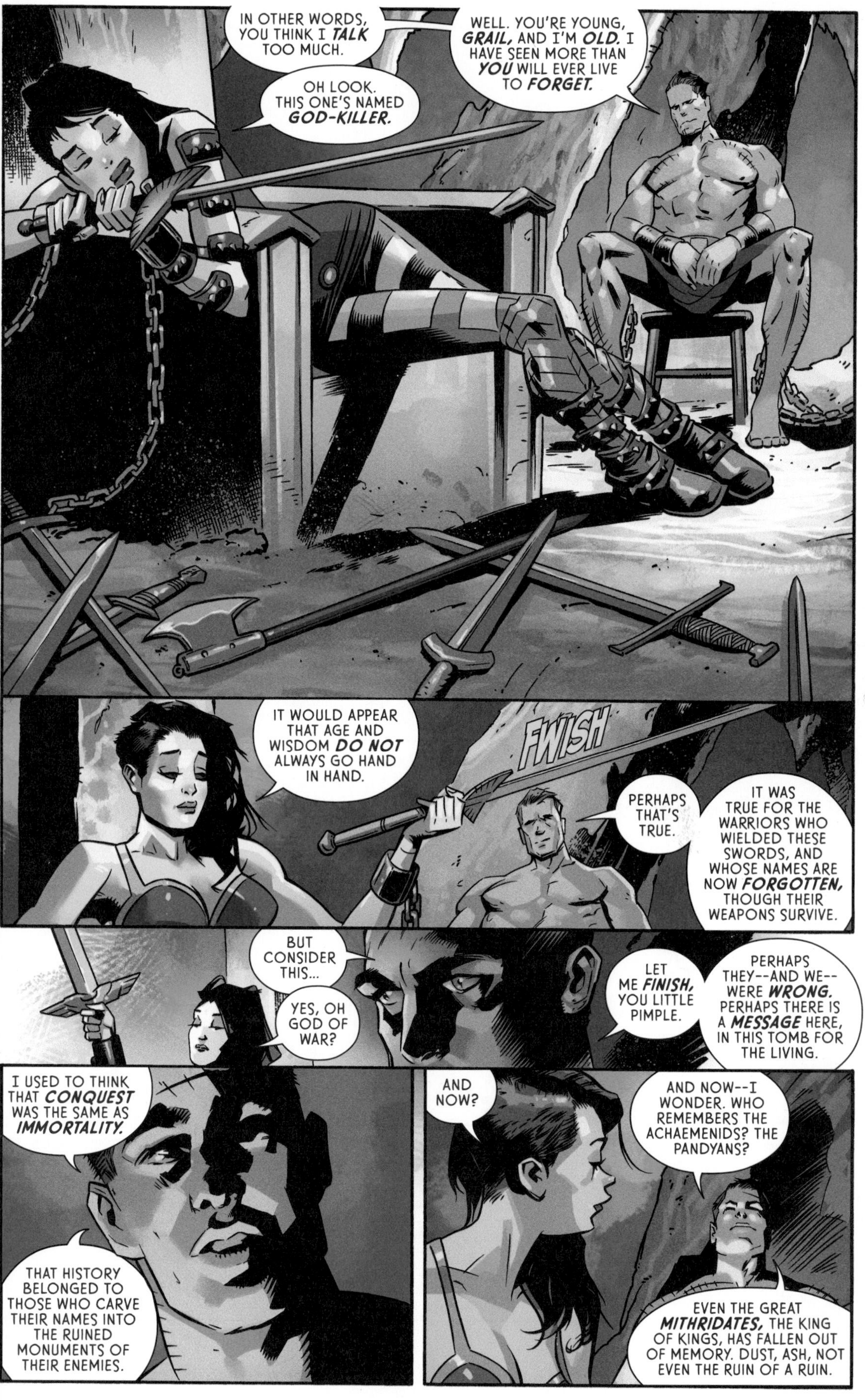
IN OTHER WORDS, YOU THINK I TALK TOO MUCH.
WELL. YOU'RE YOUNG, GRAIL, AND I'M OLD. I HAVE SEEN MORE THAN YOU WILL EVER LIVE TO FORGET.
OH LOOK. THIS ONE'S NAMED GOD-KILLER.
IT WOULD APPEAR THAT AGE AND WISDOM DO NOT ALWAYS GO HAND IN HAND.
FWISH
PERHAPS THAT'S TRUE.
IT WAS TRUE FOR THE WARRIORS WHO WIELDED THESE SWORDS, AND WHOSE NAMES ARE NOW FORGOTTEN, THOUGH THEIR WEAPONS SURVIVE.
BUT CONSIDER THIS...
YES, OH GOD OF WAR?
LET ME FINISH, YOU LITTLE PIMPLE.
PERHAPS THEY--AND WE--WERE WRONG. PERHAPS THERE IS A MESSAGE HERE, IN THIS TOMB FOR THE LIVING.
I USED TO THINK THAT CONQUEST WAS THE SAME AS IMMORTALITY.
THAT HISTORY BELONGED TO THOSE WHO CARVE THEIR NAMES INTO THE RUINED MONUMENTS OF THEIR ENEMIES.
AND NOW?
AND NOW--I WONDER. WHO REMEMBERS THE ACHAEMENIDS? THE PANDYANS?
EVEN THE GREAT MITHRIDATES, THE KING OF KINGS, HAS FALLEN OUT OF MEMORY. DUST, ASH, NOT EVEN THE RUIN OF A RUIN.

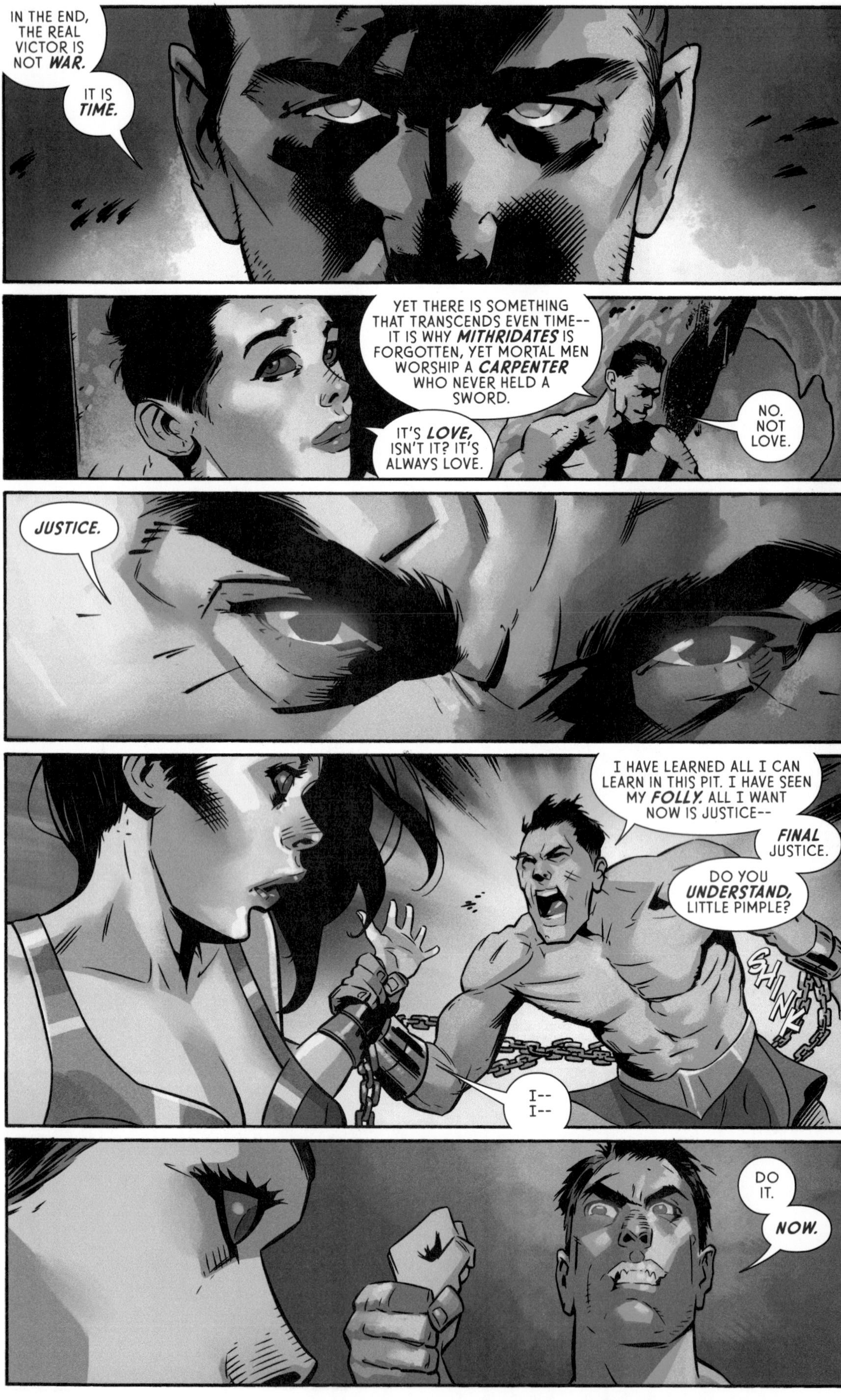
IN THE END, THE REAL VICTOR IS NOT *WAR.*
IT IS *TIME.*
YET THERE IS SOMETHING THAT TRANSCENDS EVEN TIME-- IT IS WHY *MITHRIDATES* IS FORGOTTEN, YET MORTAL MEN WORSHIP A *CARPENTER* WHO NEVER HELD A SWORD.
IT'S *LOVE,* ISN'T IT? IT'S ALWAYS LOVE.
NO. NOT LOVE.
JUSTICE.
I HAVE LEARNED ALL I CAN LEARN IN THIS PIT. I HAVE SEEN MY *FOLLY.* ALL I WANT NOW IS JUSTICE--
FINAL JUSTICE.
DO YOU *UNDERSTAND,* LITTLE PIMPLE?
SHINK
I-- I--
DO IT.
NOW.

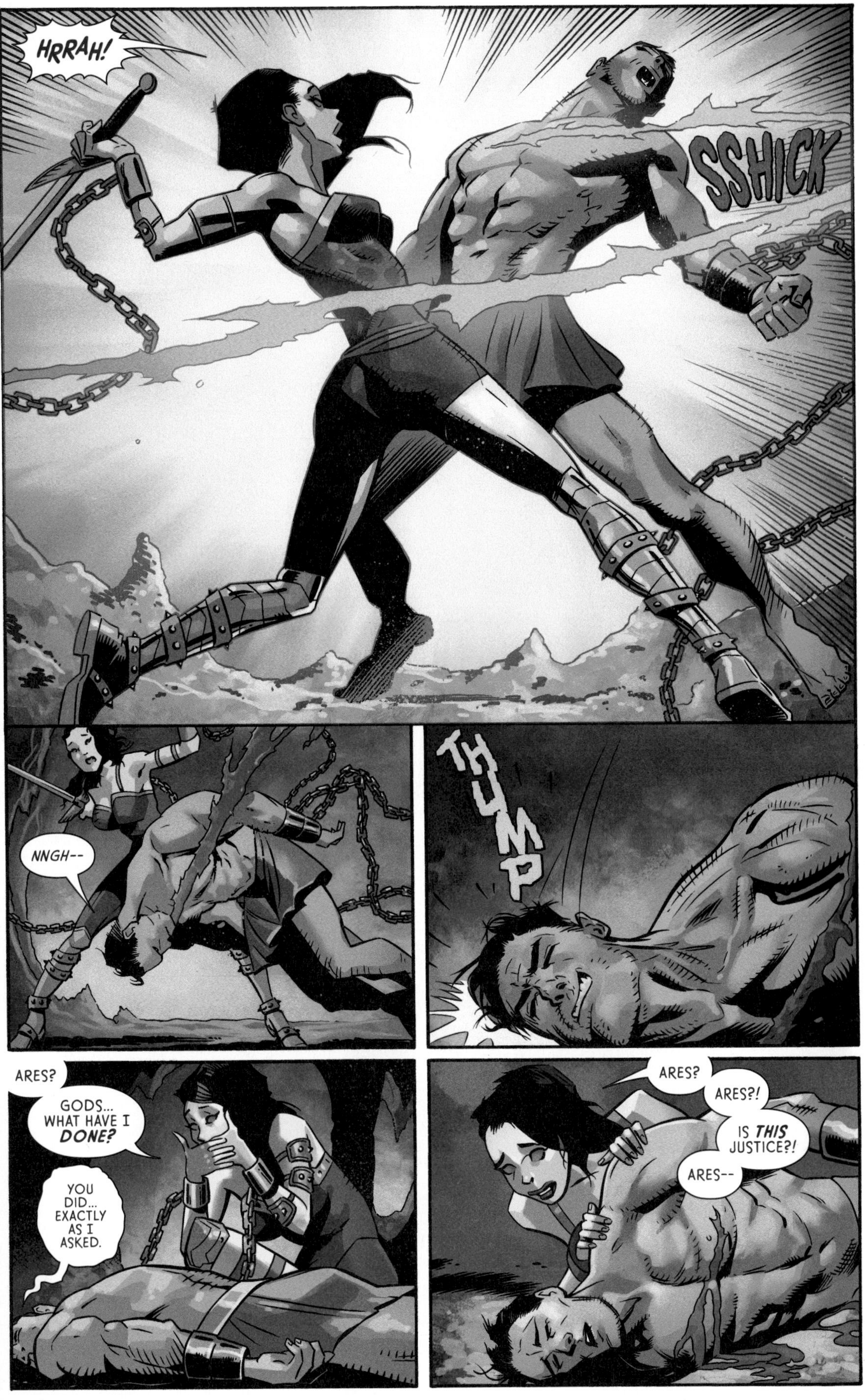
HRRAH!
SSHICK
NNGH--
THUMP
ARES?
GODS... WHAT HAVE I DONE?
YOU DID... EXACTLY AS I ASKED.
ARES?
ARES?!
IS THIS JUSTICE?!
ARES--

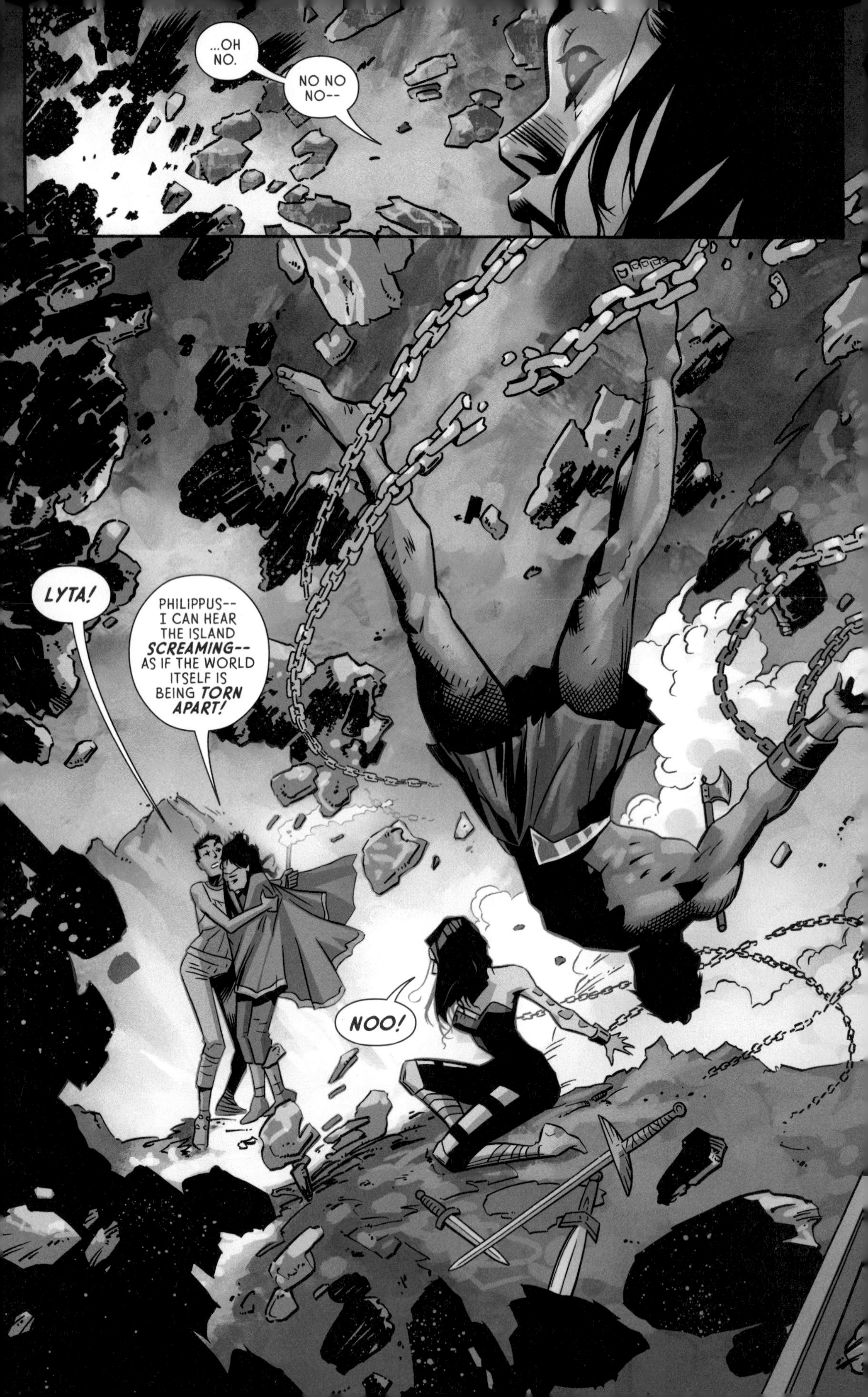
...OH NO.
NO NO NO--
LYTA!
PHILIPPUS-- I CAN HEAR THE ISLAND SCREAMING-- AS IF THE WORLD ITSELF IS BEING TORN APART!
NOO!

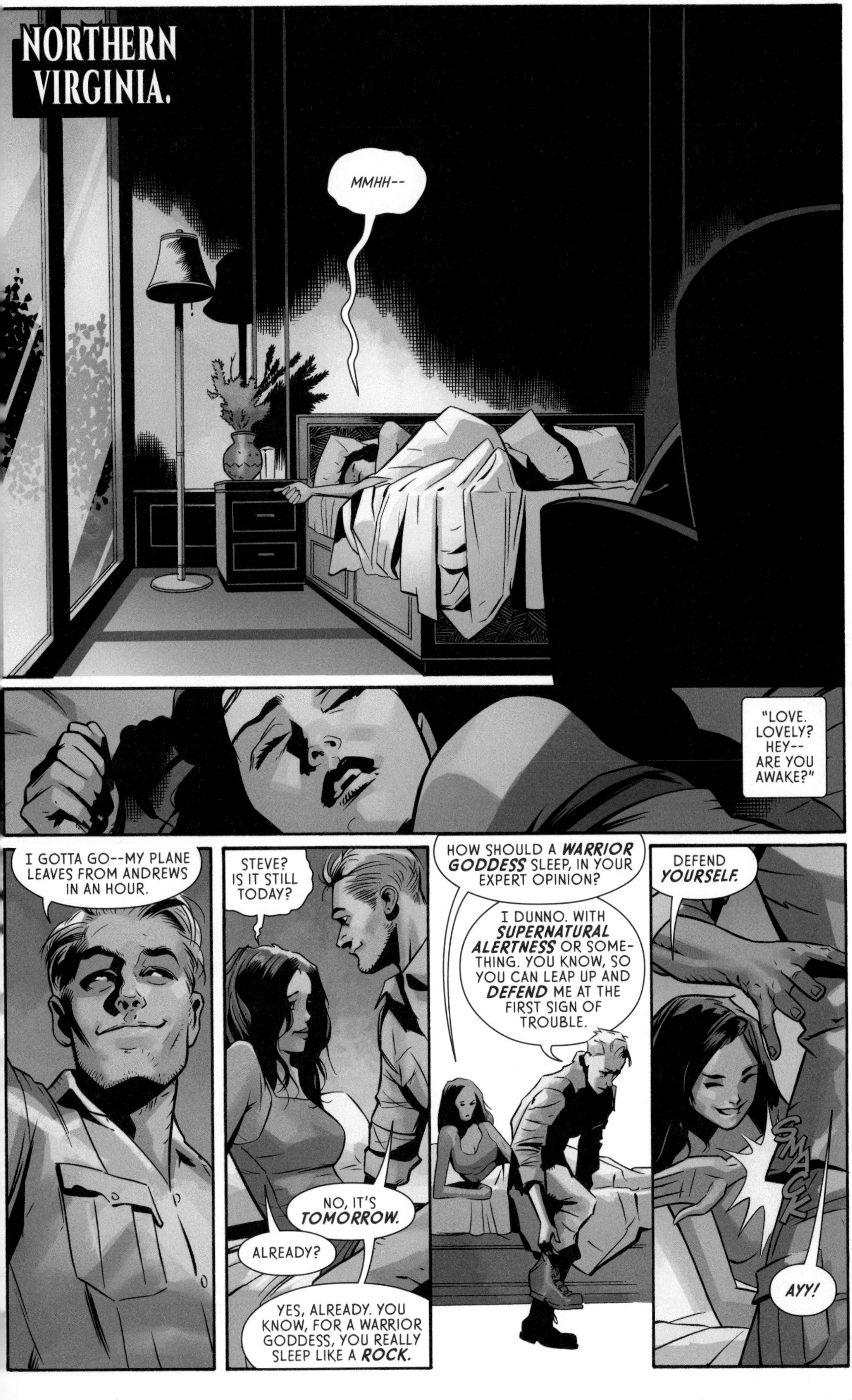
NORTHERN VIRGINIA.
MMHH--
"LOVE. LOVELY? HEY-- ARE YOU AWAKE?"
I GOTTA GO--MY PLANE LEAVES FROM ANDREWS IN AN HOUR.
STEVE? IS IT STILL TODAY?
NO, IT'S TOMORROW.
ALREADY?
YES, ALREADY. YOU KNOW, FOR A WARRIOR GODDESS, YOU REALLY SLEEP LIKE A ROCK.
HOW SHOULD A WARRIOR GODDESS SLEEP, IN YOUR EXPERT OPINION?
I DUNNO. WITH SUPERNATURAL ALERTNESS OR SOMETHING. YOU KNOW, SO YOU CAN LEAP UP AND DEFEND ME AT THE FIRST SIGN OF TROUBLE.
DEFEND YOURSELF.
SMACK
AYY!

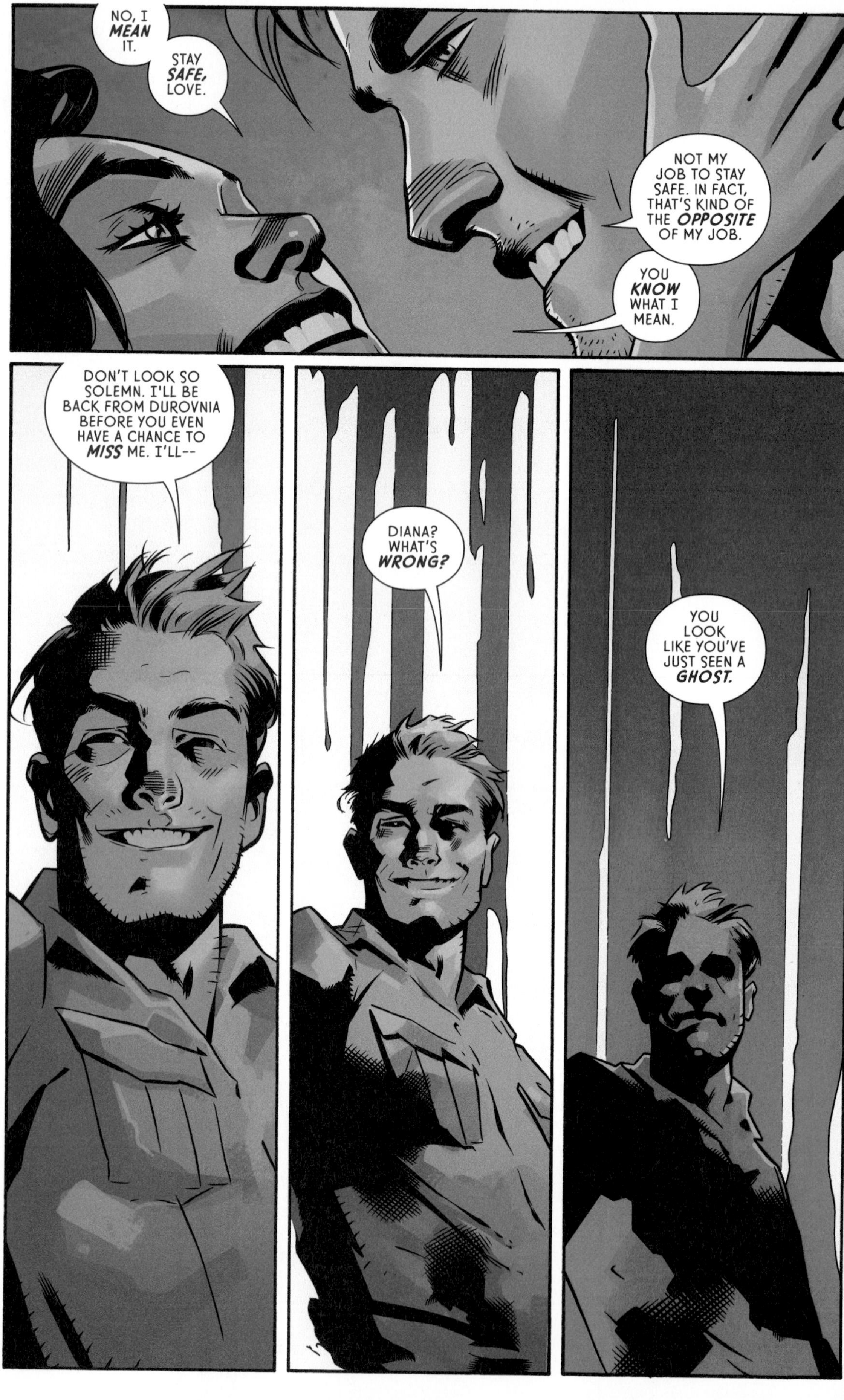
NO, I MEAN IT.
STAY SAFE, LOVE.
NOT MY JOB TO STAY SAFE. IN FACT, THAT'S KIND OF THE OPPOSITE OF MY JOB.
YOU KNOW WHAT I MEAN.
DON'T LOOK SO SOLEMN. I'LL BE BACK FROM DUROVNIA BEFORE YOU EVEN HAVE A CHANCE TO MISS ME. I'LL--
DIANA? WHAT'S WRONG?
YOU LOOK LIKE YOU'VE JUST SEEN A GHOST.

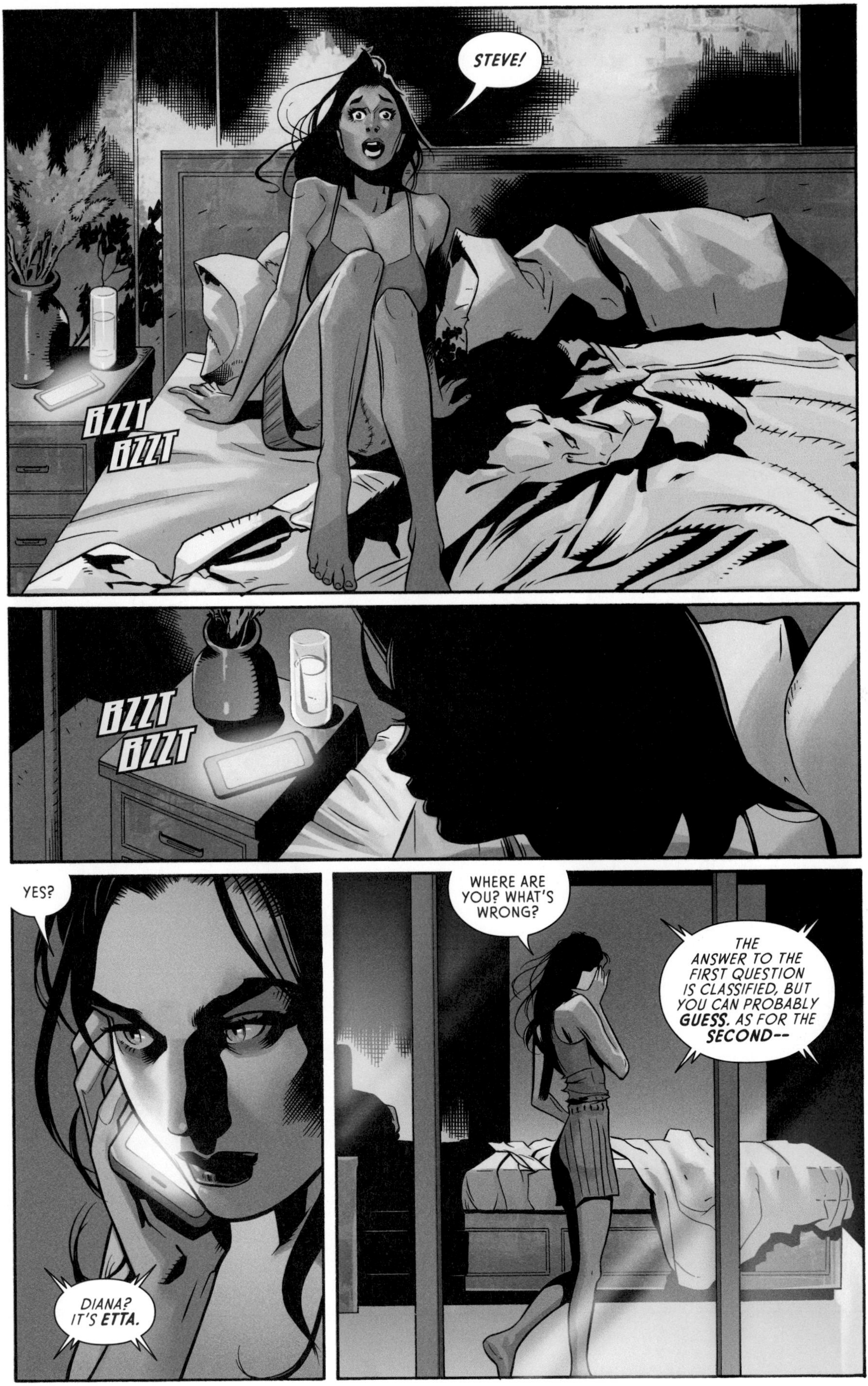
STEVE!
BZZT BZZT
BZZT BZZT
YES?
DIANA? IT'S ETTA.
WHERE ARE YOU? WHAT'S WRONG?
THE ANSWER TO THE FIRST QUESTION IS CLASSIFIED, BUT YOU CAN PROBABLY GUESS. AS FOR THE SECOND--

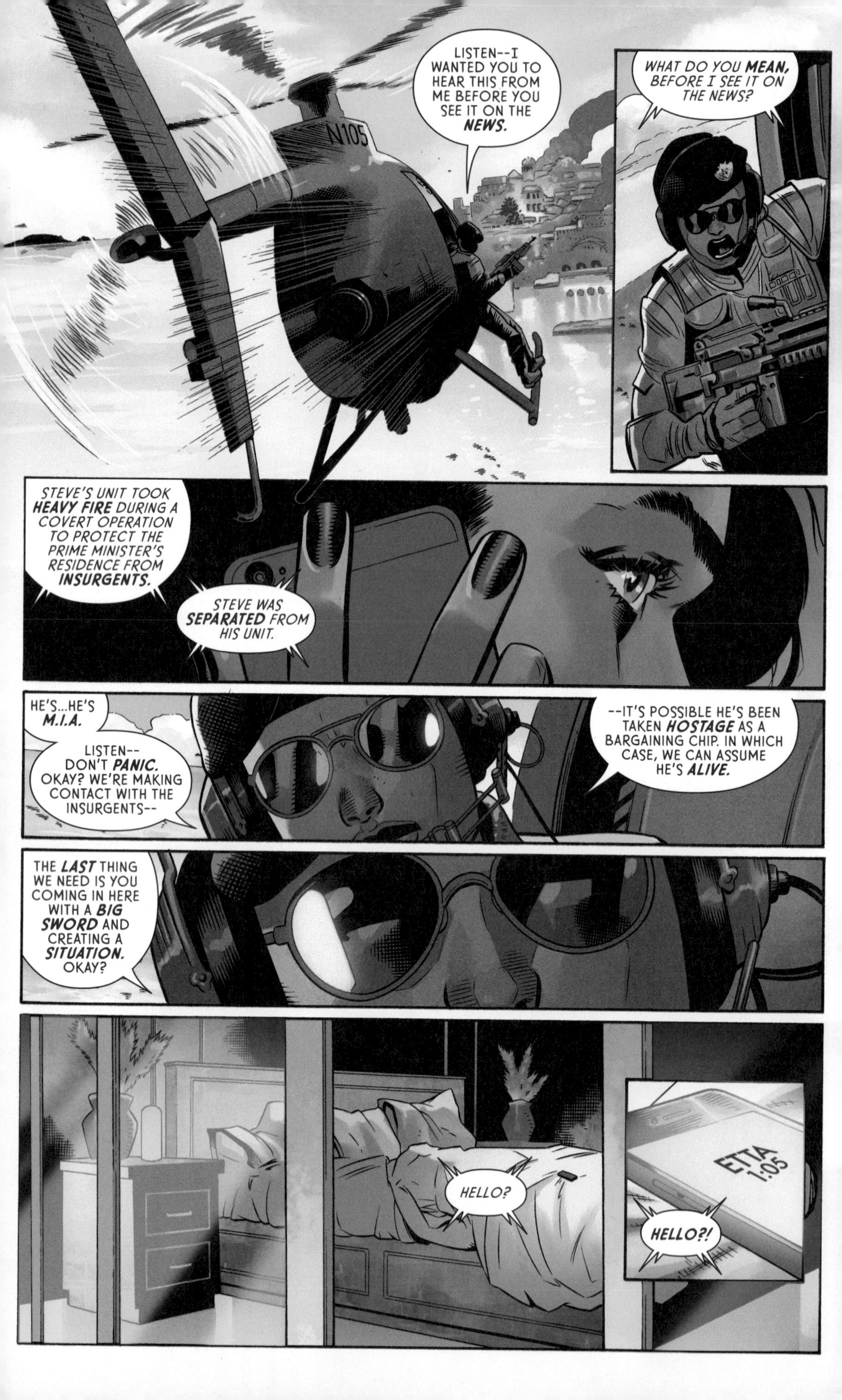

N105
LISTEN--I WANTED YOU TO HEAR THIS FROM ME BEFORE YOU SEE IT ON THE ***NEWS.***
*WHAT DO YOU **MEAN,** BEFORE I SEE IT ON THE NEWS?*
*STEVE'S UNIT TOOK **HEAVY FIRE** DURING A COVERT OPERATION TO PROTECT THE PRIME MINISTER'S RESIDENCE FROM **INSURGENTS.***
*STEVE WAS **SEPARATED** FROM HIS UNIT.*
HE'S...HE'S ***M.I.A.***
LISTEN-- DON'T ***PANIC.*** OKAY? WE'RE MAKING CONTACT WITH THE INSURGENTS--
--IT'S POSSIBLE HE'S BEEN TAKEN ***HOSTAGE*** AS A BARGAINING CHIP. IN WHICH CASE, WE CAN ASSUME HE'S ***ALIVE.***
THE ***LAST*** THING WE NEED IS YOU COMING IN HERE WITH A ***BIG SWORD*** AND CREATING A ***SITUATION.*** OKAY?
HELLO?
ETTA 1:05
HELLO?!

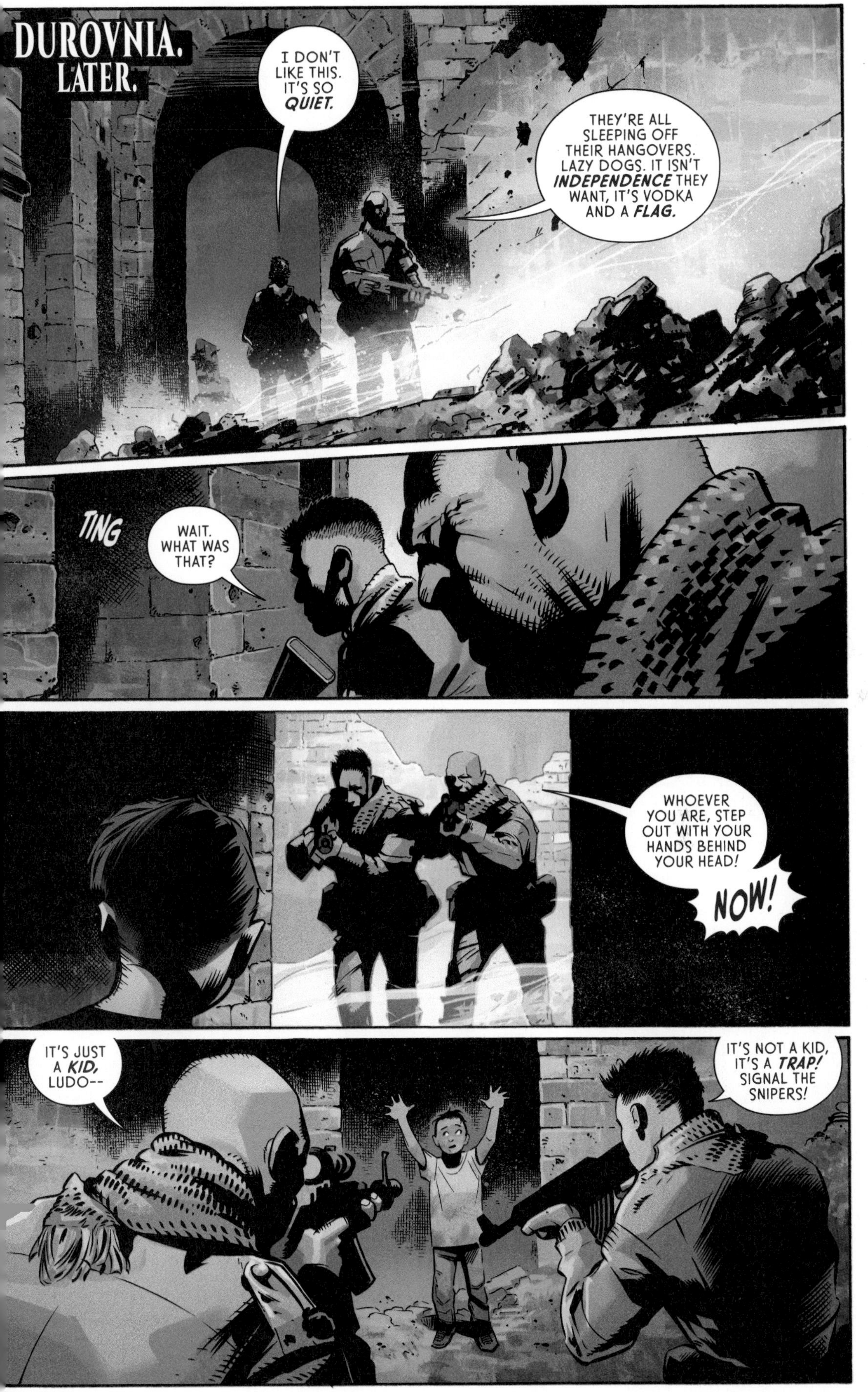
DUROVNIA. LATER.
I DON'T LIKE THIS. IT'S SO *QUIET.*
THEY'RE ALL SLEEPING OFF THEIR HANGOVERS. LAZY DOGS. IT ISN'T *INDEPENDENCE* THEY WANT, IT'S VODKA AND A *FLAG.*
TING
WAIT. WHAT WAS THAT?
WHOEVER YOU ARE, STEP OUT WITH YOUR HANDS BEHIND YOUR HEAD!
NOW!
IT'S JUST A *KID,* LUDO--
IT'S NOT A KID, IT'S A *TRAP!* SIGNAL THE SNIPERS!

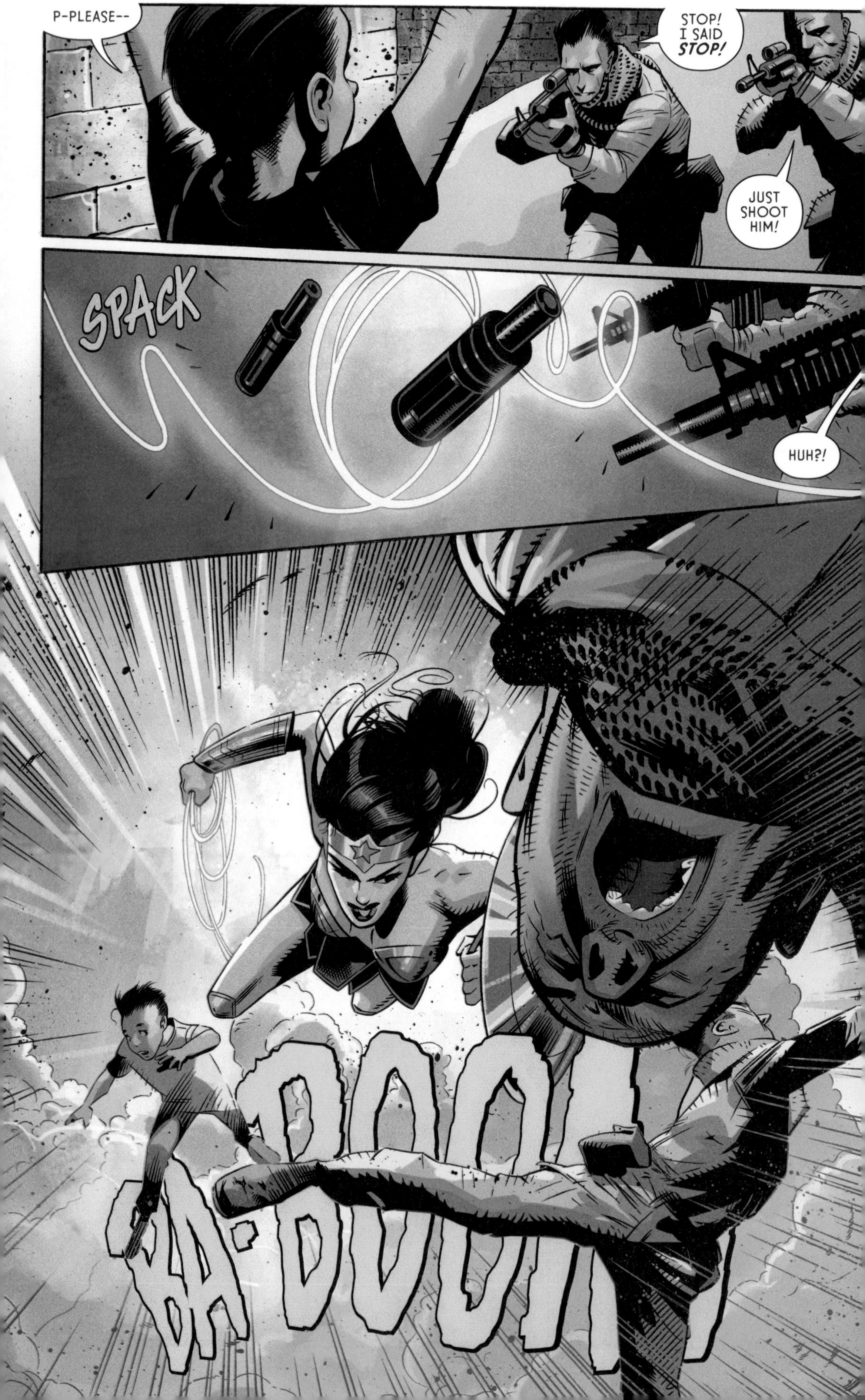
P-PLEASE--
STOP! I SAID STOP!
JUST SHOOT HIM!
SPACK
HUH?!
KA-BOOM

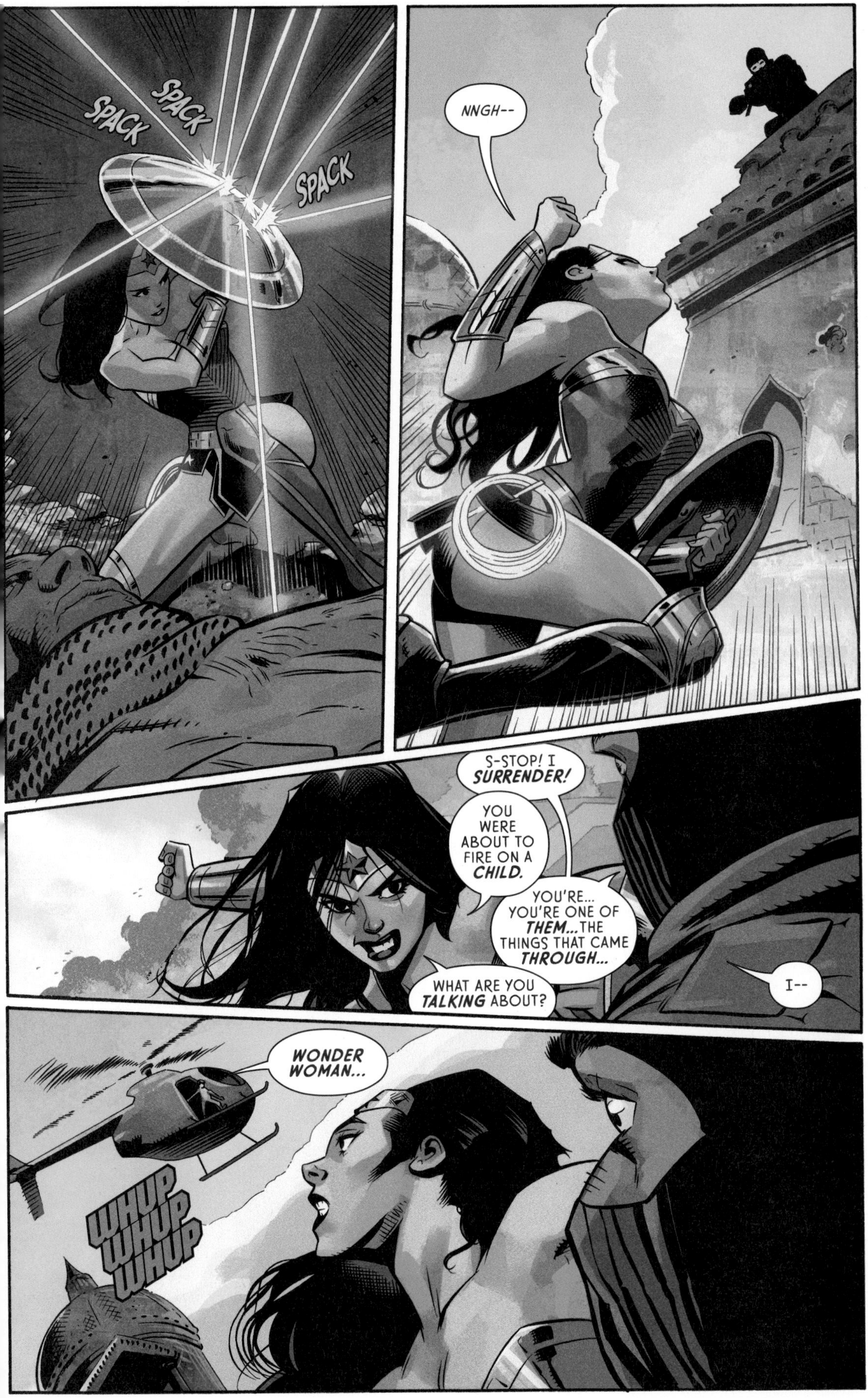
SPACK
SPACK
SPACK
NNGH--
S-STOP! I SURRENDER!
YOU WERE ABOUT TO FIRE ON A CHILD.
YOU'RE... YOU'RE ONE OF THEM... THE THINGS THAT CAME THROUGH...
WHAT ARE YOU TALKING ABOUT?
I--
WONDER WOMAN...
WHUP WHUP WHUP

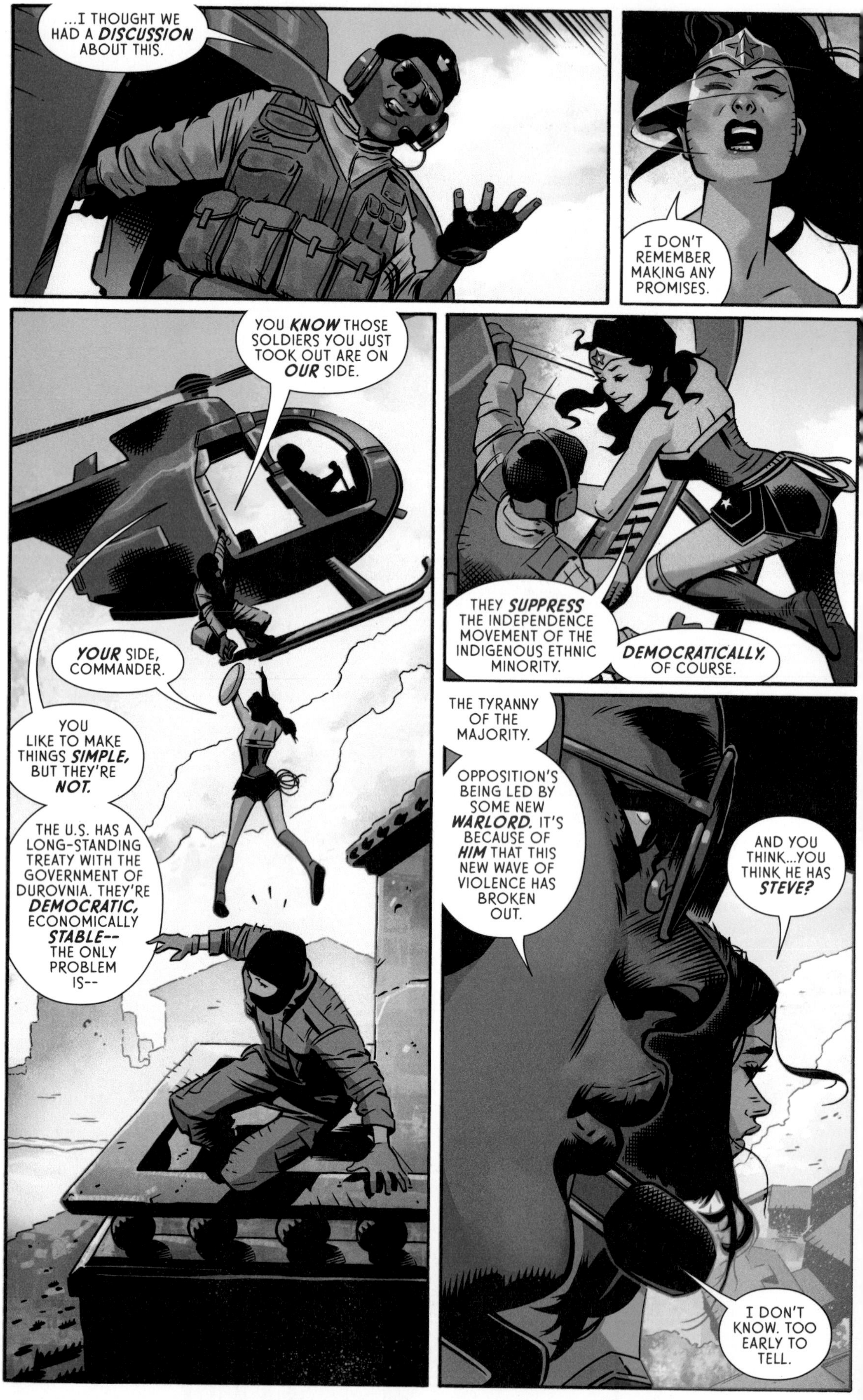

...I THOUGHT WE HAD A DISCUSSION ABOUT THIS.
I DON'T REMEMBER MAKING ANY PROMISES.
YOU KNOW THOSE SOLDIERS YOU JUST TOOK OUT ARE ON OUR SIDE.
YOUR SIDE, COMMANDER.
YOU LIKE TO MAKE THINGS SIMPLE, BUT THEY'RE NOT.
THE U.S. HAS A LONG-STANDING TREATY WITH THE GOVERNMENT OF DUROVNIA. THEY'RE DEMOCRATIC, ECONOMICALLY STABLE-- THE ONLY PROBLEM IS--
THEY SUPPRESS THE INDEPENDENCE MOVEMENT OF THE INDIGENOUS ETHNIC MINORITY.
DEMOCRATICALLY, OF COURSE.
THE TYRANNY OF THE MAJORITY.
OPPOSITION'S BEING LED BY SOME NEW WARLORD. IT'S BECAUSE OF HIM THAT THIS NEW WAVE OF VIOLENCE HAS BROKEN OUT.
AND YOU THINK...YOU THINK HE HAS STEVE?
I DON'T KNOW. TOO EARLY TO TELL.

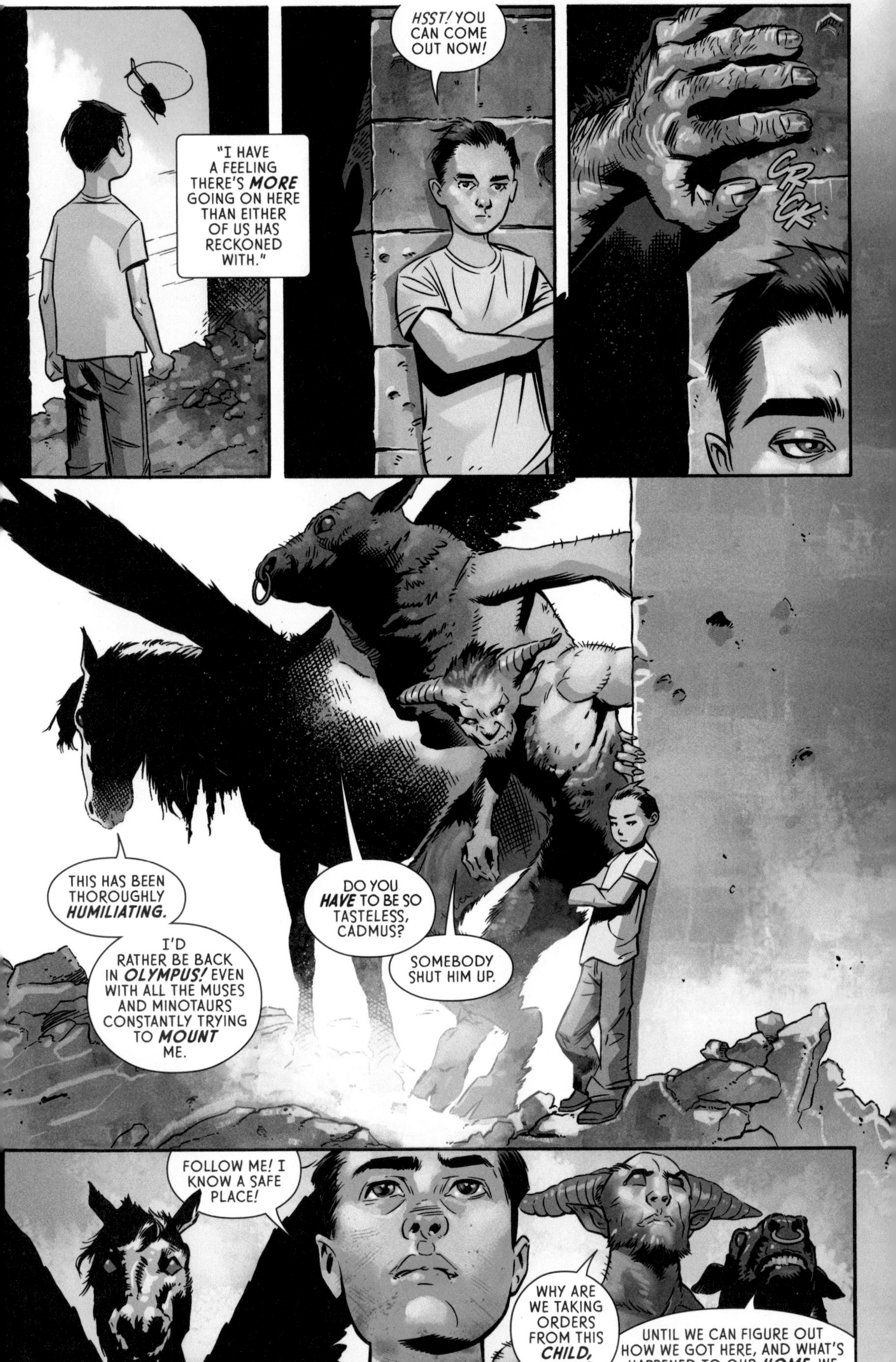
"I HAVE A FEELING THERE'S MORE GOING ON HERE THAN EITHER OF US HAS RECKONED WITH."
HSST! YOU CAN COME OUT NOW!
CRICK
THIS HAS BEEN THOROUGHLY HUMILIATING.
I'D RATHER BE BACK IN OLYMPUS! EVEN WITH ALL THE MUSES AND MINOTAURS CONSTANTLY TRYING TO MOUNT ME.
DO YOU HAVE TO BE SO TASTELESS, CADMUS?
SOMEBODY SHUT HIM UP.
FOLLOW ME! I KNOW A SAFE PLACE!
WHY ARE WE TAKING ORDERS FROM THIS CHILD, EIRENE?
UNTIL WE CAN FIGURE OUT HOW WE GOT HERE, AND WHAT'S HAPPENED TO OUR HOME, WE DON'T HAVE MUCH OF A CHOICE.

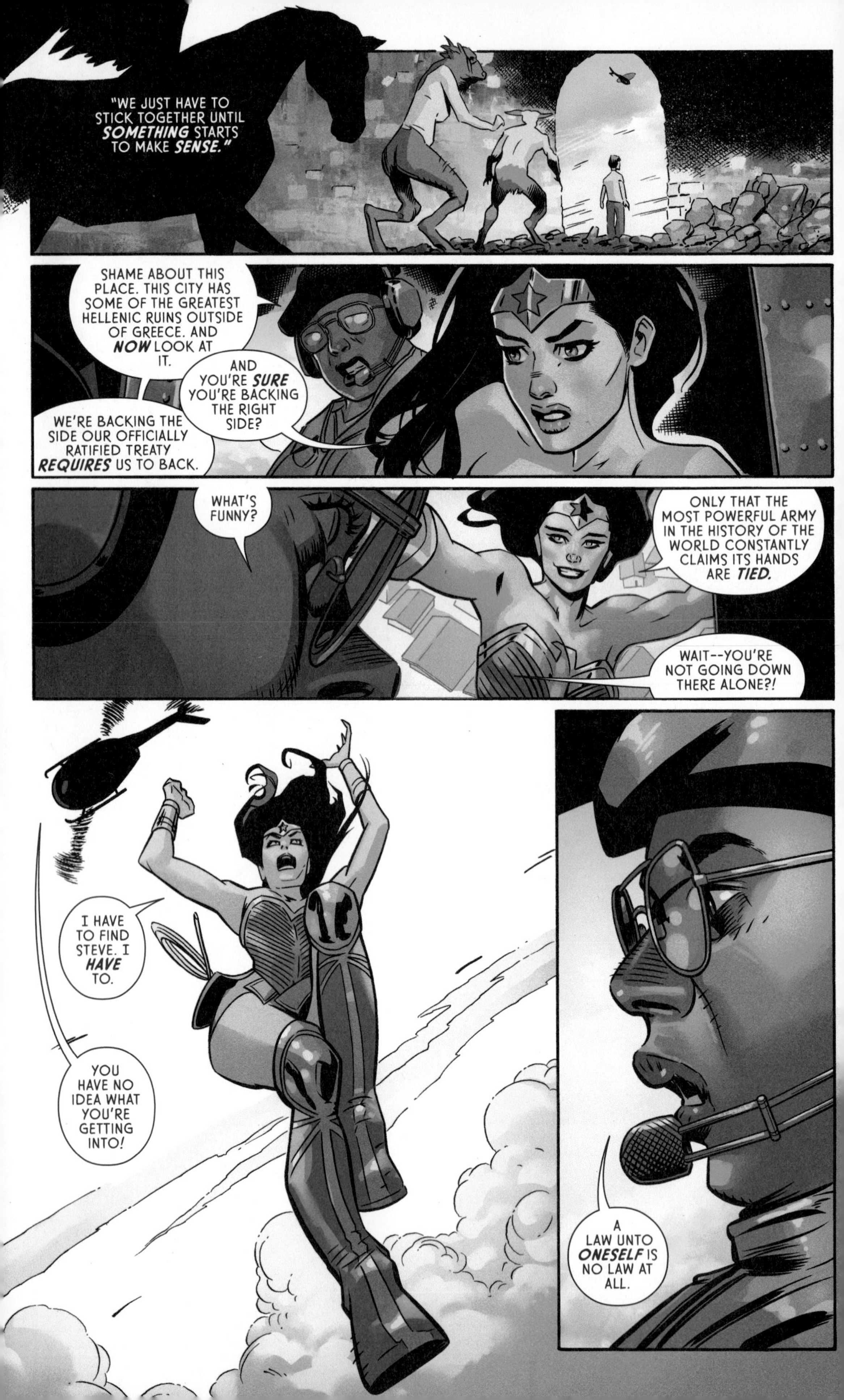
"WE JUST HAVE TO STICK TOGETHER UNTIL SOMETHING STARTS TO MAKE SENSE."
SHAME ABOUT THIS PLACE. THIS CITY HAS SOME OF THE GREATEST HELLENIC RUINS OUTSIDE OF GREECE. AND NOW LOOK AT IT.
AND YOU'RE SURE YOU'RE BACKING THE RIGHT SIDE?
WE'RE BACKING THE SIDE OUR OFFICIALLY RATIFIED TREATY REQUIRES US TO BACK.
WHAT'S FUNNY?
ONLY THAT THE MOST POWERFUL ARMY IN THE HISTORY OF THE WORLD CONSTANTLY CLAIMS ITS HANDS ARE TIED.
WAIT--YOU'RE NOT GOING DOWN THERE ALONE?!
I HAVE TO FIND STEVE. I HAVE TO.
YOU HAVE NO IDEA WHAT YOU'RE GETTING INTO!
A LAW UNTO ONESELF IS NO LAW AT ALL.

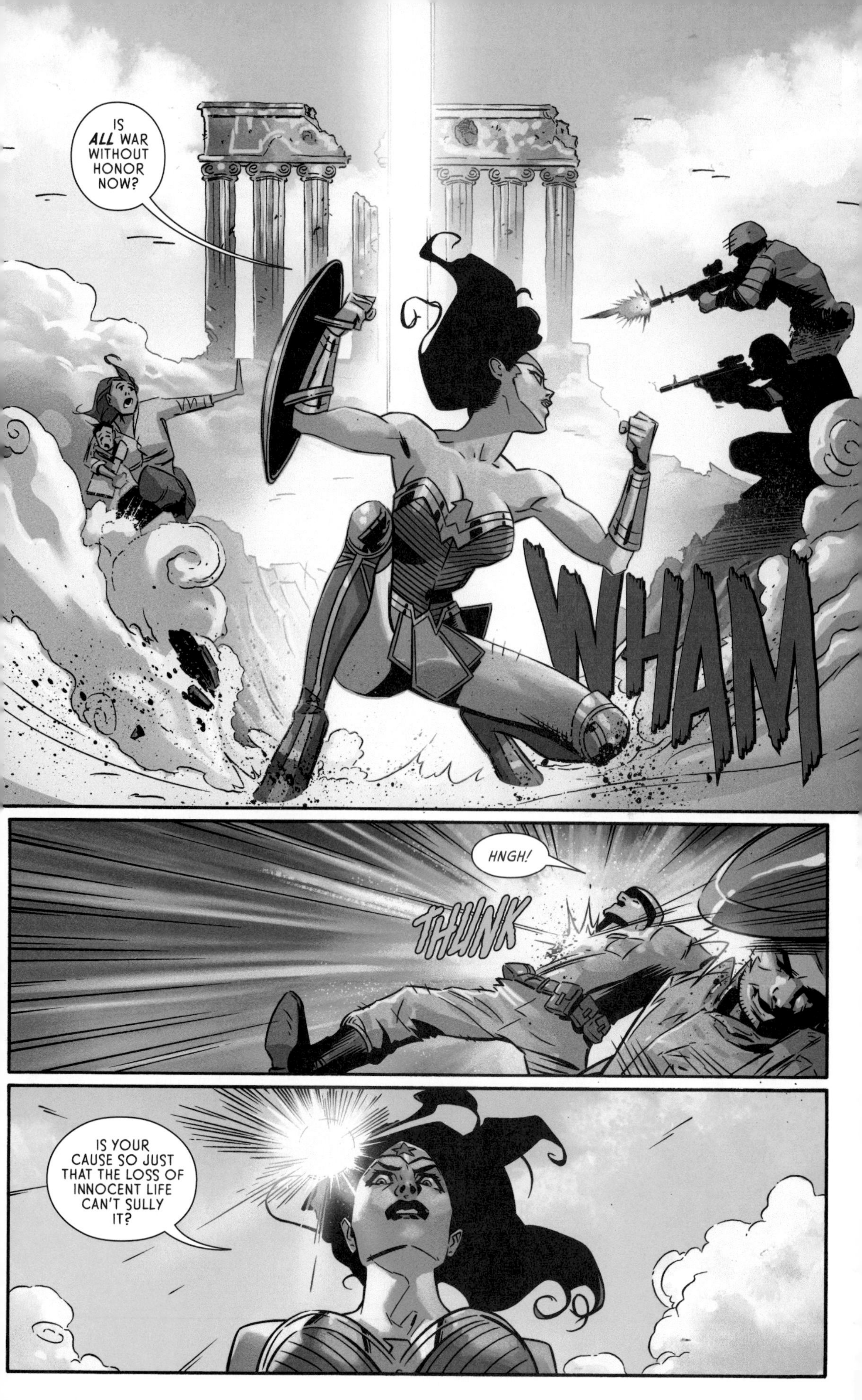
IS ALL WAR WITHOUT HONOR NOW?
WHAM
HNGH!
THUNK
IS YOUR CAUSE SO JUST THAT THE LOSS OF INNOCENT LIFE CAN'T SULLY IT?

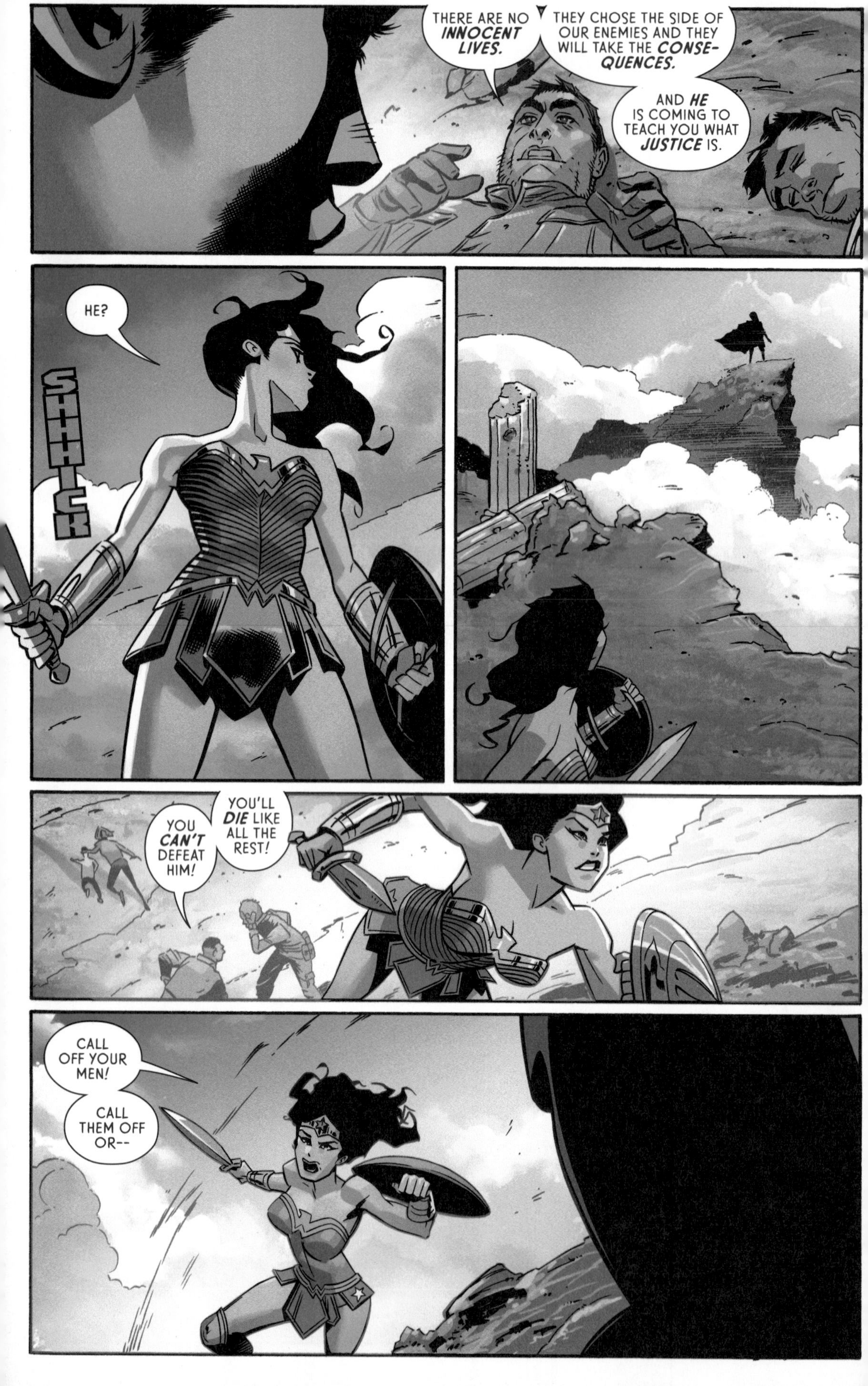

THERE ARE NO INNOCENT LIVES.
THEY CHOSE THE SIDE OF OUR ENEMIES AND THEY WILL TAKE THE CONSE-QUENCES.
AND HE IS COMING TO TEACH YOU WHAT JUSTICE IS.
HE?
SHHHICK
YOU CAN'T DEFEAT HIM!
YOU'LL DIE LIKE ALL THE REST!
CALL OFF YOUR MEN!
CALL THEM OFF OR--

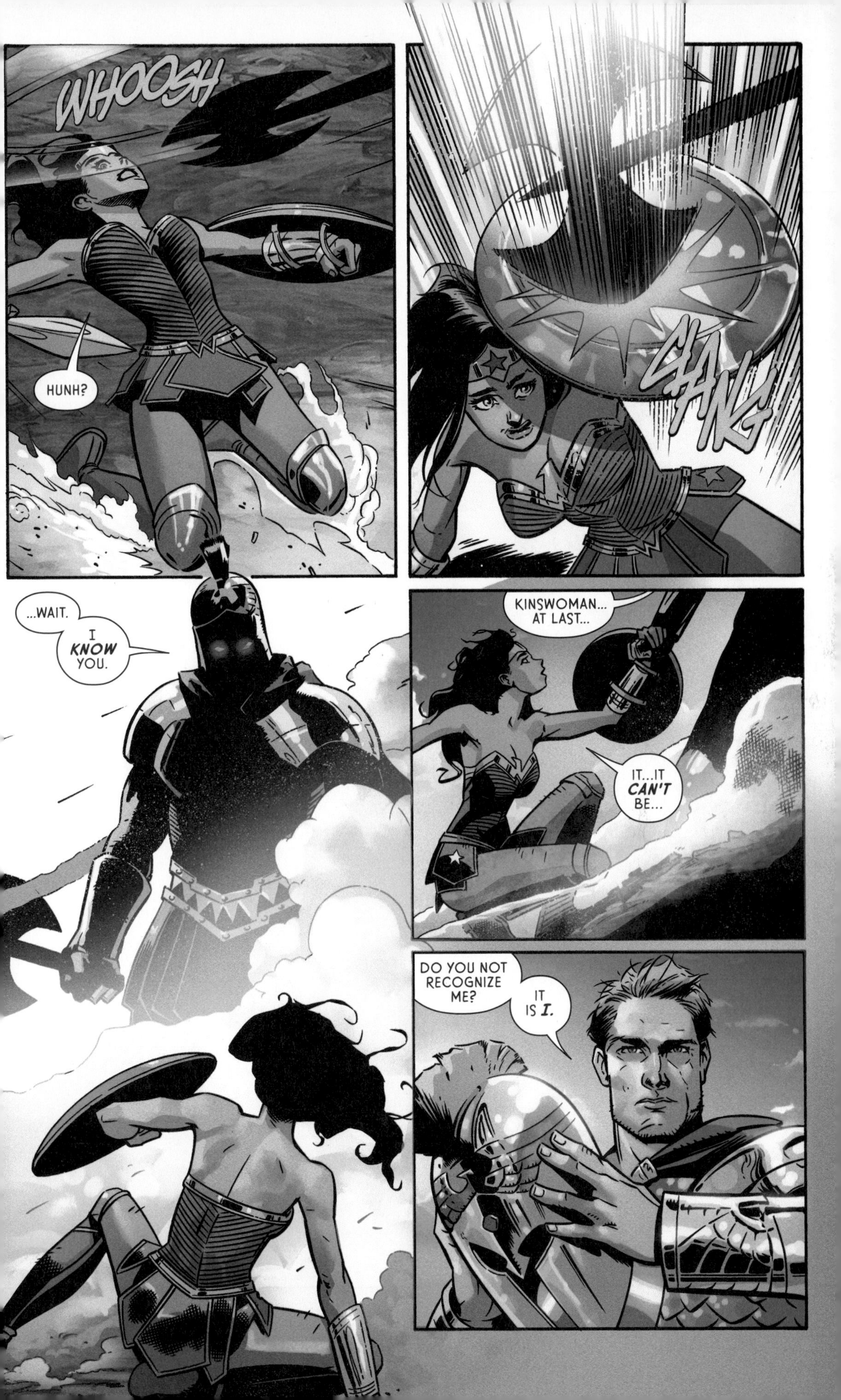
WHOOSH
HUNH?
CLANG
...WAIT.
I KNOW YOU.
KINSWOMAN... AT LAST...
IT...IT CAN'T BE...
DO YOU NOT RECOGNIZE ME?
IT IS I.

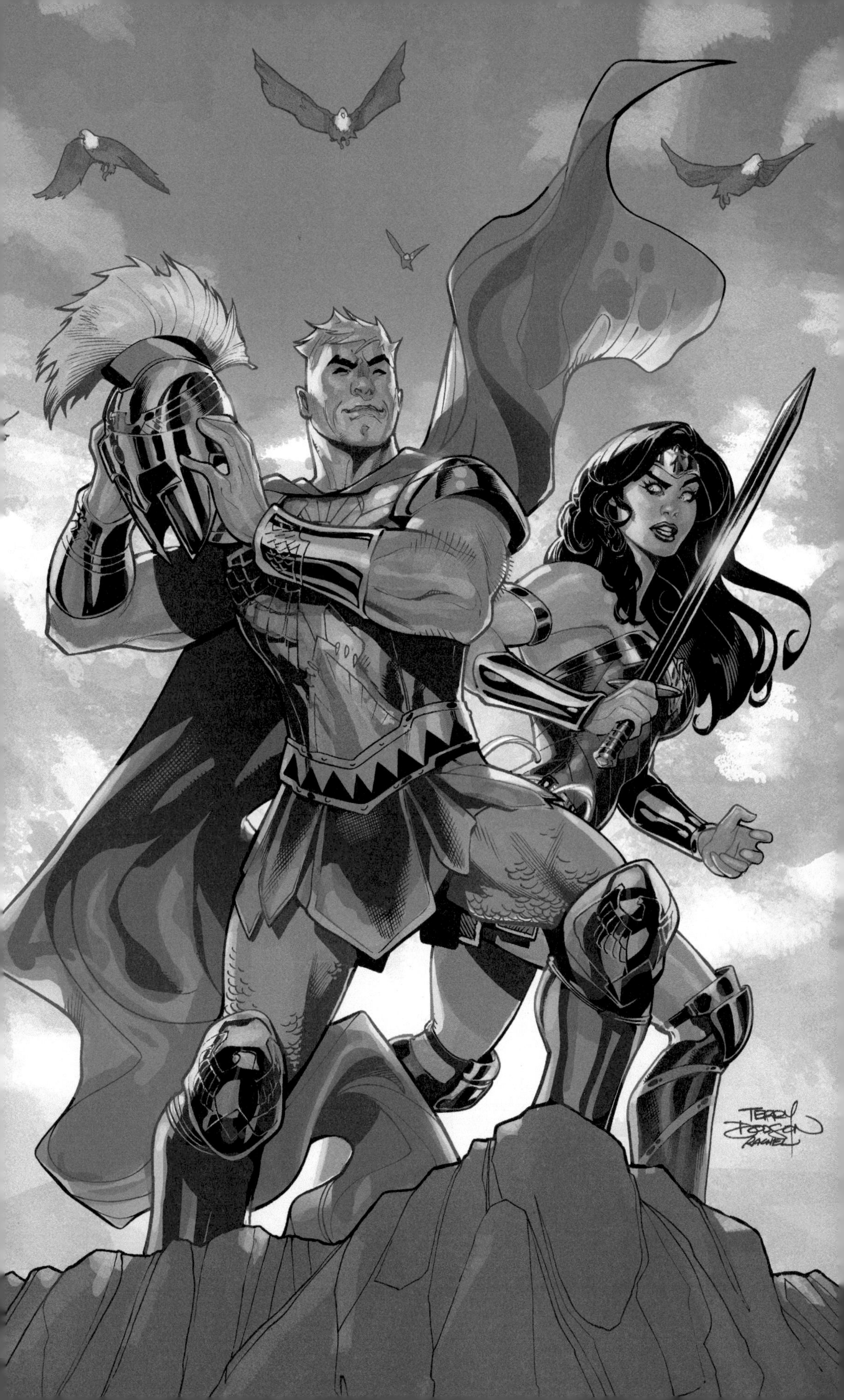
TERRY
DODSON
RACHEL

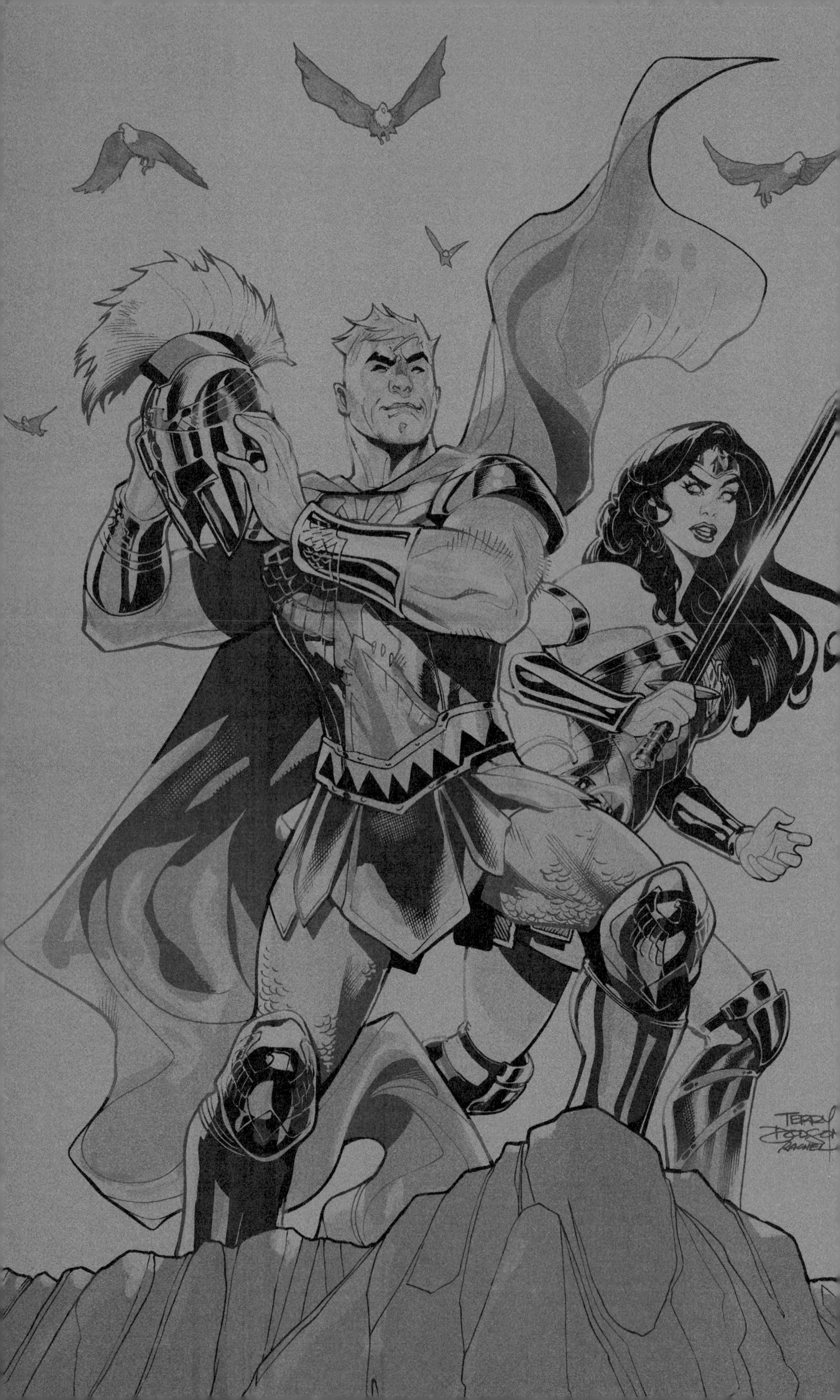
TERRY DODSON
RACHEL

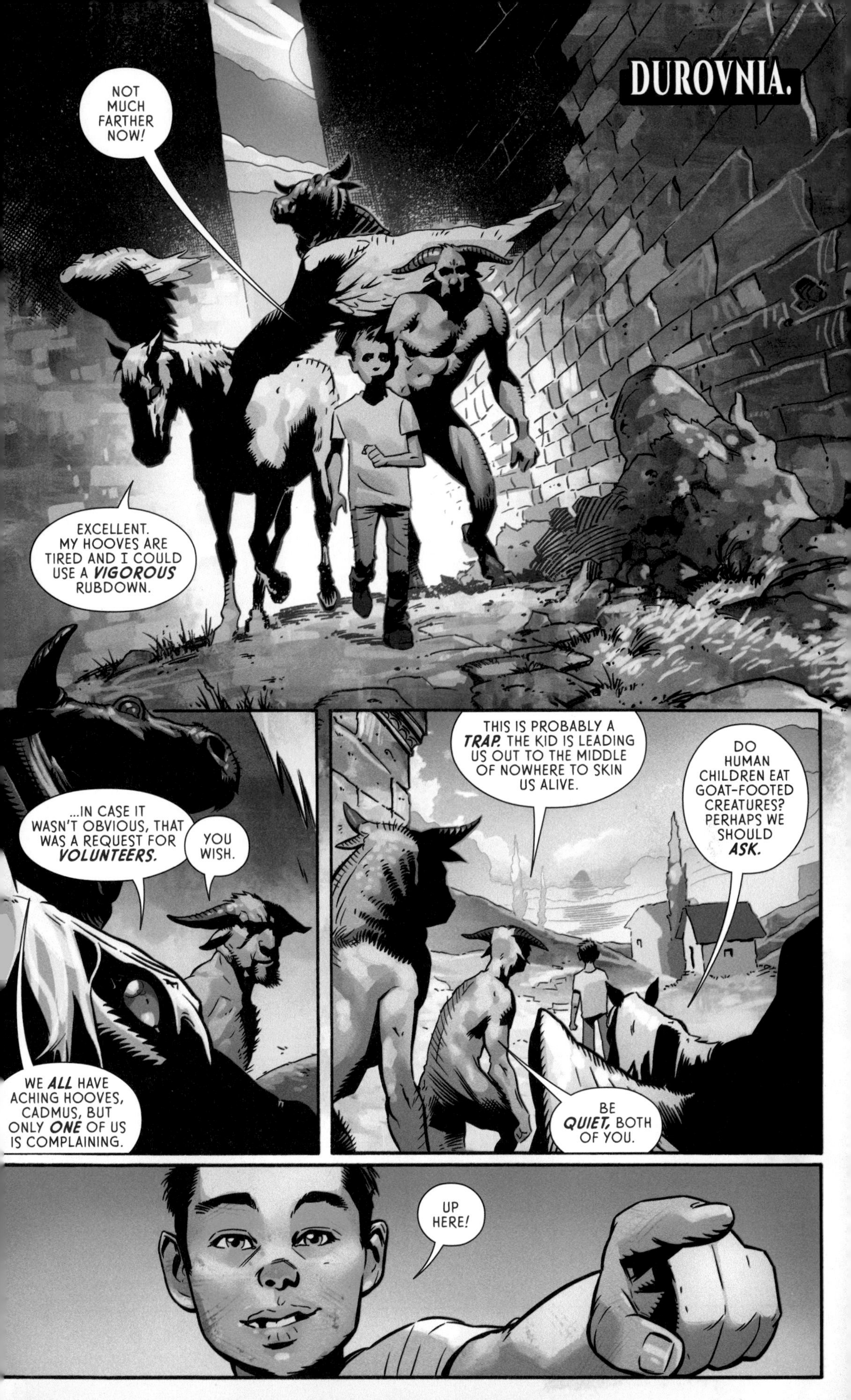
DUROVNIA.
NOT MUCH FARTHER NOW!
EXCELLENT. MY HOOVES ARE TIRED AND I COULD USE A *VIGOROUS* RUBDOWN.
...IN CASE IT WASN'T OBVIOUS, THAT WAS A REQUEST FOR *VOLUNTEERS.*
YOU WISH.
WE *ALL* HAVE ACHING HOOVES, CADMUS, BUT ONLY *ONE* OF US IS COMPLAINING.
THIS IS PROBABLY A *TRAP.* THE KID IS LEADING US OUT TO THE MIDDLE OF NOWHERE TO SKIN US ALIVE.
DO HUMAN CHILDREN EAT GOAT-FOOTED CREATURES? PERHAPS WE SHOULD *ASK.*
BE *QUIET,* BOTH OF YOU.
UP HERE!

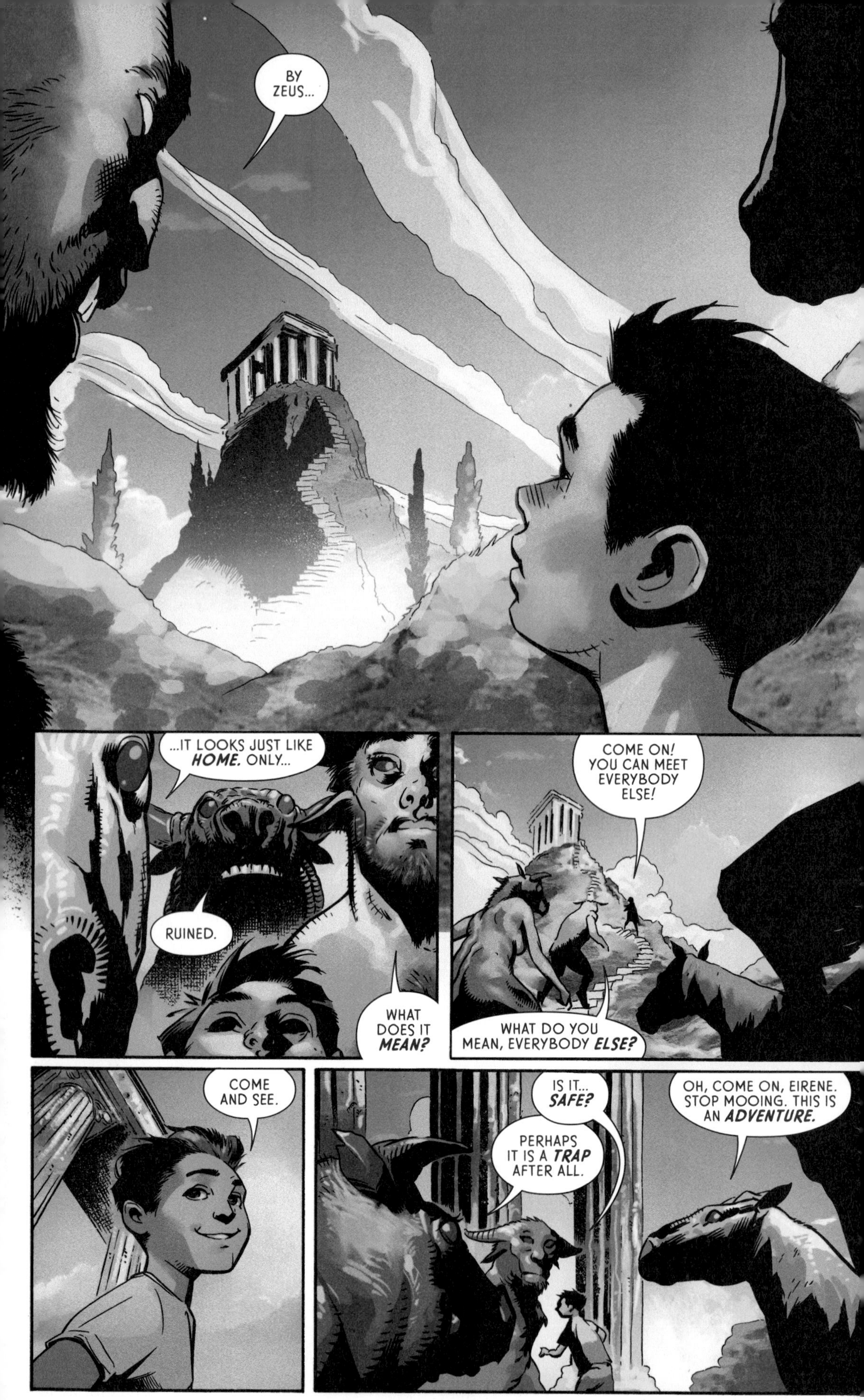
BY ZEUS...
...IT LOOKS JUST LIKE *HOME.* ONLY...
RUINED.
WHAT DOES IT *MEAN?*
COME ON! YOU CAN MEET EVERYBODY ELSE!
WHAT DO YOU MEAN, EVERYBODY *ELSE?*
COME AND SEE.
IS IT... *SAFE?*
PERHAPS IT IS A *TRAP* AFTER ALL.
OH, COME ON, EIRENE. STOP MOOING. THIS IS AN *ADVENTURE.*

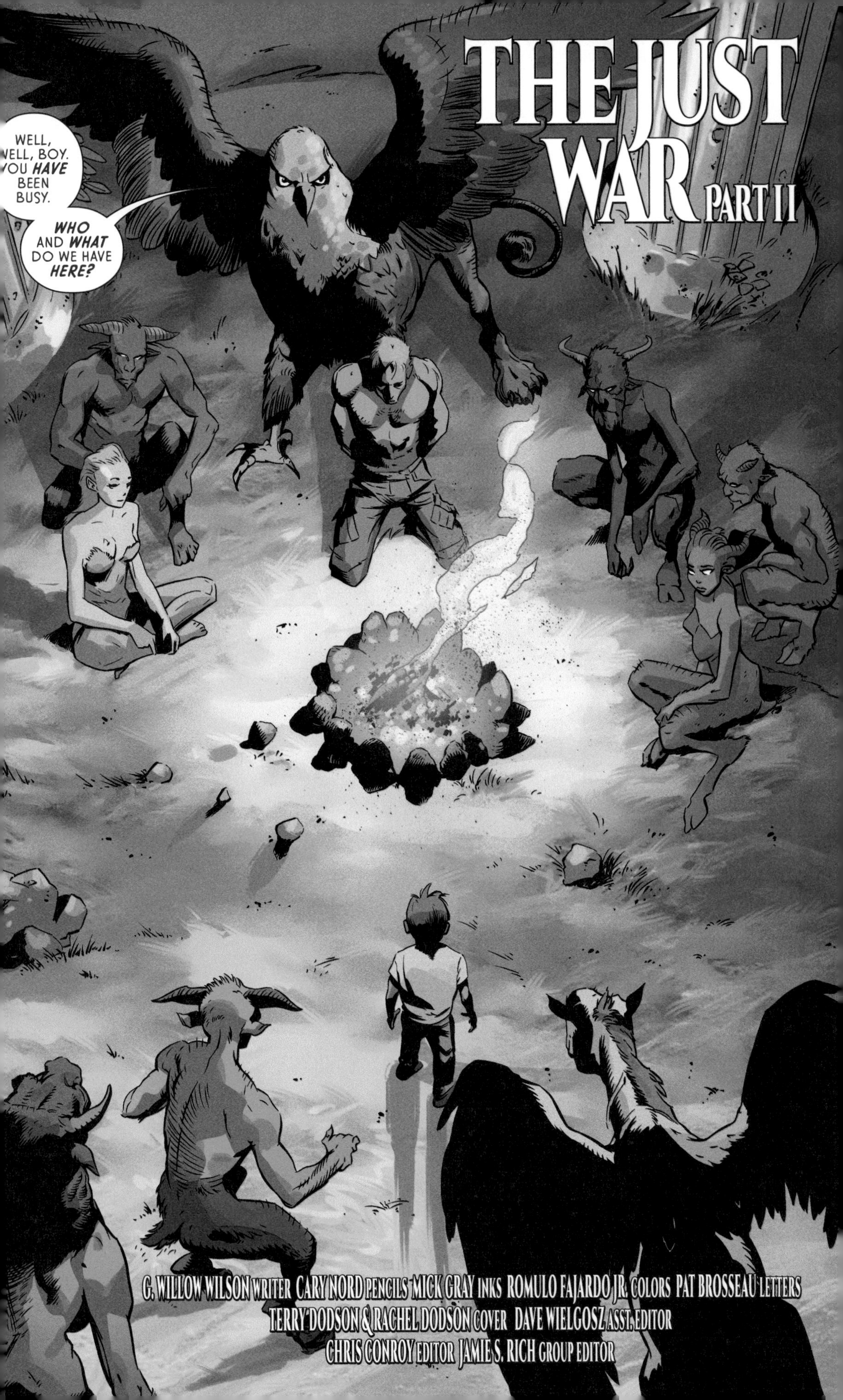
THE JUST WAR PART II
WELL, ELL, BOY. OU *HAVE* BEEN BUSY.
WHO AND *WHAT* DO WE HAVE *HERE?*
G. WILLOW WILSON WRITER CARY NORD PENCILS MICK GRAY INKS ROMULO FAJARDO JR. COLORS PAT BROSSEAU LETTERS
TERRY DODSON & RACHEL DODSON COVER DAVE WIELGOSZ ASST. EDITOR
CHRIS CONROY EDITOR JAMIE S. RICH GROUP EDITOR

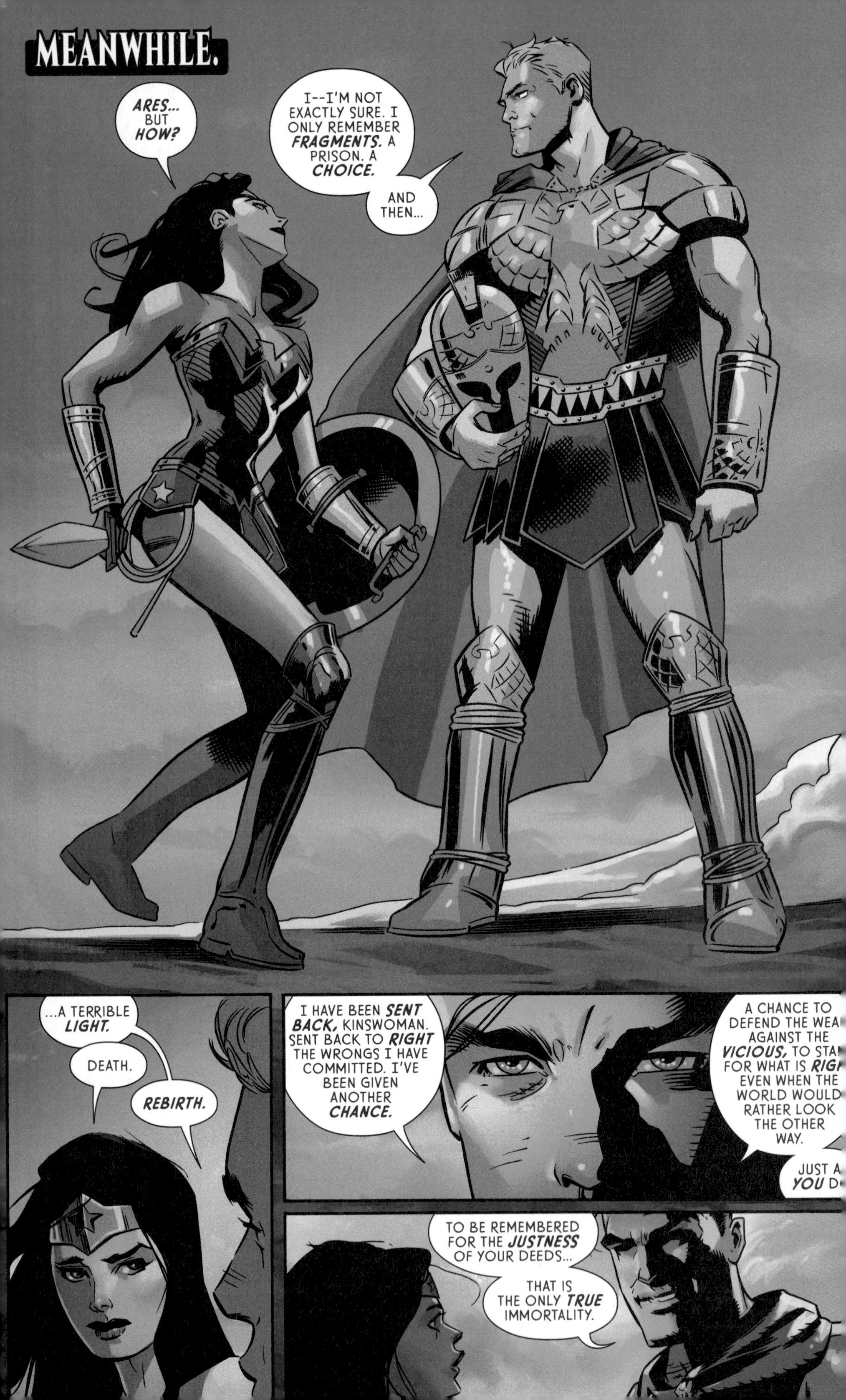
MEANWHILE.
ARES... BUT HOW?
I--I'M NOT EXACTLY SURE. I ONLY REMEMBER FRAGMENTS. A PRISON. A CHOICE.
AND THEN...
...A TERRIBLE LIGHT.
DEATH.
REBIRTH.
I HAVE BEEN SENT BACK, KINSWOMAN. SENT BACK TO RIGHT THE WRONGS I HAVE COMMITTED. I'VE BEEN GIVEN ANOTHER CHANCE.
A CHANCE TO DEFEND THE WEA AGAINST THE VICIOUS, TO STA FOR WHAT IS RIG EVEN WHEN THE WORLD WOULD RATHER LOOK THE OTHER WAY.
JUST A YOU D
TO BE REMEMBERED FOR THE JUSTNESS OF YOUR DEEDS...
THAT IS THE ONLY TRUE IMMORTALITY.

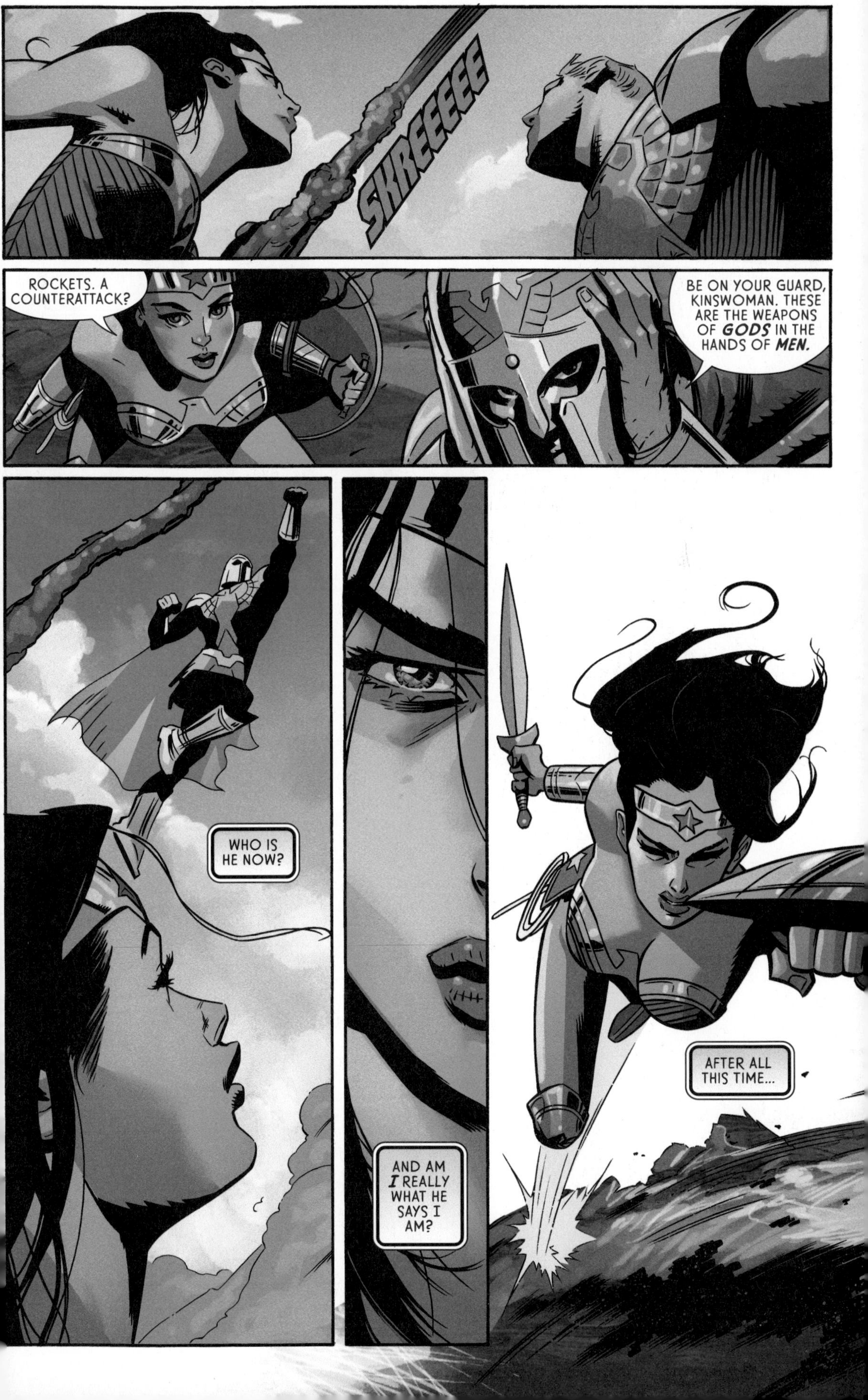
SKREEEEE
ROCKETS. A COUNTERATTACK?
BE ON YOUR GUARD, KINSWOMAN. THESE ARE THE WEAPONS OF GODS IN THE HANDS OF MEN.
WHO IS HE NOW?
AND AM I REALLY WHAT HE SAYS I AM?
AFTER ALL THIS TIME...

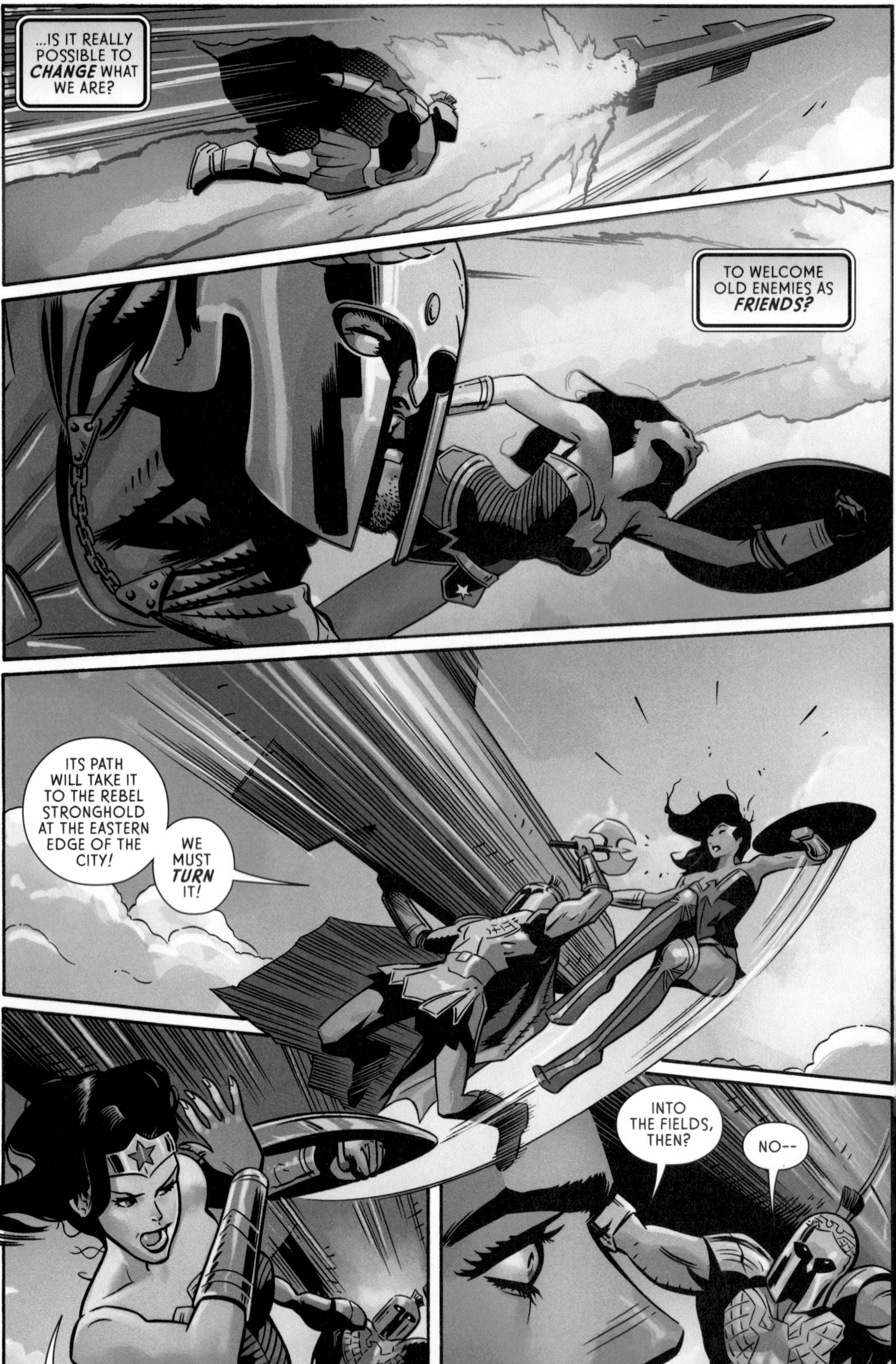
...IS IT REALLY POSSIBLE TO *CHANGE* WHAT WE ARE?
TO WELCOME OLD ENEMIES AS *FRIENDS?*
ITS PATH WILL TAKE IT TO THE REBEL STRONGHOLD AT THE EASTERN EDGE OF THE CITY!
WE MUST *TURN* IT!
HNNGH!
INTO THE FIELDS, THEN?
NO--

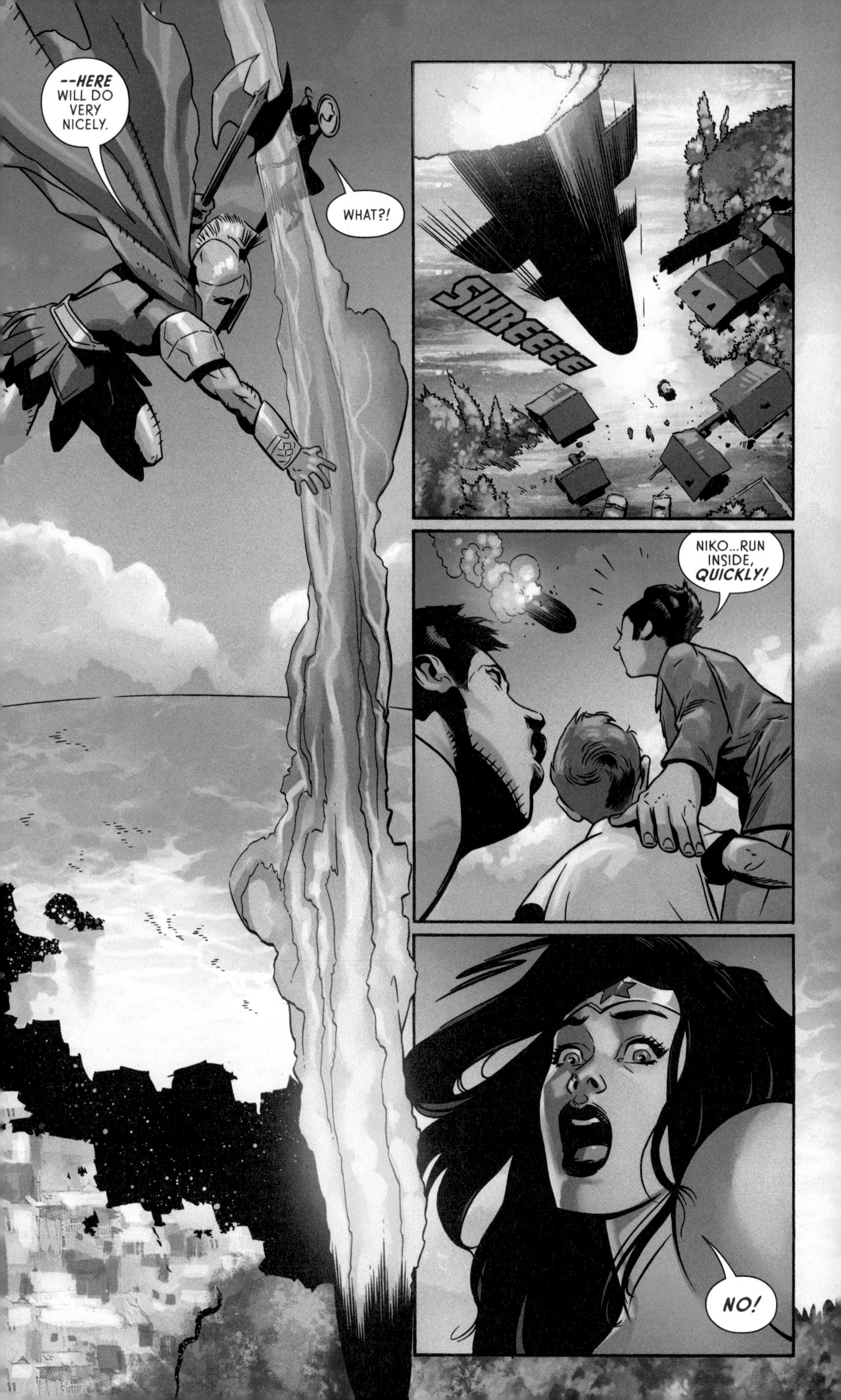
--HERE WILL DO VERY NICELY.
WHAT?!
SKREEEEE
NIKO...RUN INSIDE, QUICKLY!
NO!

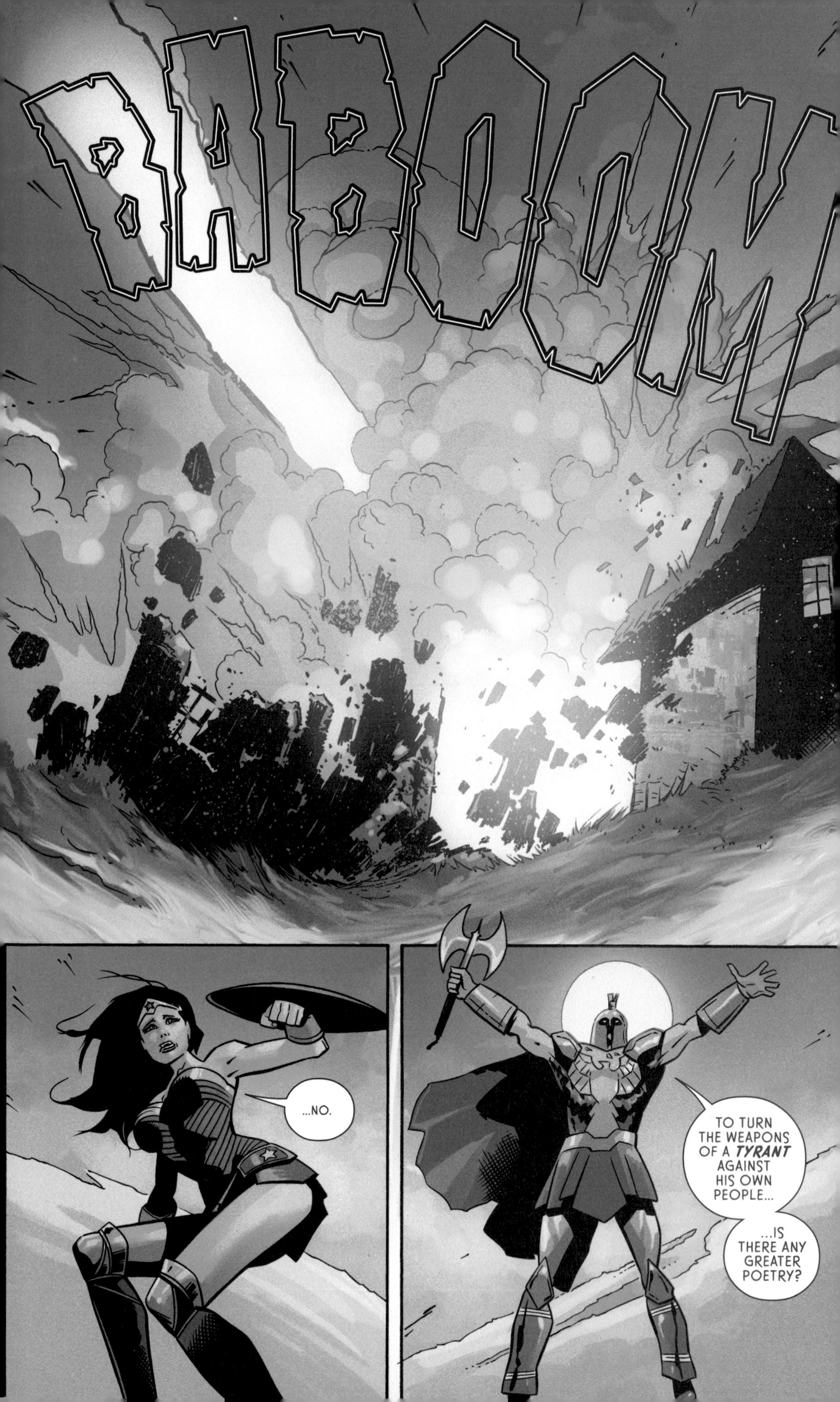
BABOOM
...NO.
TO TURN THE WEAPONS OF A *TYRANT* AGAINST HIS OWN PEOPLE...
...IS THERE ANY GREATER POETRY?

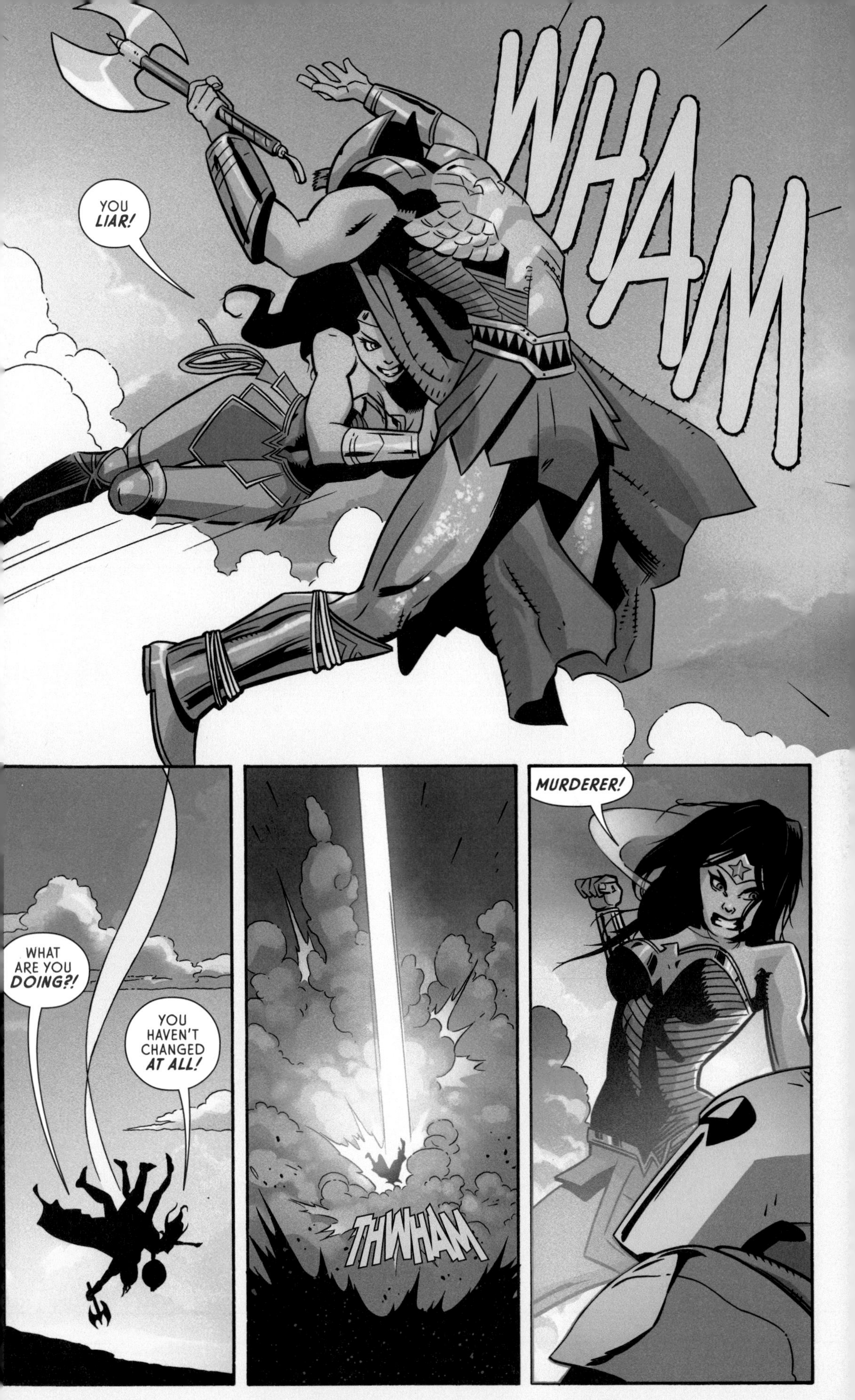

WHAM
YOU LIAR!
WHAT ARE YOU DOING?!
YOU HAVEN'T CHANGED AT ALL!
THWHAM
MURDERER!

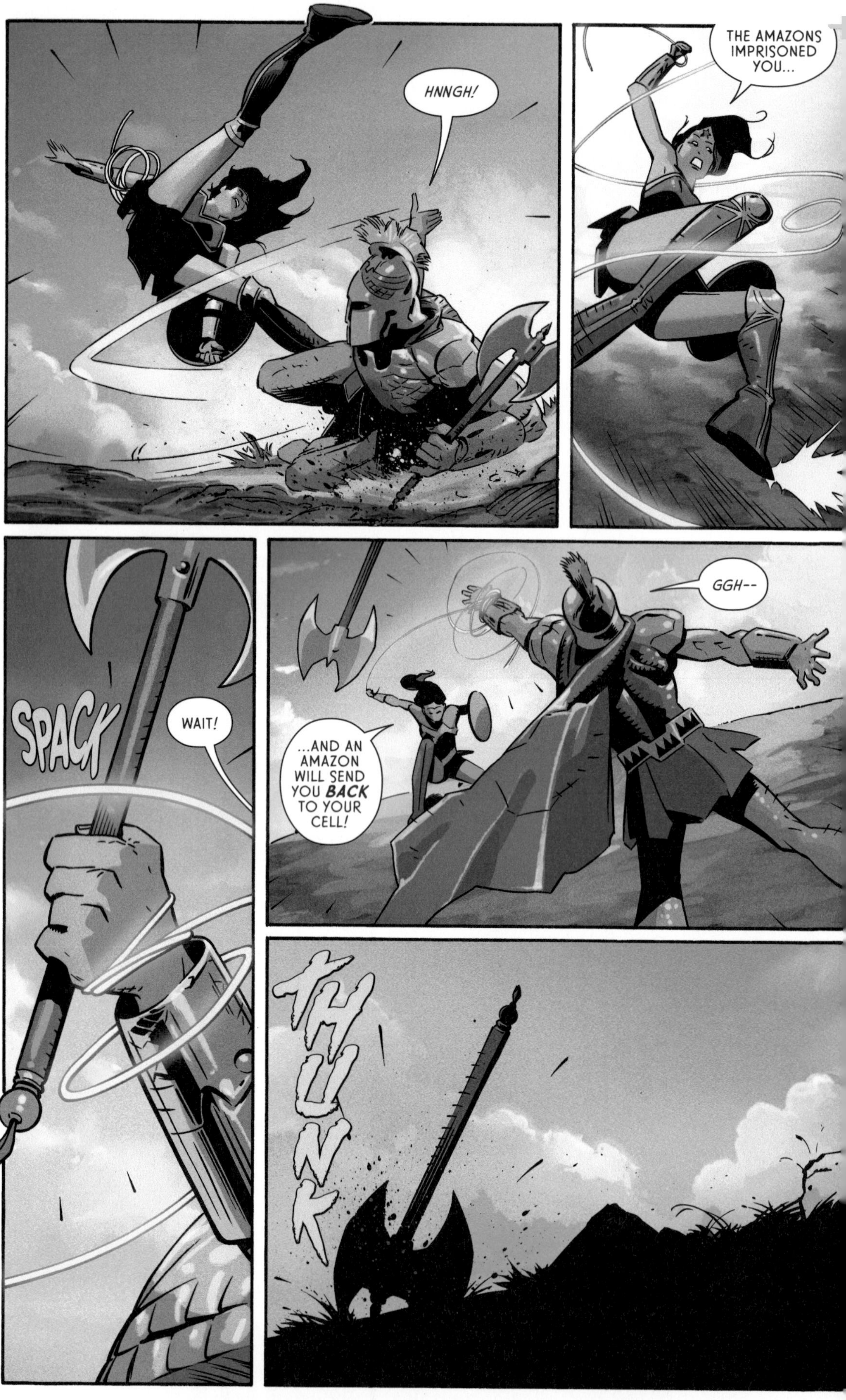
HNNGH!
THE AMAZONS IMPRISONED YOU...
SPACK
WAIT!
GGH--
...AND AN AMAZON WILL SEND YOU BACK TO YOUR CELL!
THUNK

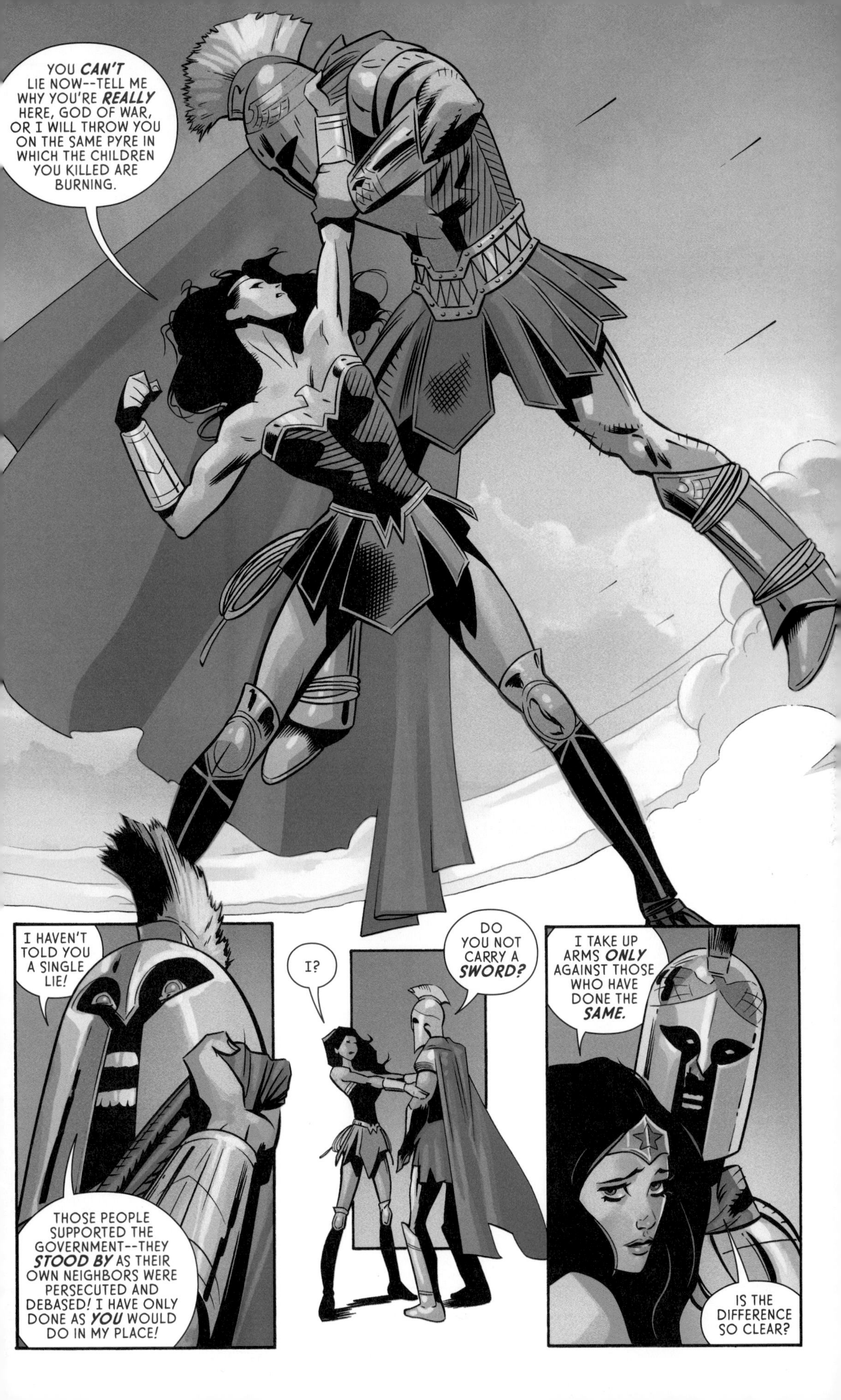
YOU CAN'T LIE NOW--TELL ME WHY YOU'RE REALLY HERE, GOD OF WAR, OR I WILL THROW YOU ON THE SAME PYRE IN WHICH THE CHILDREN YOU KILLED ARE BURNING.
I HAVEN'T TOLD YOU A SINGLE LIE!
THOSE PEOPLE SUPPORTED THE GOVERNMENT--THEY STOOD BY AS THEIR OWN NEIGHBORS WERE PERSECUTED AND DEBASED! I HAVE ONLY DONE AS YOU WOULD DO IN MY PLACE!
I?
DO YOU NOT CARRY A SWORD?
I TAKE UP ARMS ONLY AGAINST THOSE WHO HAVE DONE THE SAME.
IS THE DIFFERENCE SO CLEAR?

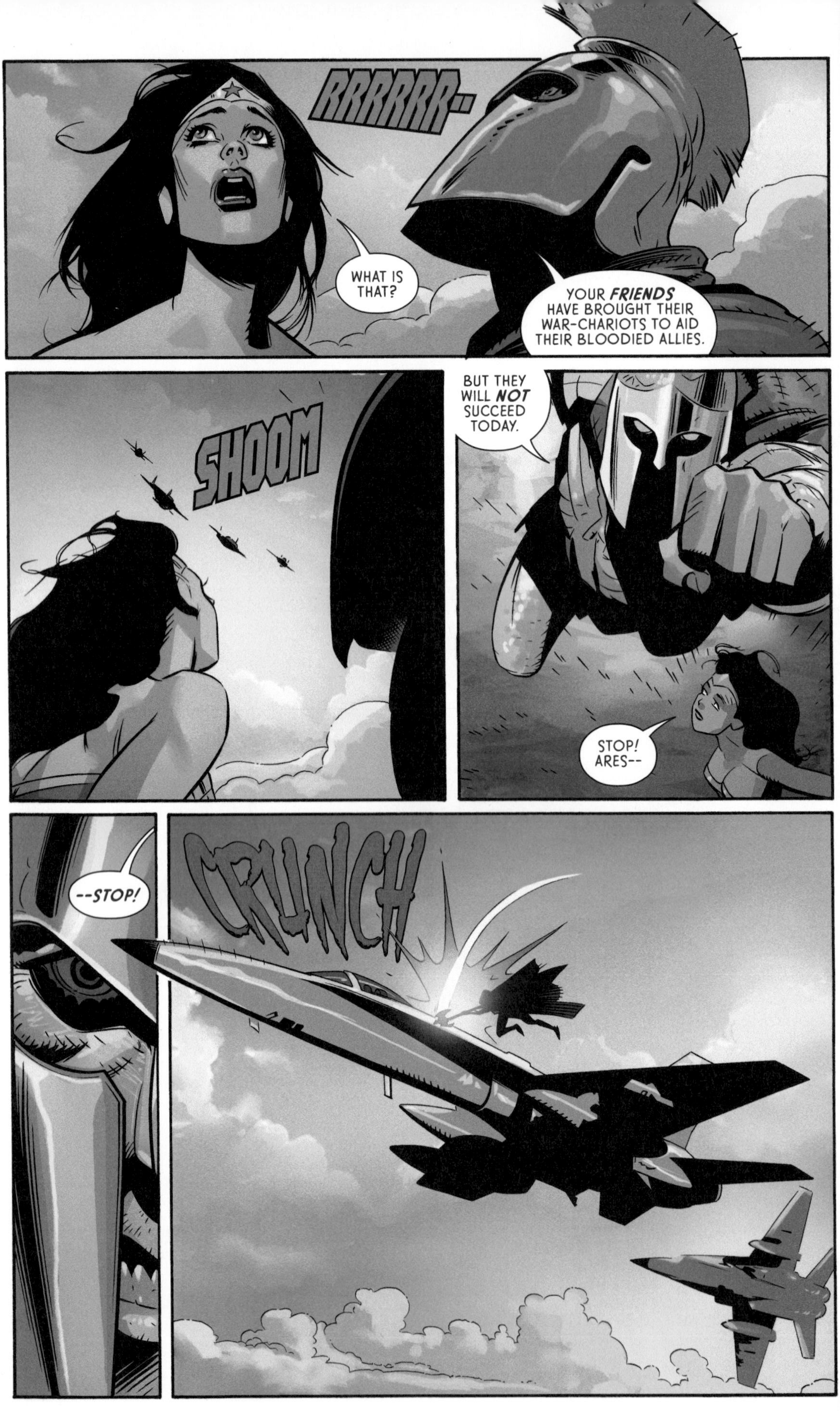
RRRRRR--
WHAT IS THAT?
YOUR FRIENDS HAVE BROUGHT THEIR WAR-CHARIOTS TO AID THEIR BLOODIED ALLIES.
SHOOM
BUT THEY WILL NOT SUCCEED TODAY.
STOP! ARES--
--STOP!
CRUNCH

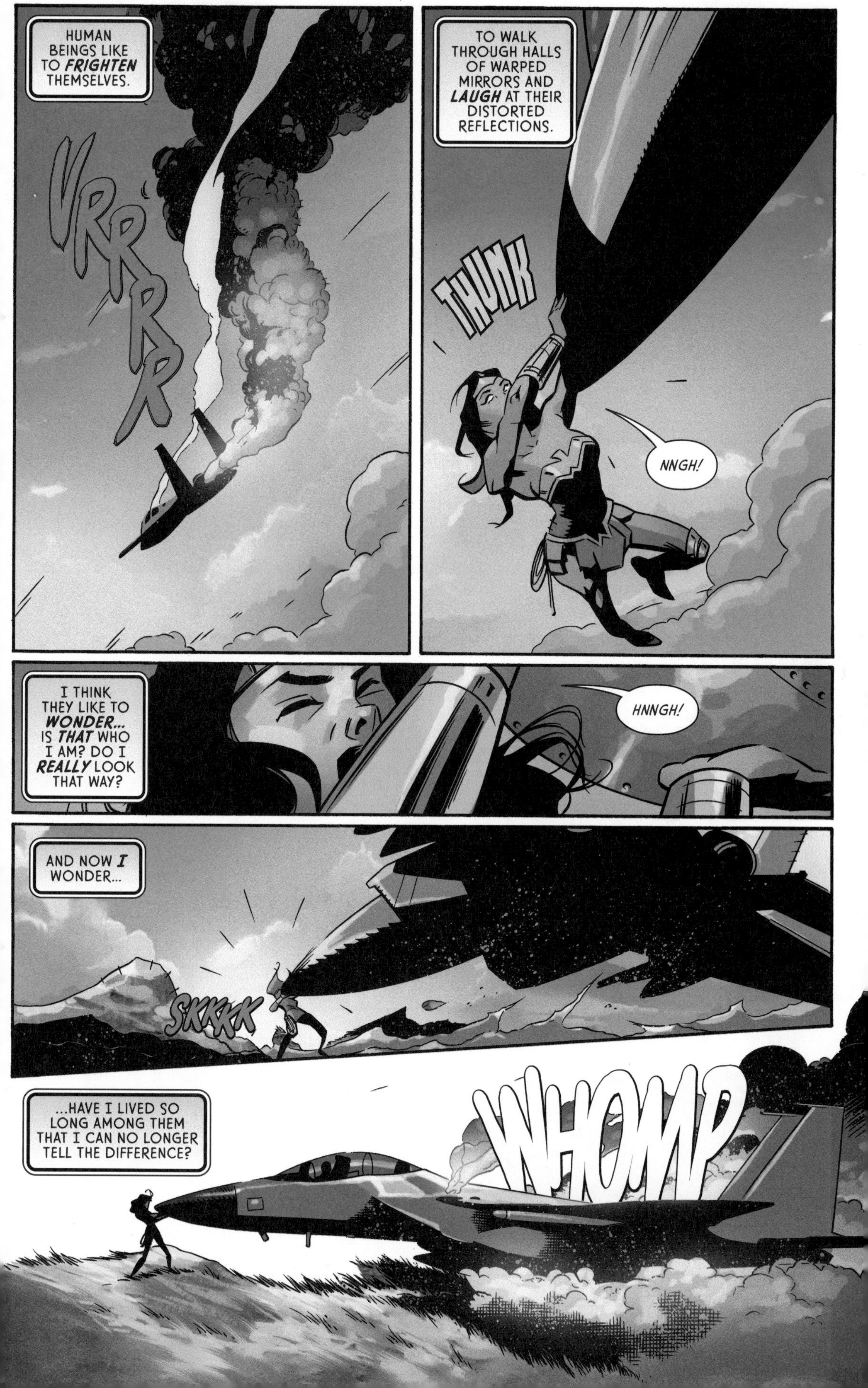
HUMAN BEINGS LIKE TO FRIGHTEN THEMSELVES.
VRRRRR
TO WALK THROUGH HALLS OF WARPED MIRRORS AND LAUGH AT THEIR DISTORTED REFLECTIONS.
THUNK
NNGH!
I THINK THEY LIKE TO WONDER... IS THAT WHO I AM? DO I REALLY LOOK THAT WAY?
HNNGH!
AND NOW I WONDER...
SKKKK
...HAVE I LIVED SO LONG AMONG THEM THAT I CAN NO LONGER TELL THE DIFFERENCE?
WHOMP

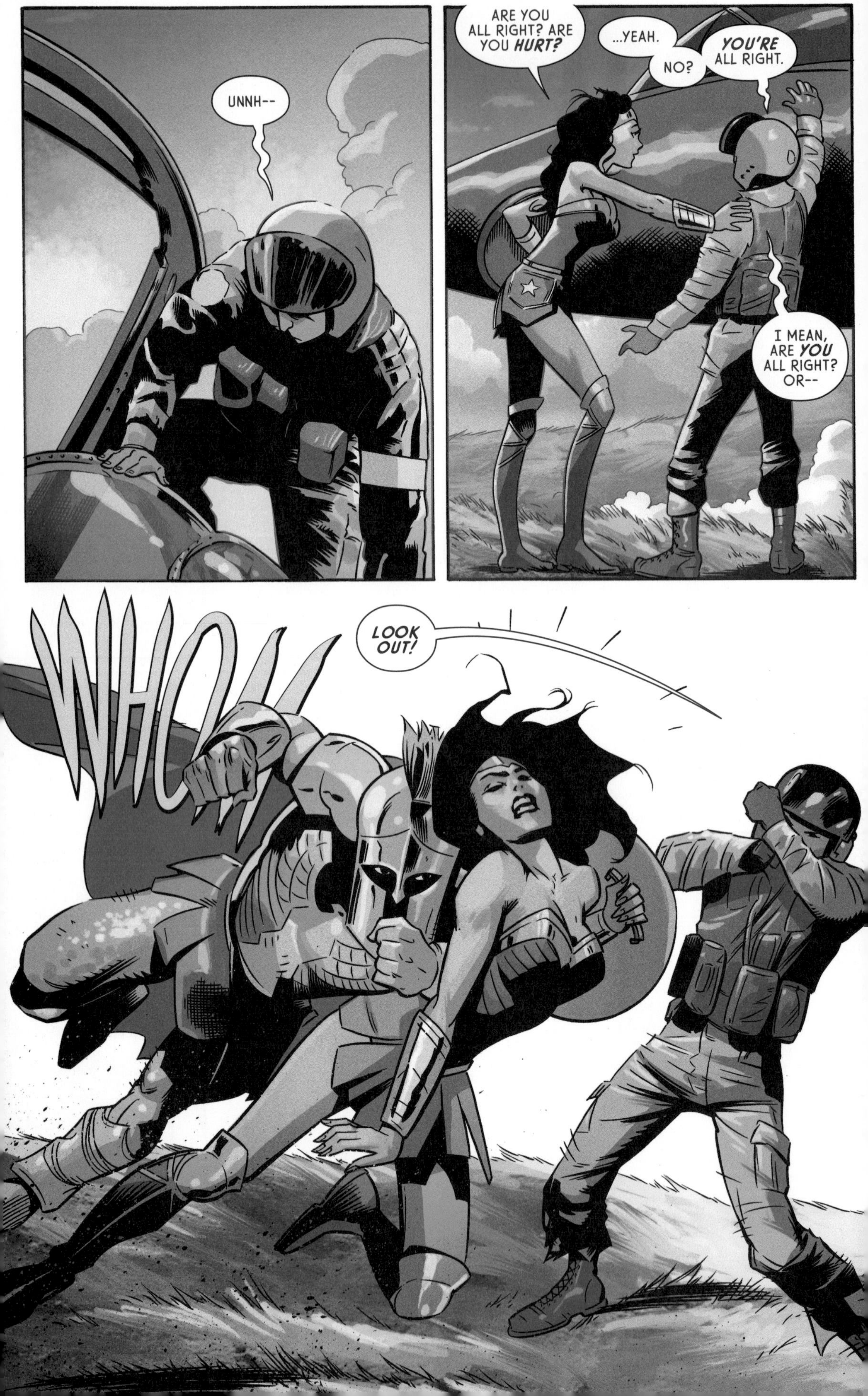
UNNH--
ARE YOU ALL RIGHT? ARE YOU HURT?
...YEAH.
NO?
YOU'RE ALL RIGHT.
I MEAN, ARE YOU ALL RIGHT? OR--
WHOOM
LOOK OUT!

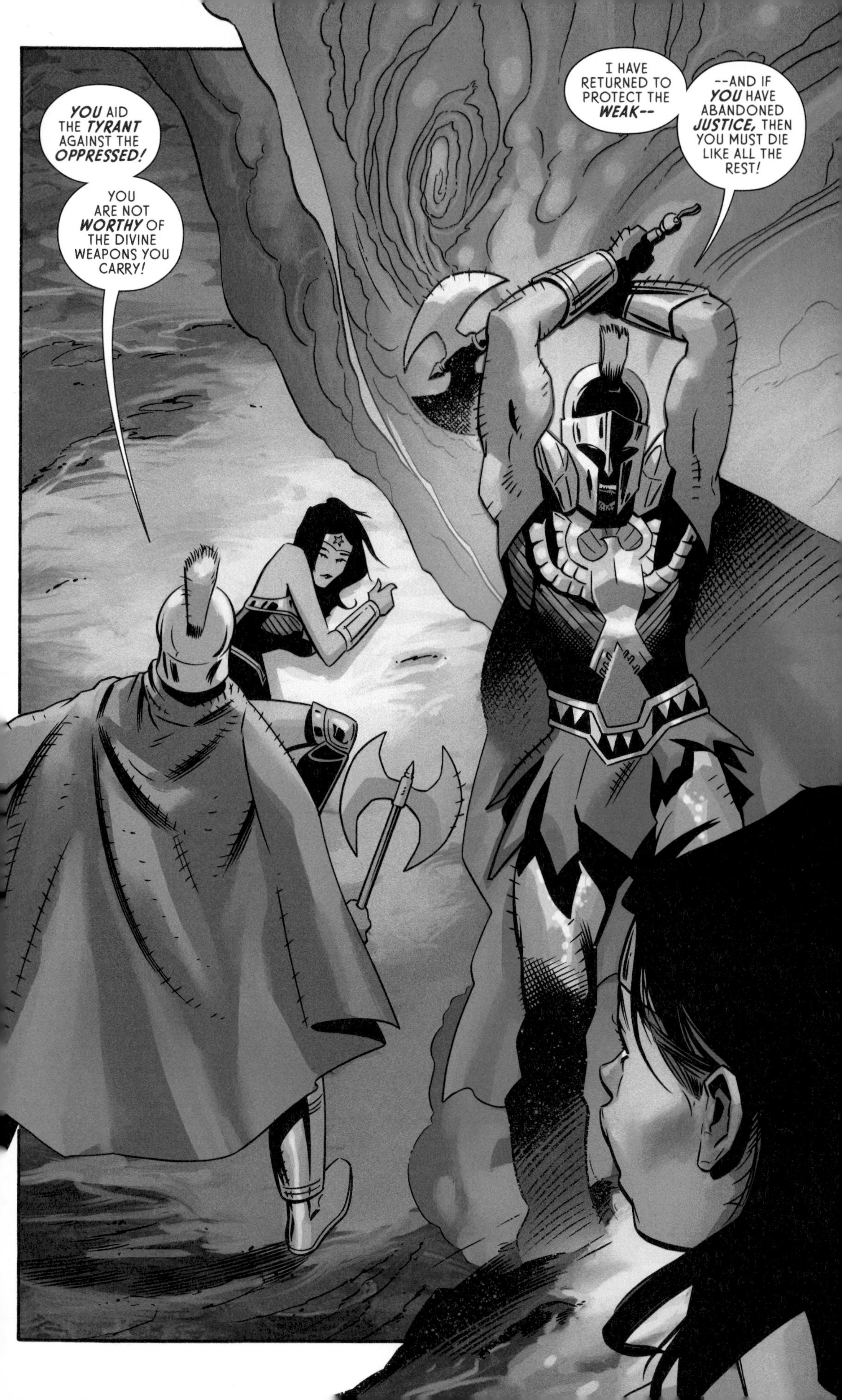
YOU AID THE TYRANT AGAINST THE OPPRESSED!
YOU ARE NOT WORTHY OF THE DIVINE WEAPONS YOU CARRY!
I HAVE RETURNED TO PROTECT THE WEAK--
--AND IF YOU HAVE ABANDONED JUSTICE, THEN YOU MUST DIE LIKE ALL THE REST!

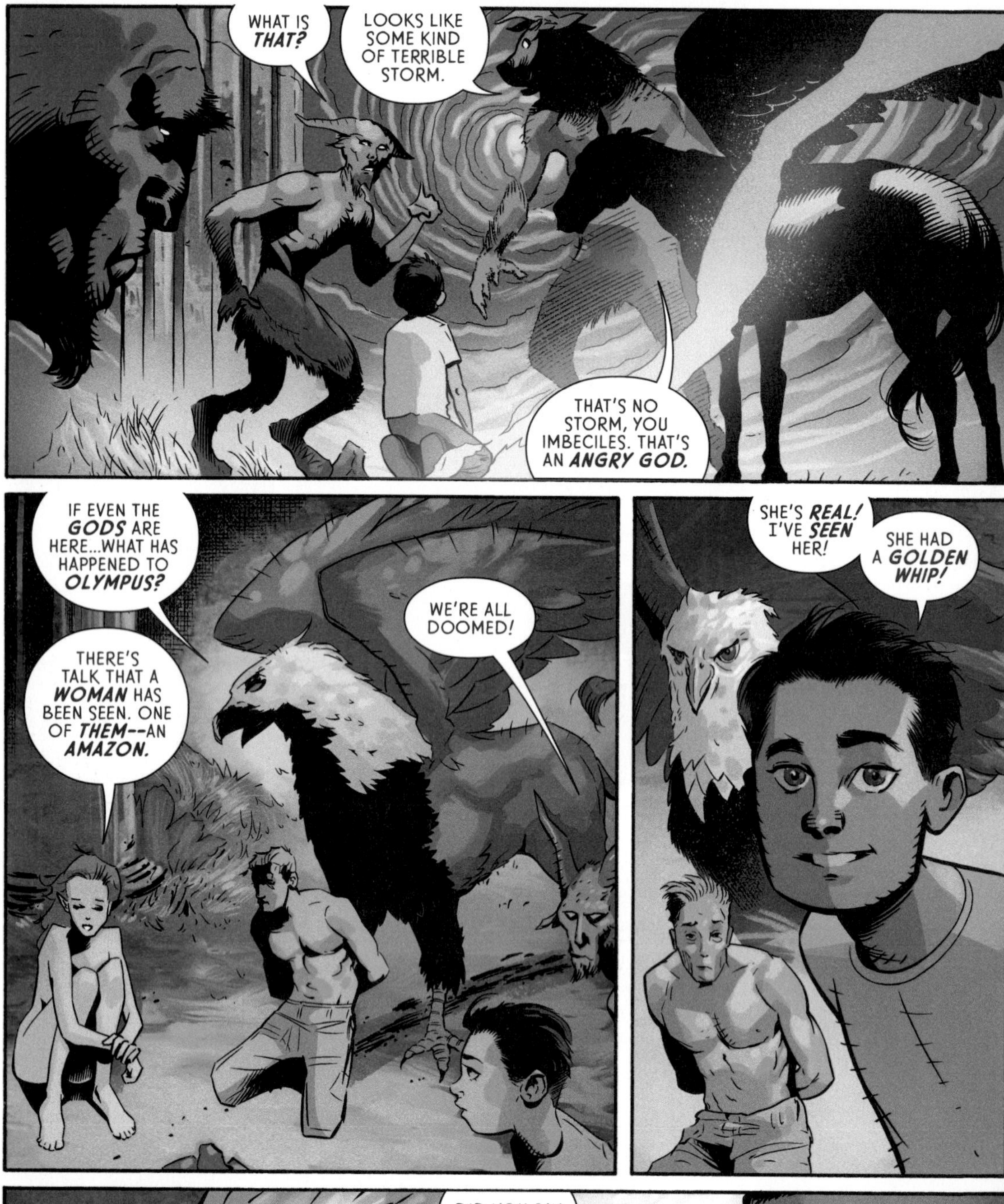
WHAT IS THAT?
LOOKS LIKE SOME KIND OF TERRIBLE STORM.
THAT'S NO STORM, YOU IMBECILES. THAT'S AN ANGRY GOD.
IF EVEN THE GODS ARE HERE...WHAT HAS HAPPENED TO OLYMPUS?
THERE'S TALK THAT A WOMAN HAS BEEN SEEN. ONE OF THEM--AN AMAZON.
WE'RE ALL DOOMED!
SHE'S REAL! I'VE SEEN HER!
SHE HAD A GOLDEN WHIP!
DID YOU SAY A GOLDEN WHIP?
DID SHE HAVE DARK HAIR, BLUE EYES--ABOUT MY HEIGHT?
SILENCE, BEAKLESS IDIOT.

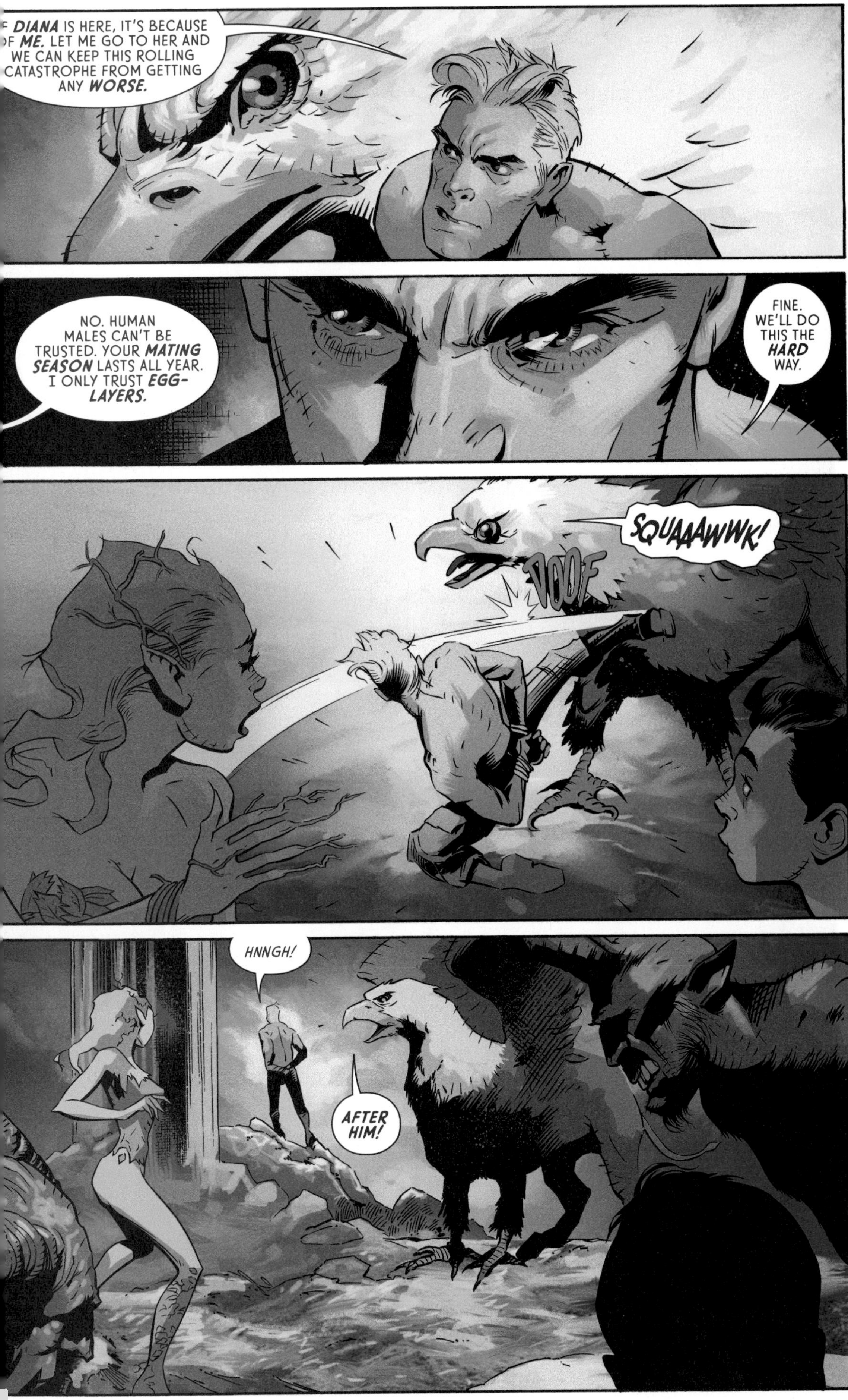
IF DIANA IS HERE, IT'S BECAUSE OF ME. LET ME GO TO HER AND WE CAN KEEP THIS ROLLING CATASTROPHE FROM GETTING ANY WORSE.
NO. HUMAN MALES CAN'T BE TRUSTED. YOUR MATING SEASON LASTS ALL YEAR. I ONLY TRUST EGG-LAYERS.
FINE. WE'LL DO THIS THE HARD WAY.
SQUAAAWWK!
DOOF
HNNGH!
AFTER HIM!

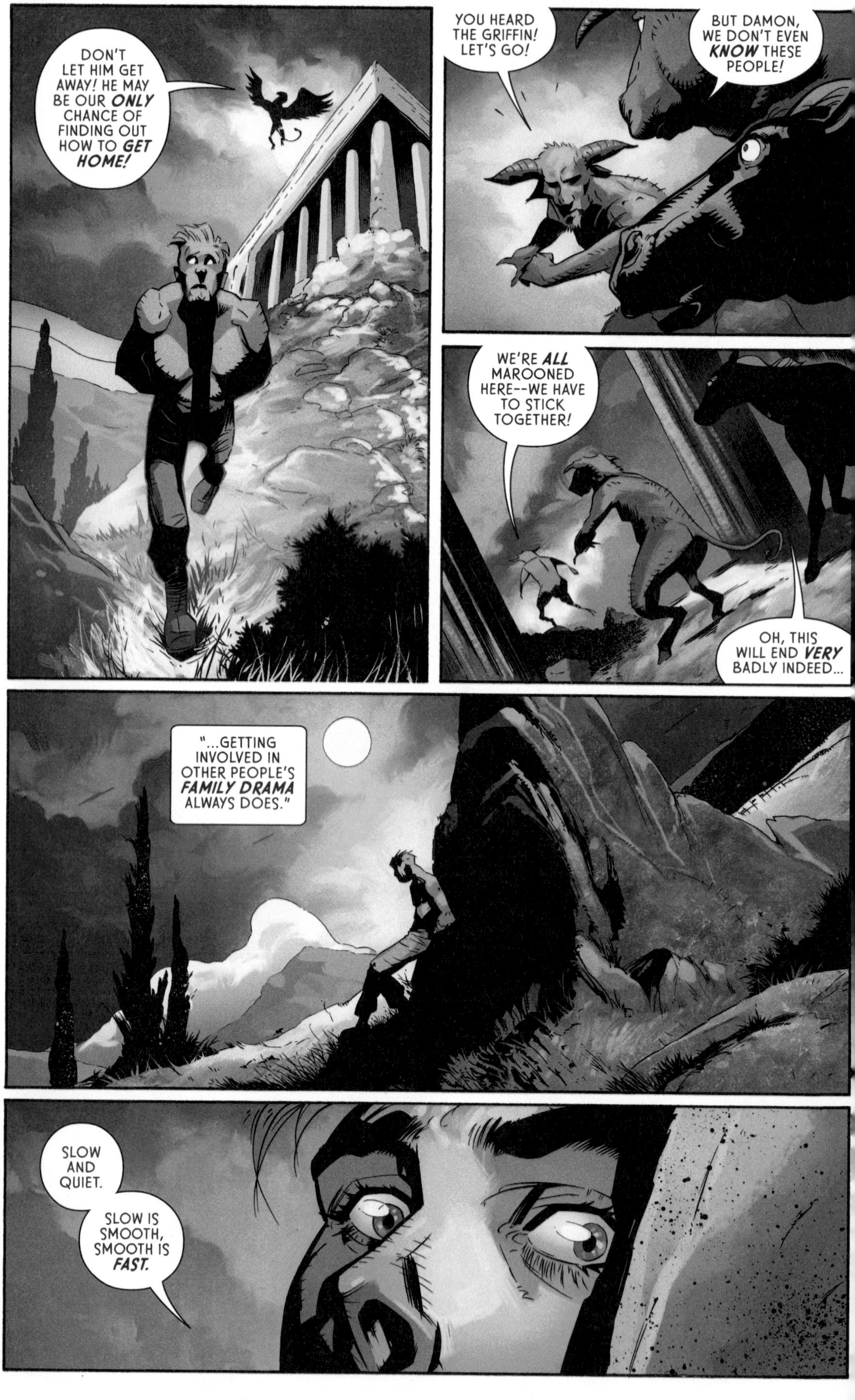
DON'T LET HIM GET AWAY! HE MAY BE OUR ONLY CHANCE OF FINDING OUT HOW TO GET HOME!
YOU HEARD THE GRIFFIN! LET'S GO!
BUT DAMON, WE DON'T EVEN KNOW THESE PEOPLE!
WE'RE ALL MAROONED HERE--WE HAVE TO STICK TOGETHER!
OH, THIS WILL END VERY BADLY INDEED...
"...GETTING INVOLVED IN OTHER PEOPLE'S FAMILY DRAMA ALWAYS DOES."
SLOW AND QUIET.
SLOW IS SMOOTH, SMOOTH IS FAST.

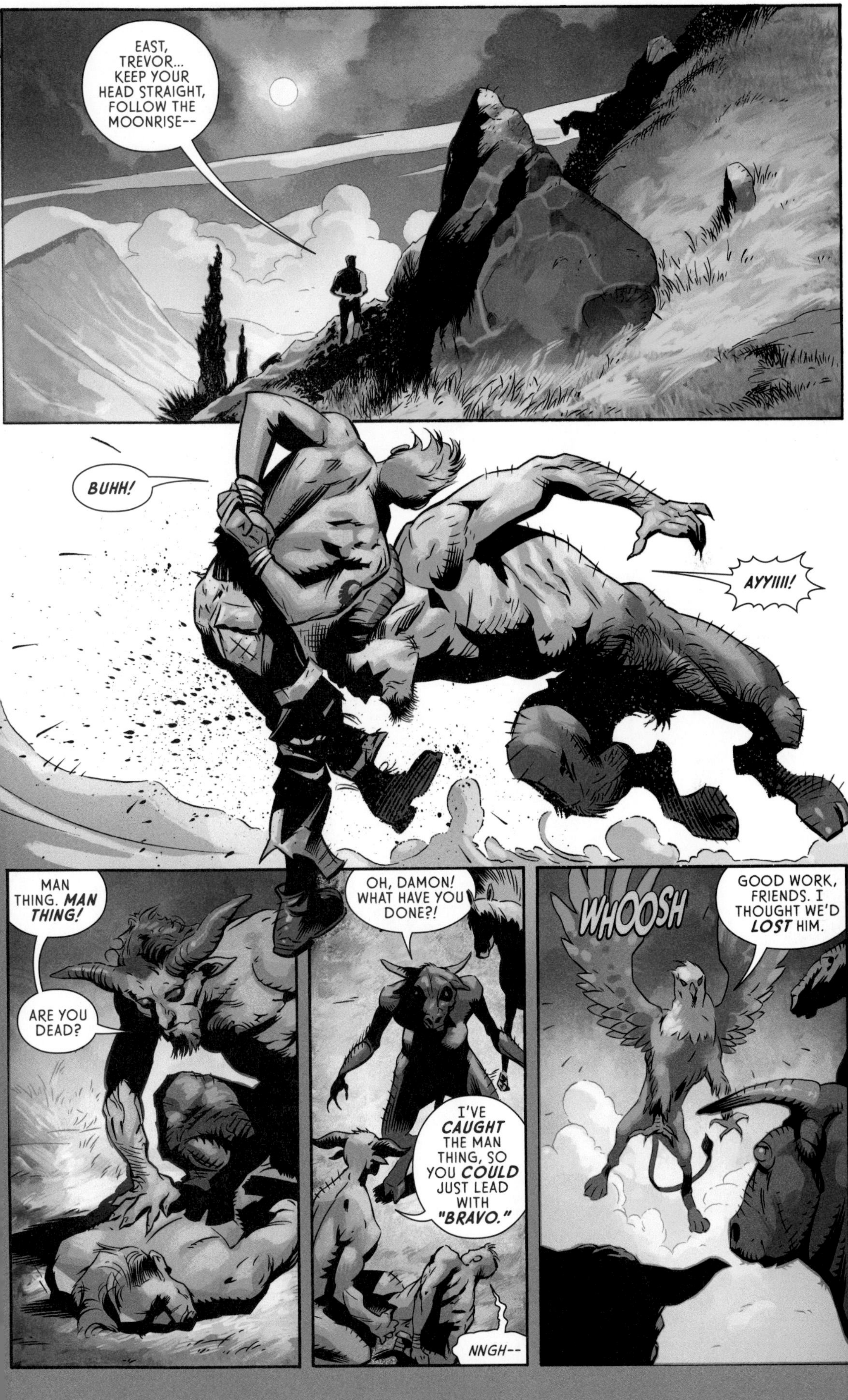
EAST, TREVOR... KEEP YOUR HEAD STRAIGHT, FOLLOW THE MOONRISE--
BUHH!
AYYIIII!
MAN THING. MAN THING!
ARE YOU DEAD?
OH, DAMON! WHAT HAVE YOU DONE?!
I'VE CAUGHT THE MAN THING, SO YOU COULD JUST LEAD WITH "BRAVO."
NNGH--
WHOOSH
GOOD WORK, FRIENDS. I THOUGHT WE'D LOST HIM.

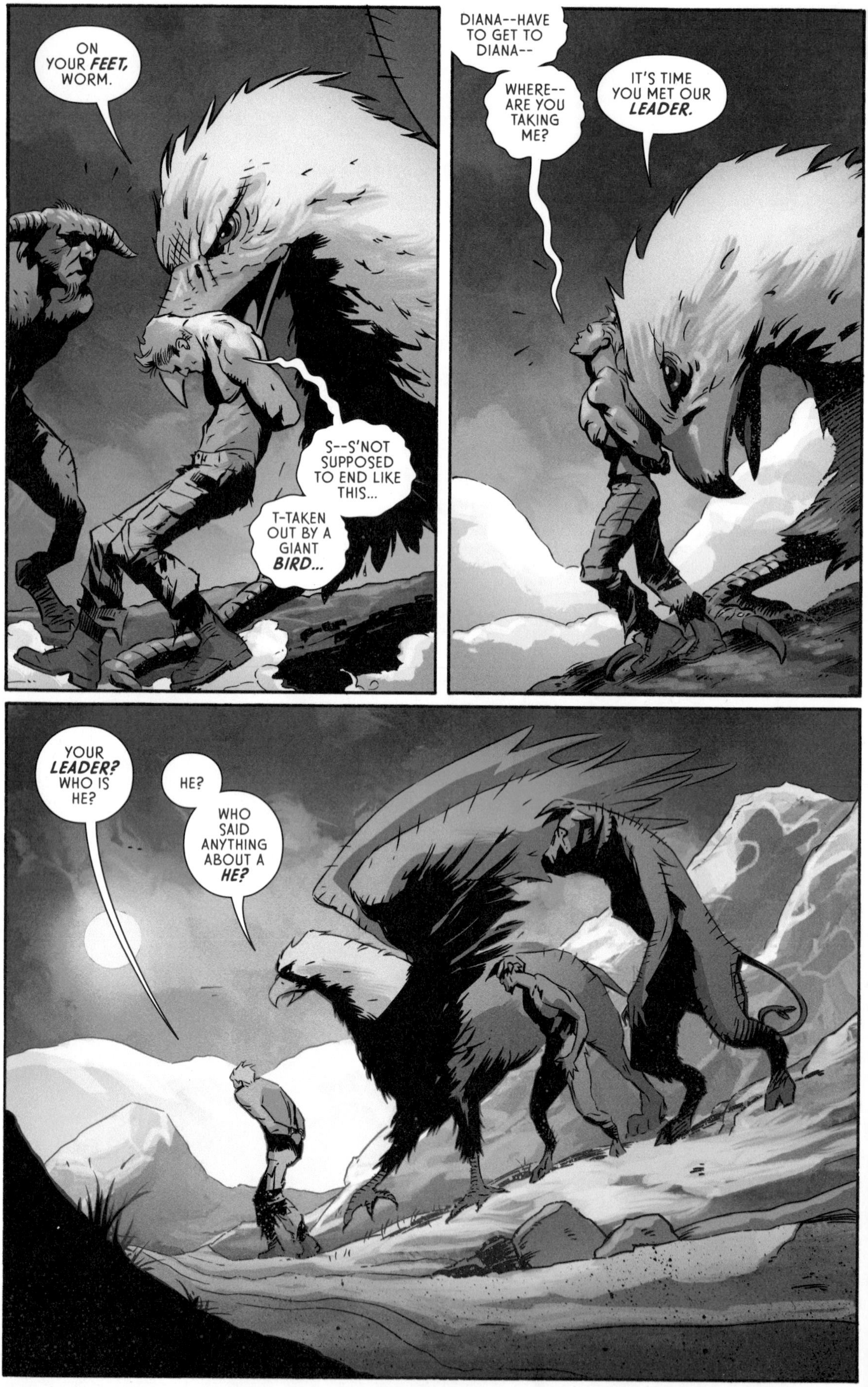

ON YOUR ***FEET,*** WORM.
S--S'NOT SUPPOSED TO END LIKE THIS...
T-TAKEN OUT BY A GIANT ***BIRD...***
DIANA--HAVE TO GET TO DIANA--
WHERE-- ARE YOU TAKING ME?
IT'S TIME YOU MET OUR ***LEADER.***
YOUR ***LEADER?*** WHO IS HE?
HE?
WHO SAID ANYTHING ABOUT A ***HE?***

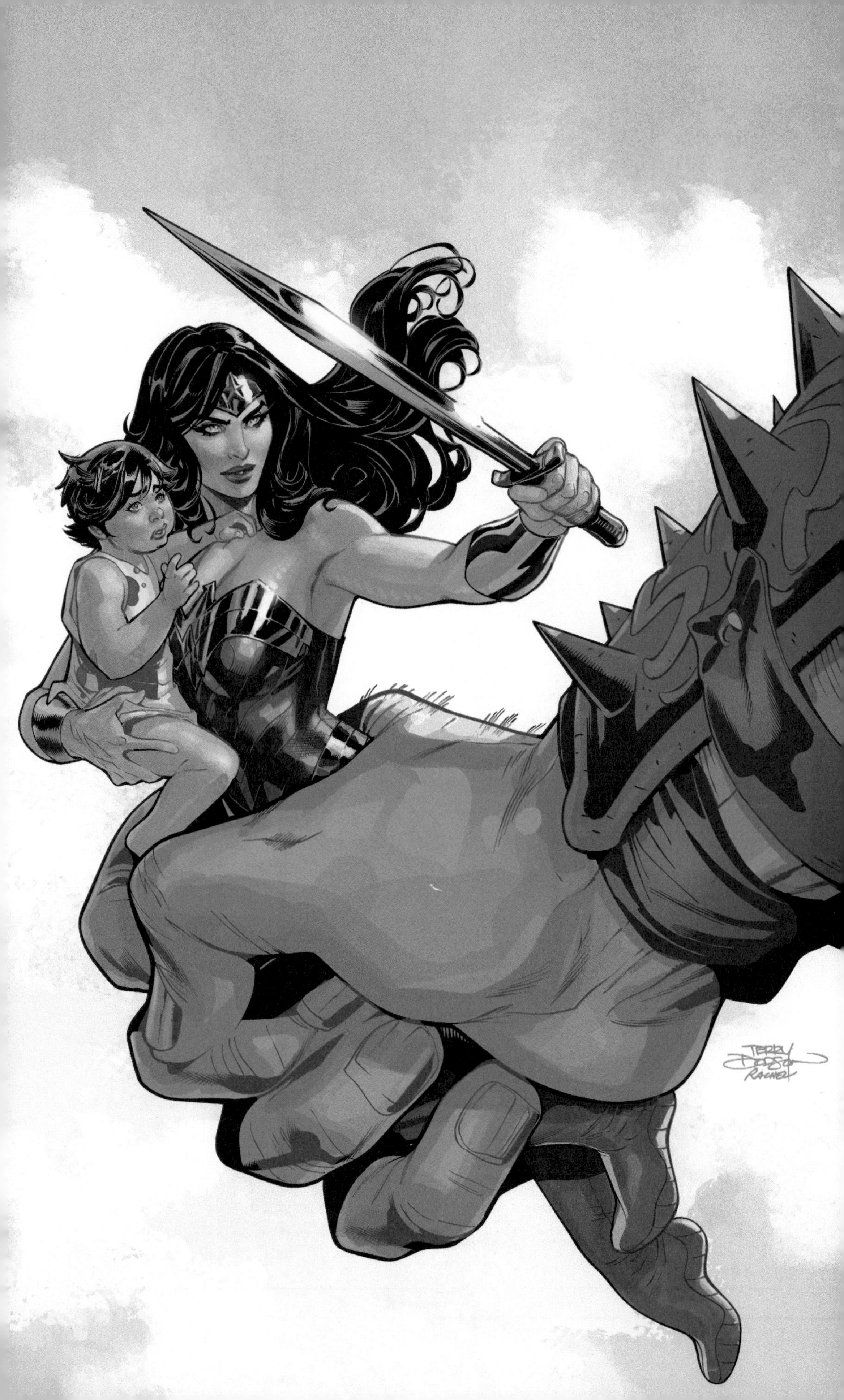
TERRY DODSON RACHEL

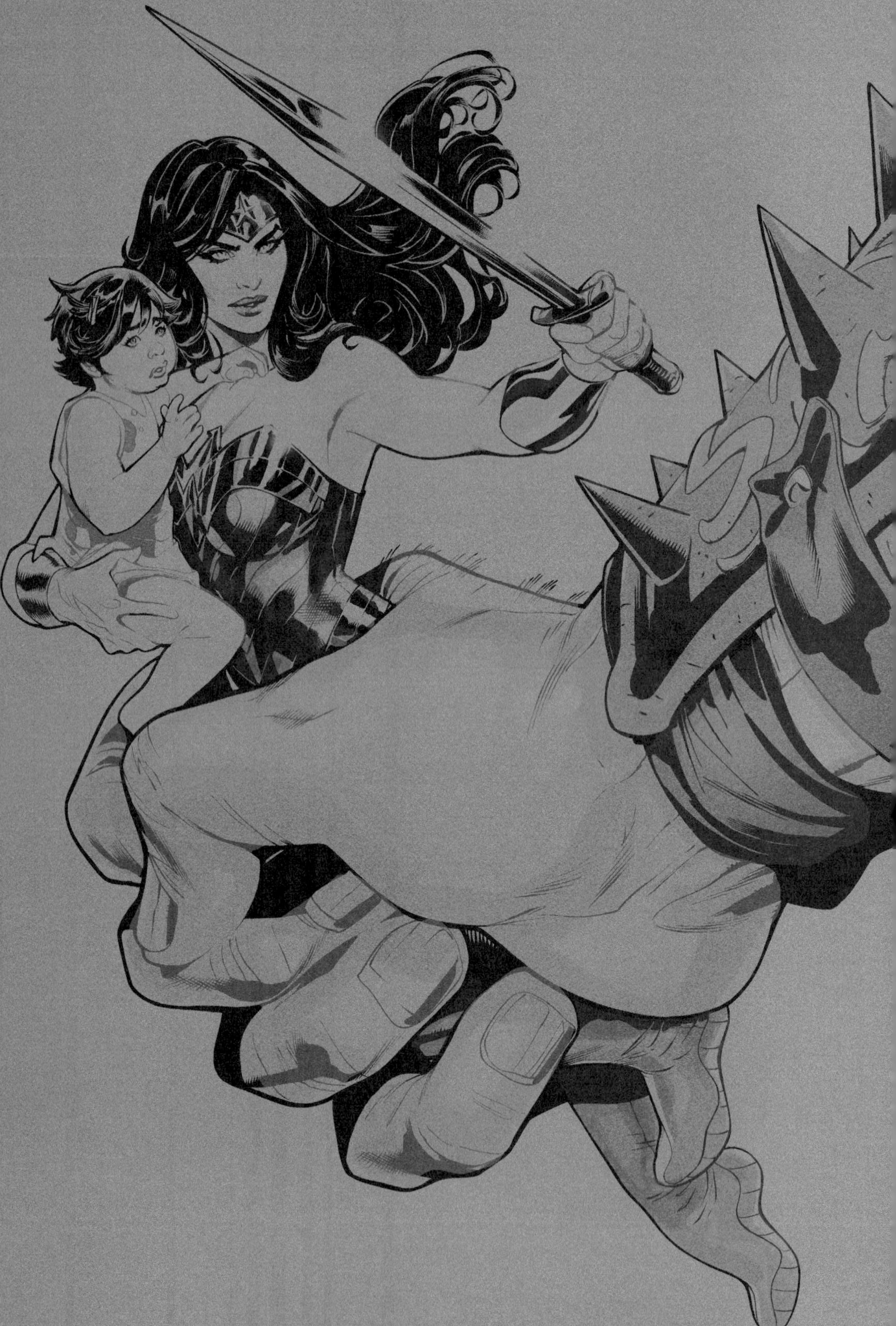

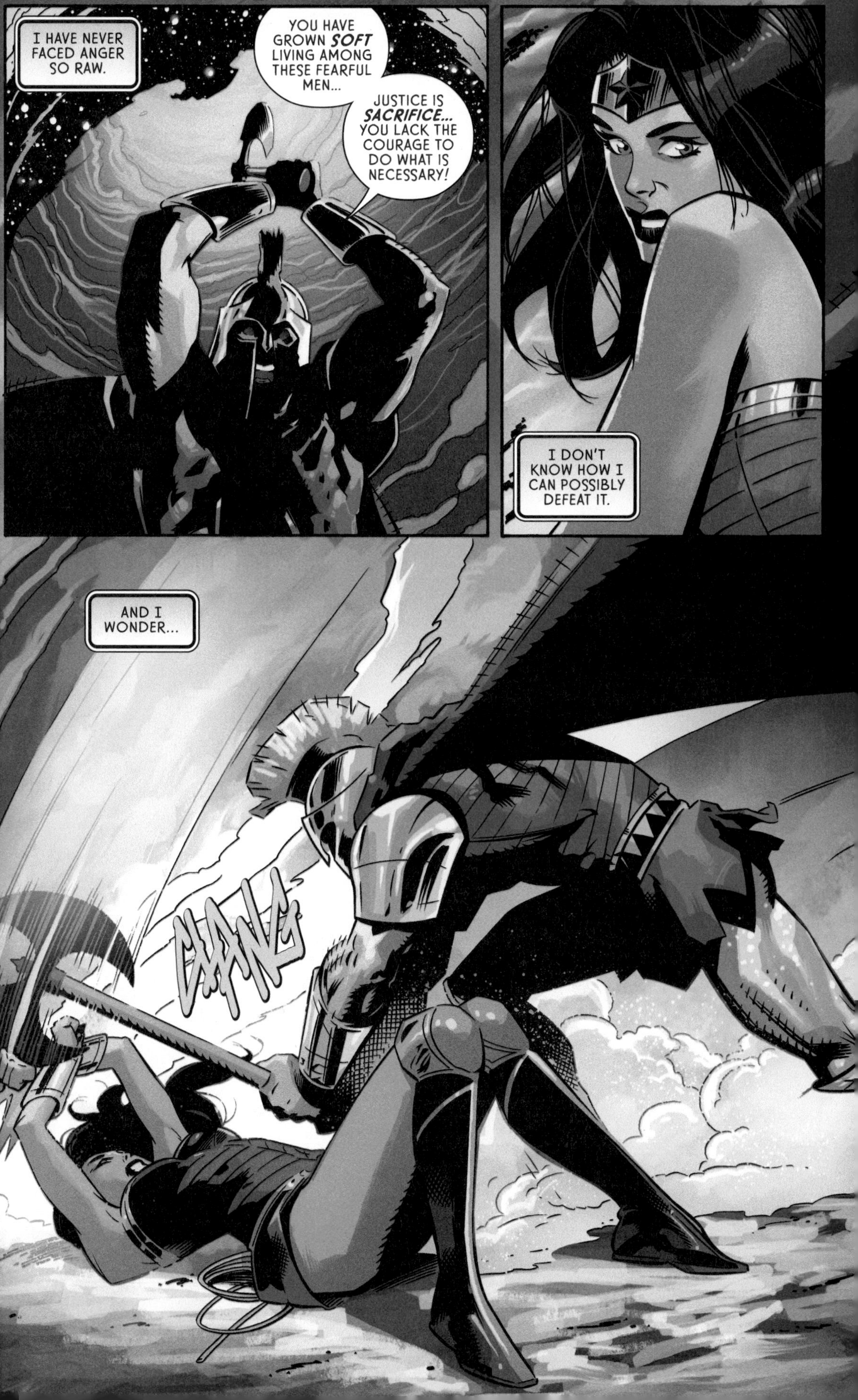
I HAVE NEVER FACED ANGER SO RAW.
YOU HAVE GROWN **SOFT** LIVING AMONG THESE FEARFUL MEN...
JUSTICE IS **SACRIFICE...** YOU LACK THE COURAGE TO DO WHAT IS NECESSARY!
I DON'T KNOW HOW I CAN POSSIBLY DEFEAT IT.
AND I WONDER...
CLANG

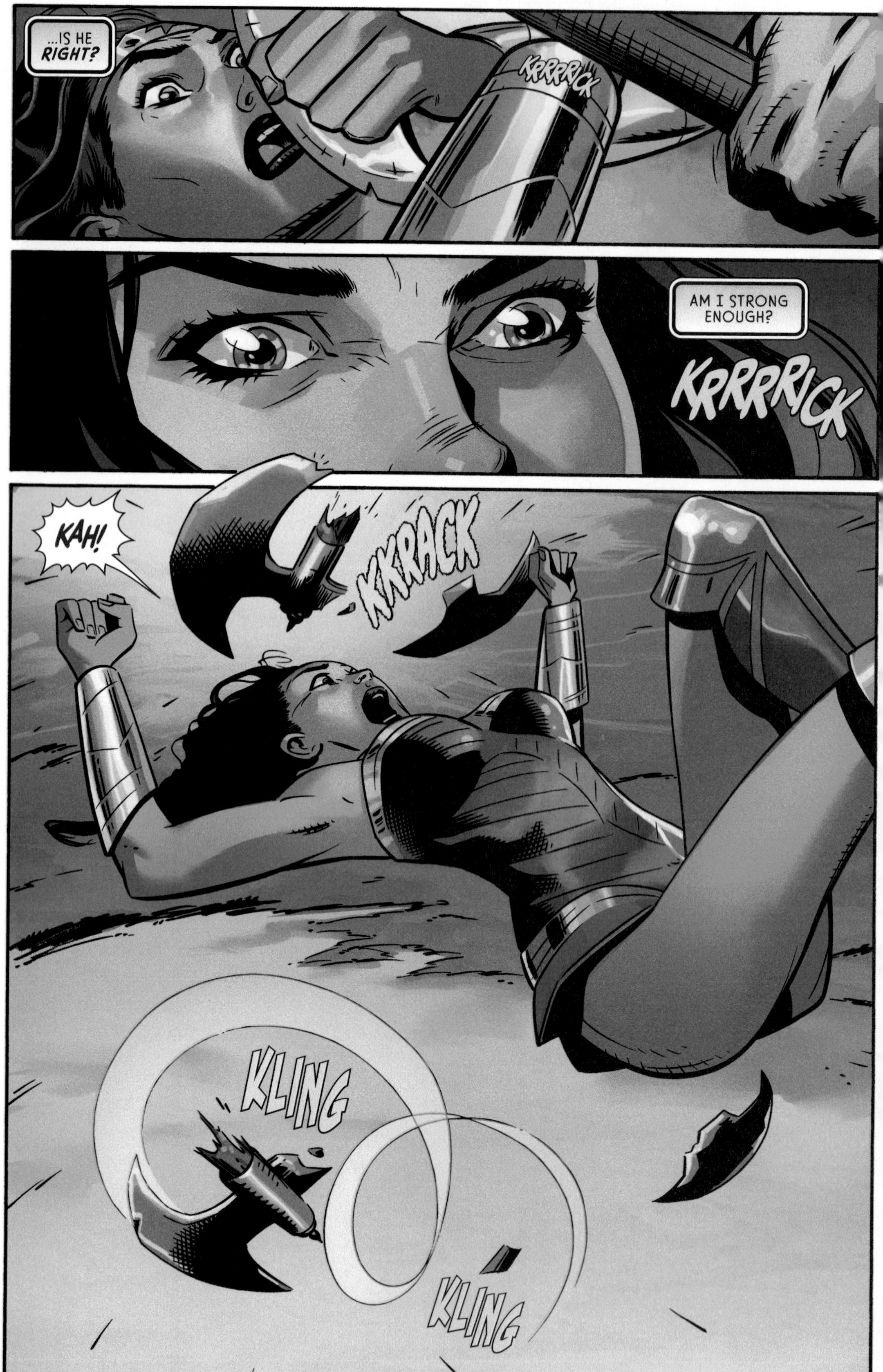
...IS HE RIGHT?
KRRRRICK
AM I STRONG ENOUGH?
KRRRRICK
KAH!
KKRACK
KLING
KLING

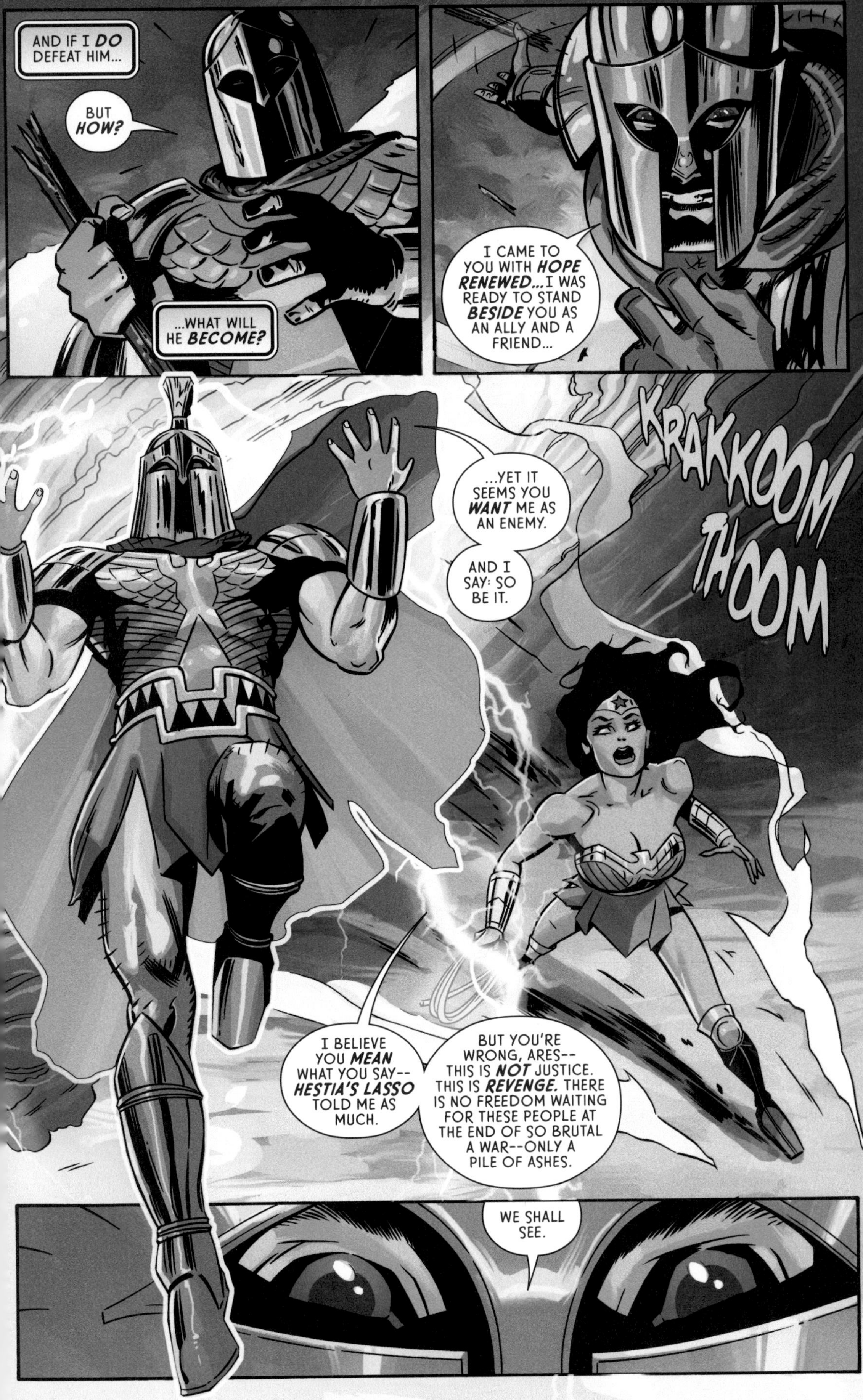
AND IF I DO DEFEAT HIM...
BUT HOW?
...WHAT WILL HE BECOME?
I CAME TO YOU WITH HOPE RENEWED...I WAS READY TO STAND BESIDE YOU AS AN ALLY AND A FRIEND...
KRAKKOOM THOOM
...YET IT SEEMS YOU WANT ME AS AN ENEMY.
AND I SAY: SO BE IT.
I BELIEVE YOU MEAN WHAT YOU SAY-- HESTIA'S LASSO TOLD ME AS MUCH.
BUT YOU'RE WRONG, ARES-- THIS IS NOT JUSTICE. THIS IS REVENGE. THERE IS NO FREEDOM WAITING FOR THESE PEOPLE AT THE END OF SO BRUTAL A WAR--ONLY A PILE OF ASHES.
WE SHALL SEE.

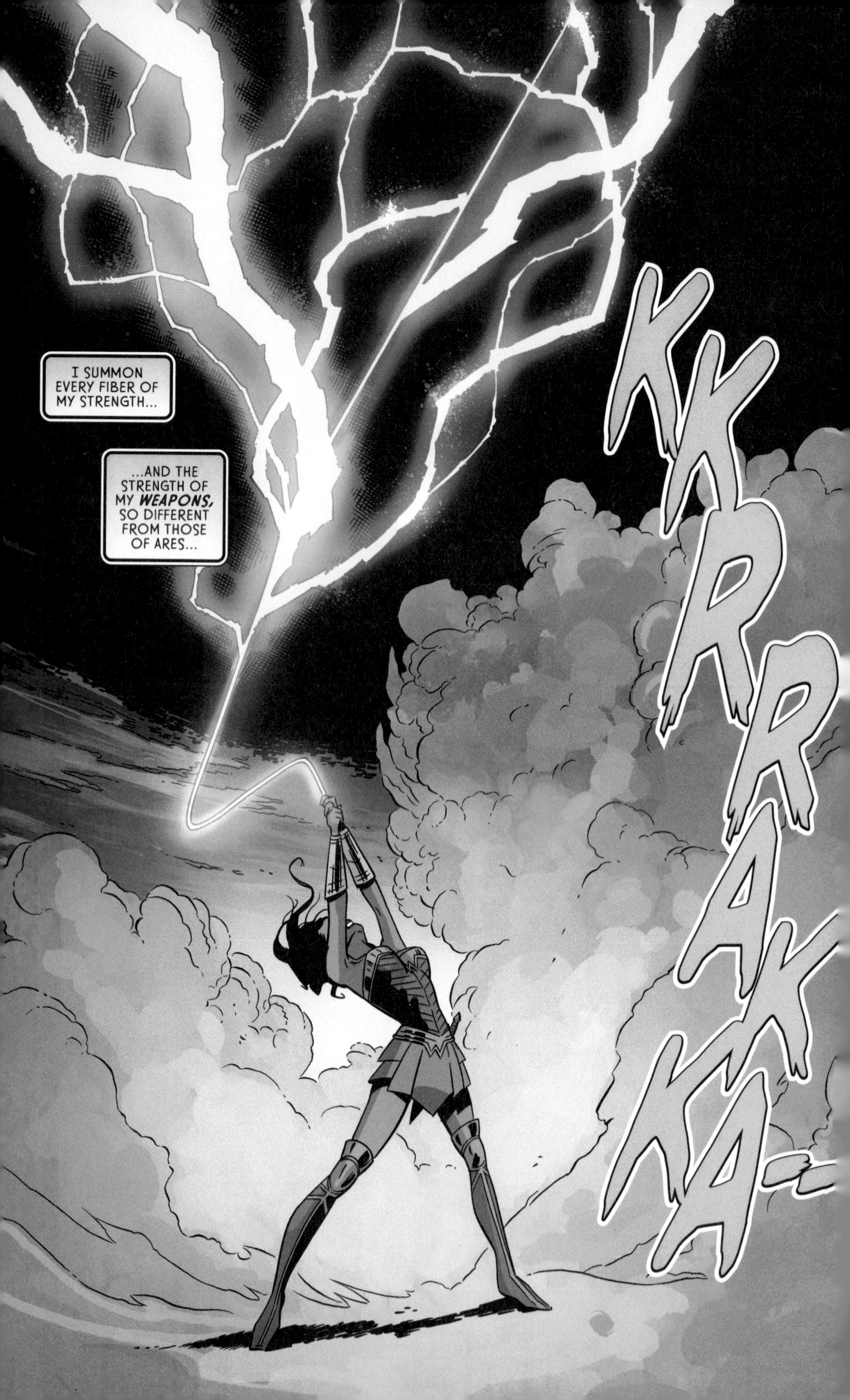
I SUMMON EVERY FIBER OF MY STRENGTH...
...AND THE STRENGTH OF MY *WEAPONS,* SO DIFFERENT FROM THOSE OF ARES...
KKRRAKKA--

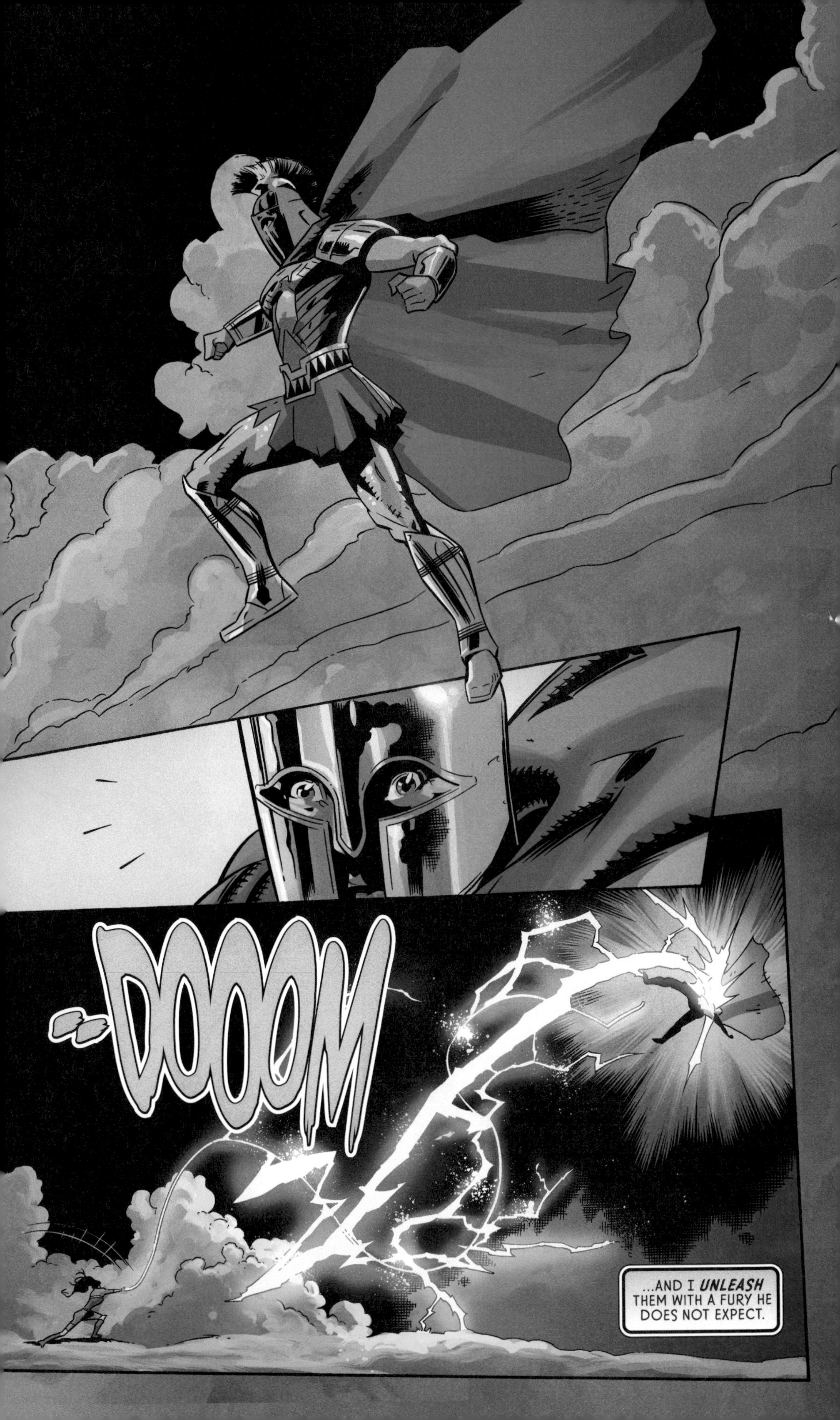

--DOOOM
...AND I UNLEASH THEM WITH A FURY HE DOES NOT EXPECT.

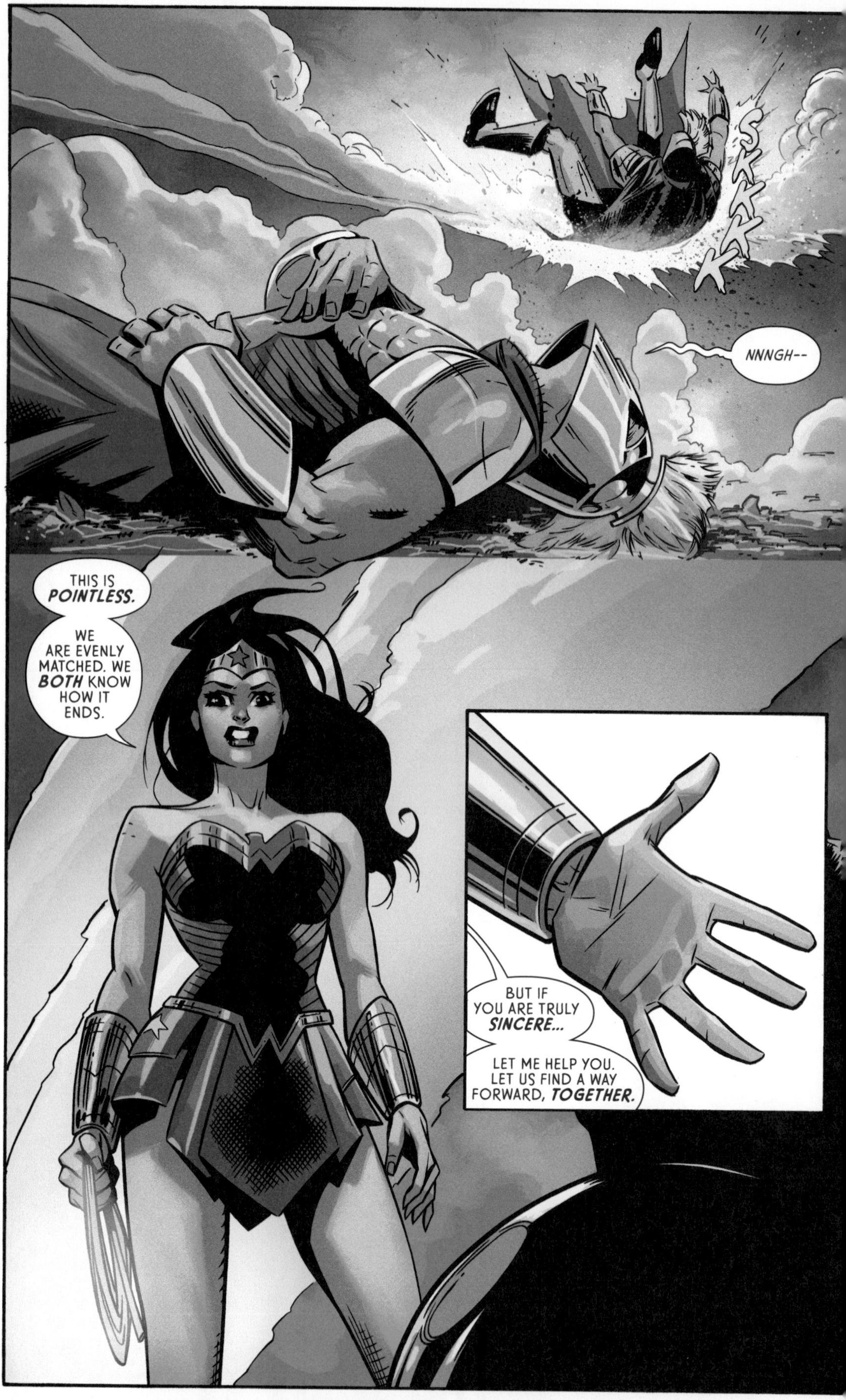
SKKKK
NNNGH--
THIS IS POINTLESS.
WE ARE EVENLY MATCHED. WE BOTH KNOW HOW IT ENDS.
BUT IF YOU ARE TRULY SINCERE...
LET ME HELP YOU. LET US FIND A WAY FORWARD, TOGETHER.

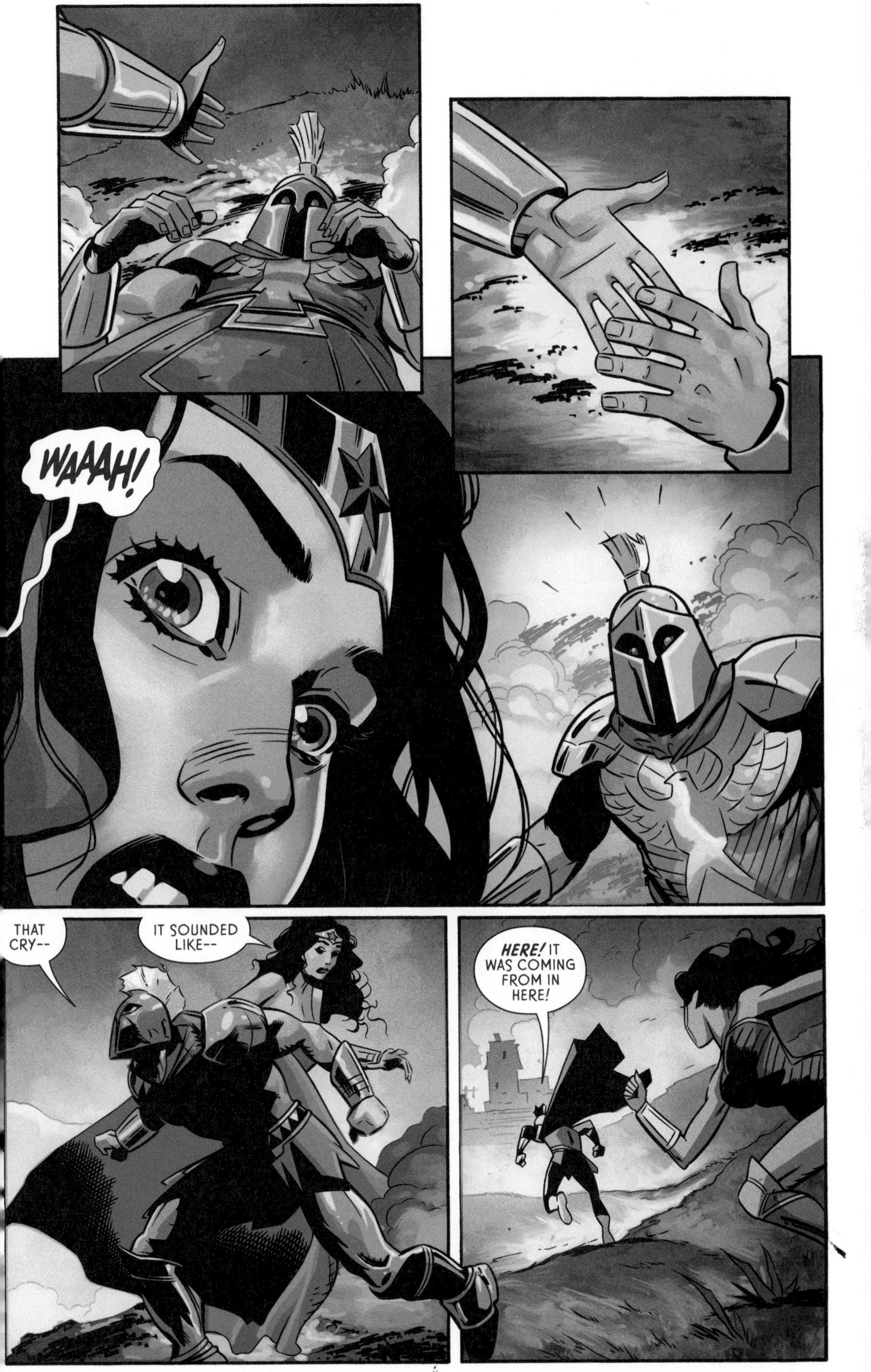
WAAAH!
THAT CRY--
IT SOUNDED LIKE--
HERE! IT WAS COMING FROM IN HERE!

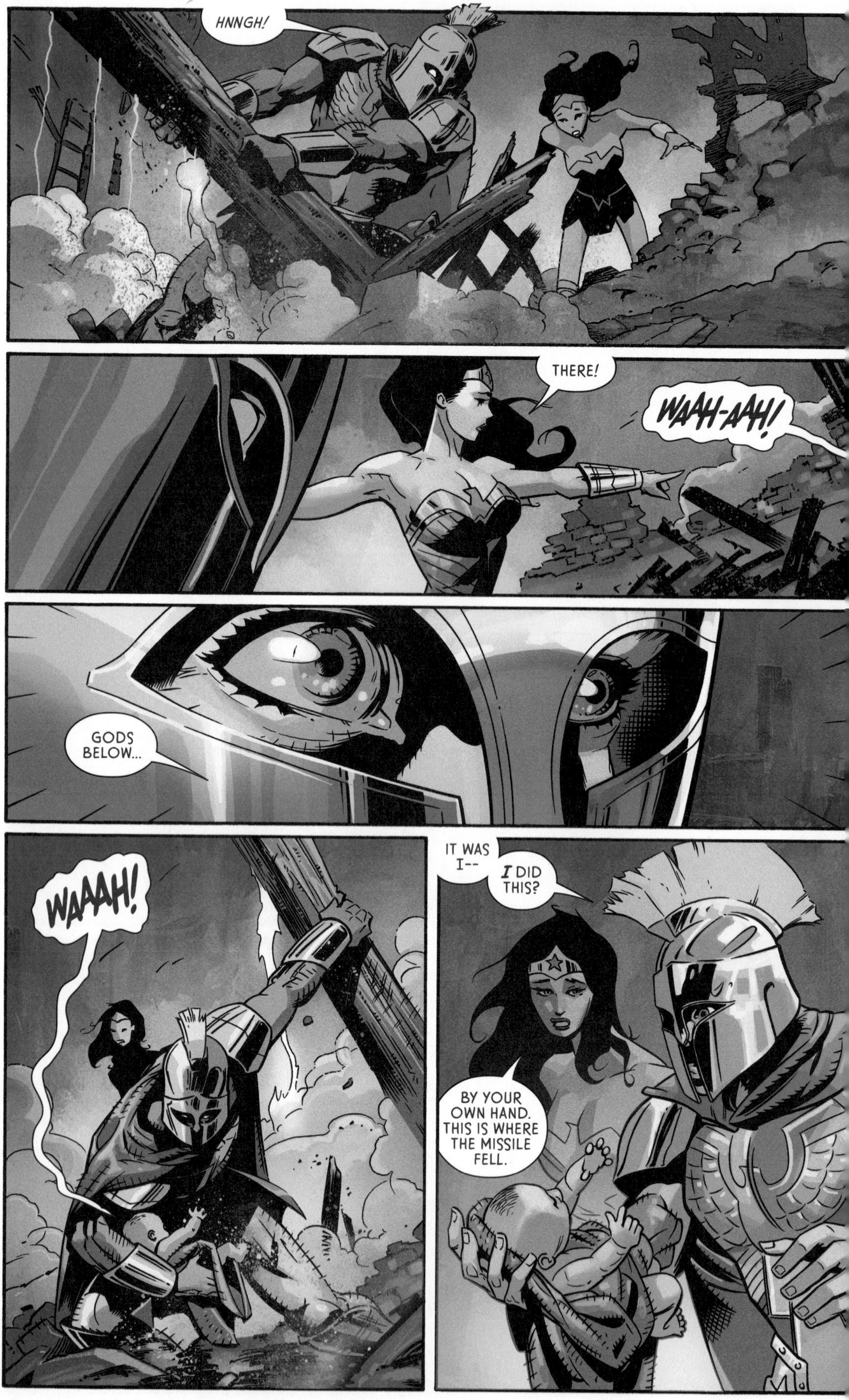

HNNGH!
THERE!
WAAH-AAH!
GODS BELOW...
WAAAH!
IT WAS I--
I DID THIS?
BY YOUR OWN HAND. THIS IS WHERE THE MISSILE FELL.

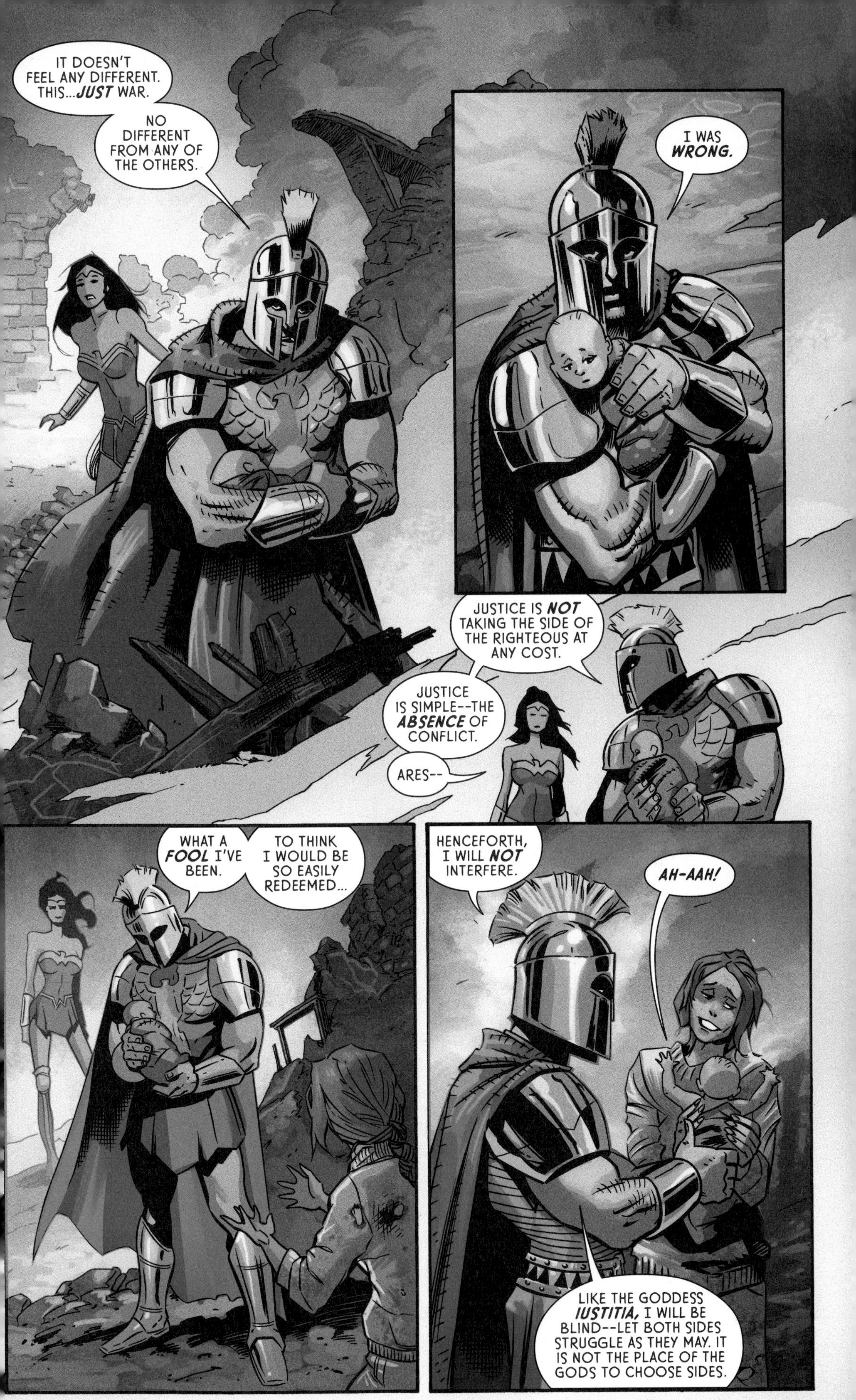
IT DOESN'T FEEL ANY DIFFERENT. THIS...JUST WAR.
NO DIFFERENT FROM ANY OF THE OTHERS.
I WAS WRONG.
JUSTICE IS NOT TAKING THE SIDE OF THE RIGHTEOUS AT ANY COST.
JUSTICE IS SIMPLE--THE ABSENCE OF CONFLICT.
ARES--
WHAT A FOOL I'VE BEEN.
TO THINK I WOULD BE SO EASILY REDEEMED...
HENCEFORTH, I WILL NOT INTERFERE.
AH-AAH!
LIKE THE GODDESS IUSTITIA, I WILL BE BLIND--LET BOTH SIDES STRUGGLE AS THEY MAY. IT IS NOT THE PLACE OF THE GODS TO CHOOSE SIDES.

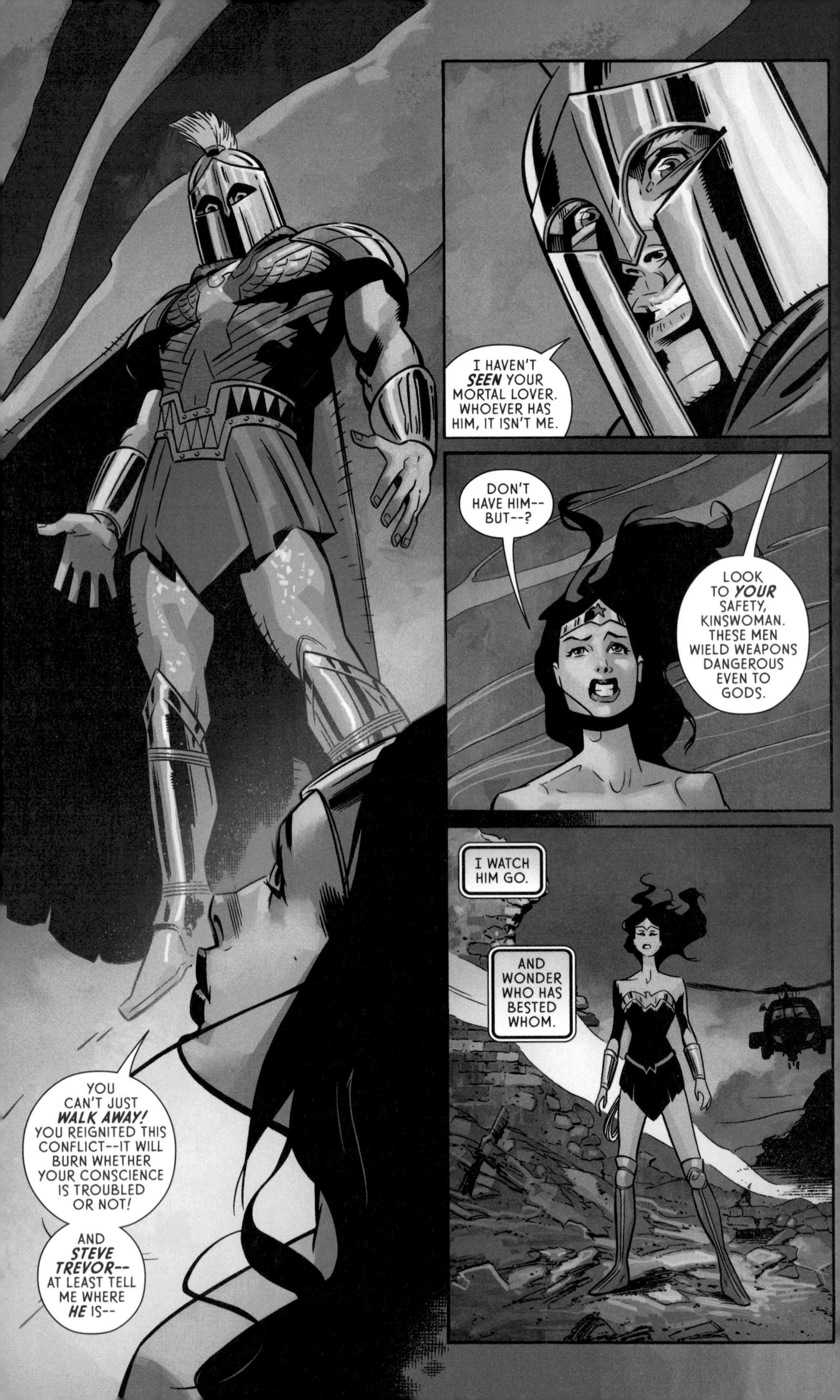
I HAVEN'T SEEN YOUR MORTAL LOVER. WHOEVER HAS HIM, IT ISN'T ME.
YOU CAN'T JUST WALK AWAY! YOU REIGNITED THIS CONFLICT--IT WILL BURN WHETHER YOUR CONSCIENCE IS TROUBLED OR NOT!
AND STEVE TREVOR-- AT LEAST TELL ME WHERE HE IS--
DON'T HAVE HIM-- BUT--?
LOOK TO YOUR SAFETY, KINSWOMAN. THESE MEN WIELD WEAPONS DANGEROUS EVEN TO GODS.
I WATCH HIM GO.
AND WONDER WHO HAS BESTED WHOM.

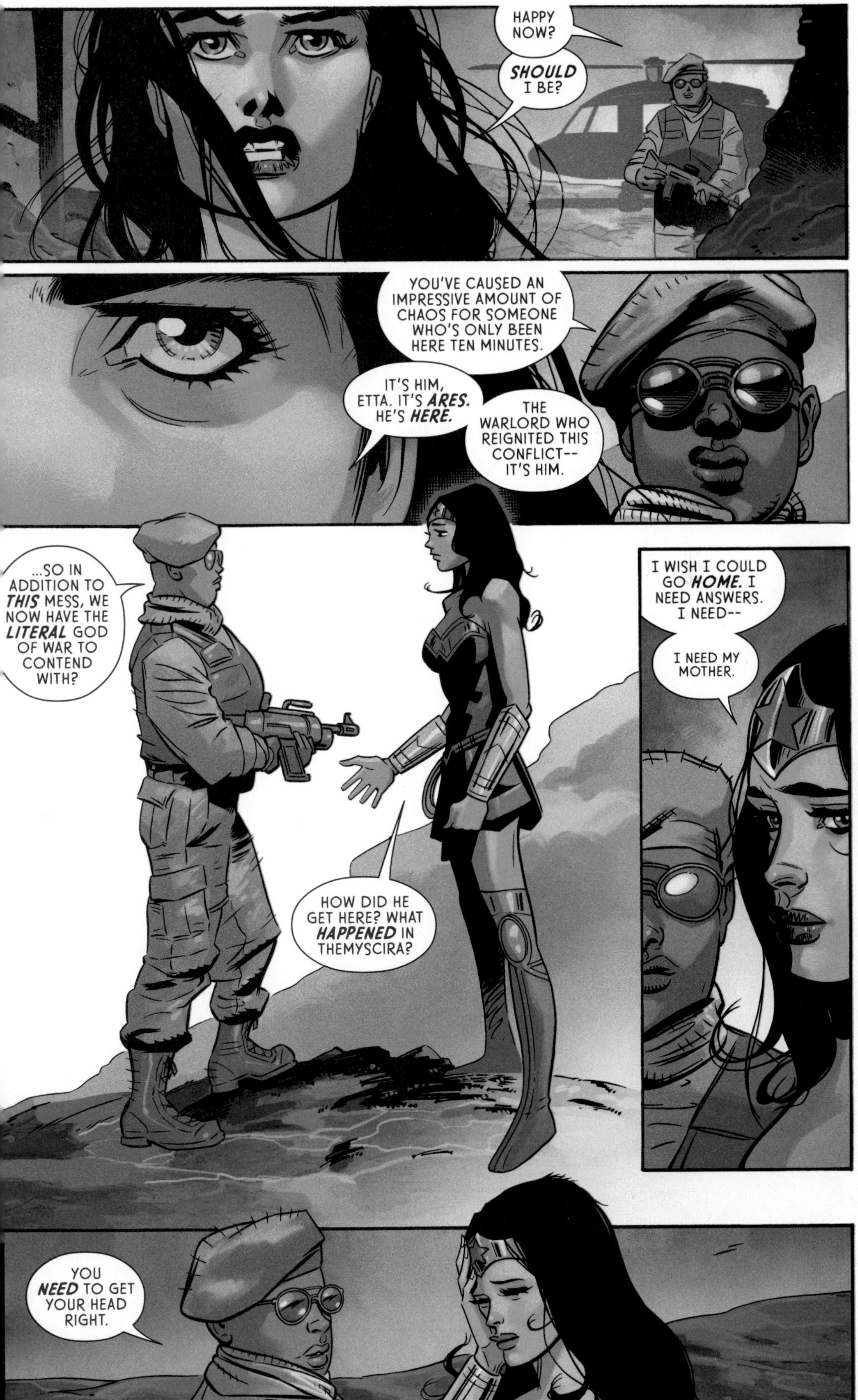

HAPPY NOW?
SHOULD I BE?
YOU'VE CAUSED AN IMPRESSIVE AMOUNT OF CHAOS FOR SOMEONE WHO'S ONLY BEEN HERE TEN MINUTES.
IT'S HIM, ETTA. IT'S ARES. HE'S HERE.
THE WARLORD WHO REIGNITED THIS CONFLICT-- IT'S HIM.
...SO IN ADDITION TO THIS MESS, WE NOW HAVE THE LITERAL GOD OF WAR TO CONTEND WITH?
HOW DID HE GET HERE? WHAT HAPPENED IN THEMYSCIRA?
I WISH I COULD GO HOME. I NEED ANSWERS. I NEED--
I NEED MY MOTHER.
YOU NEED TO GET YOUR HEAD RIGHT.

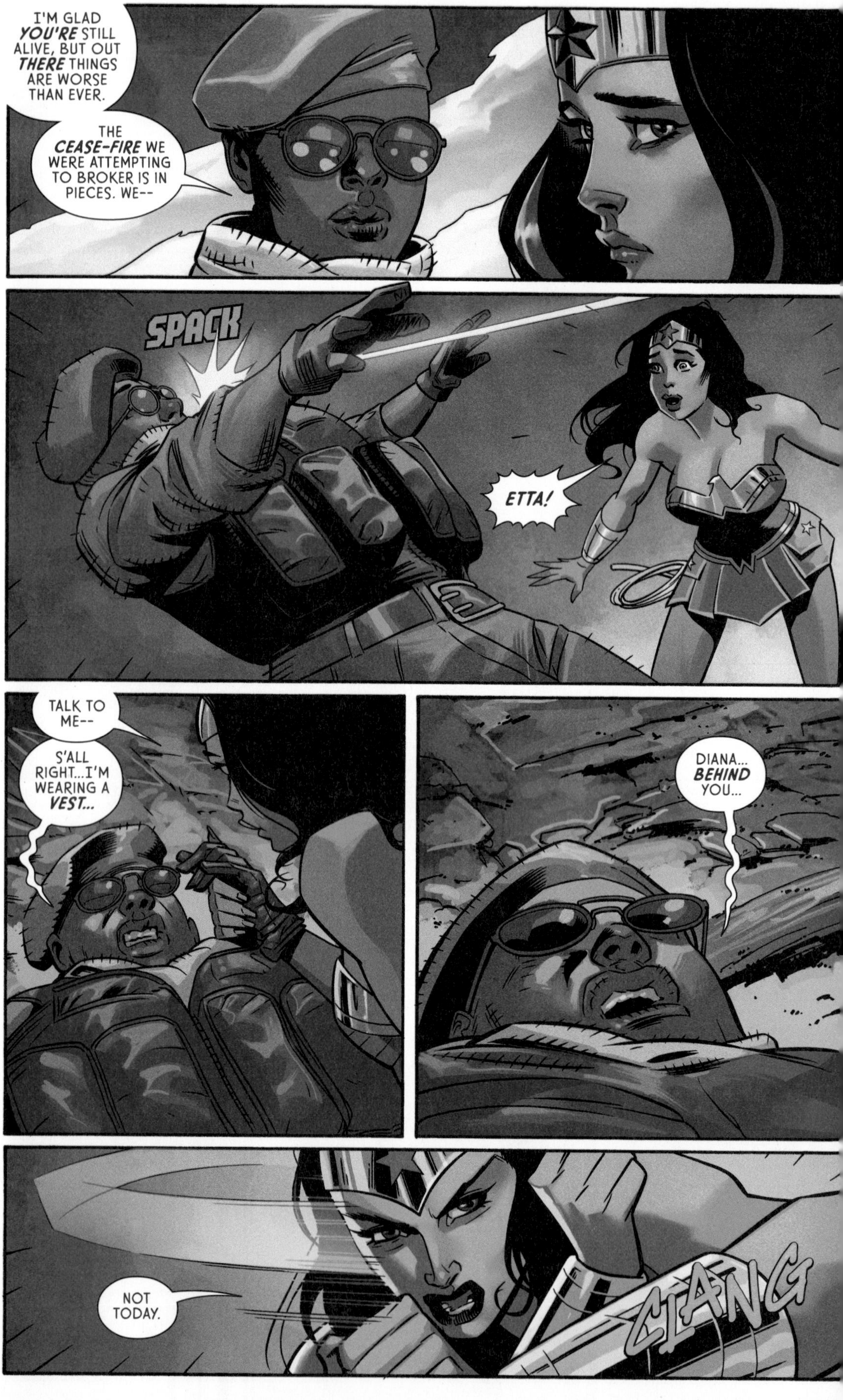

I'M GLAD *YOU'RE* STILL ALIVE, BUT OUT *THERE* THINGS ARE WORSE THAN EVER.
THE *CEASE-FIRE* WE WERE ATTEMPTING TO BROKER IS IN PIECES. WE--
SPACK
ETTA!
TALK TO ME--
S'ALL RIGHT...I'M WEARING A *VEST...*
DIANA... *BEHIND* YOU...
NOT TODAY.
CLANG

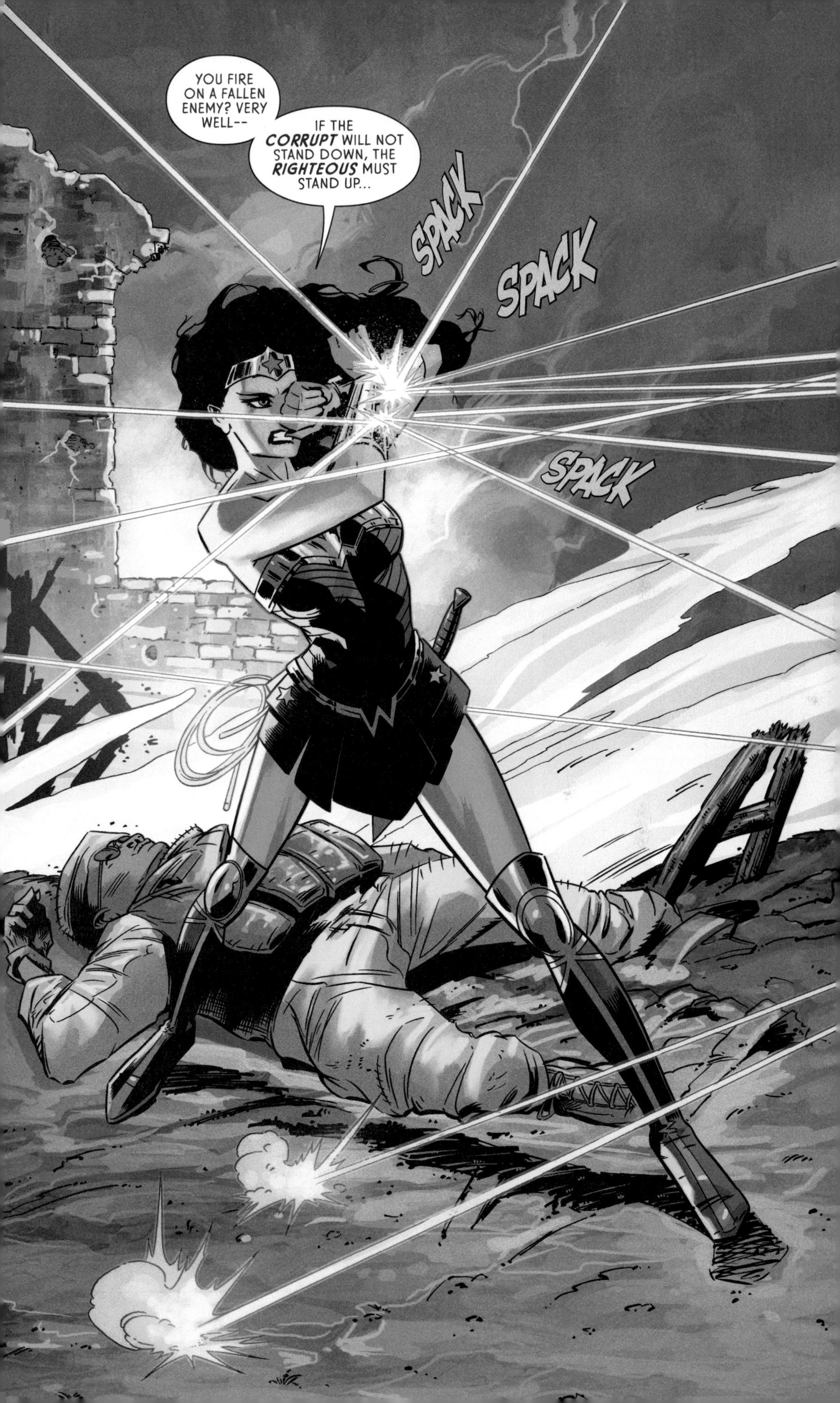

YOU FIRE ON A FALLEN ENEMY? VERY WELL--
IF THE **CORRUPT** WILL NOT STAND DOWN, THE **RIGHTEOUS** MUST STAND UP...
SPACK
SPACK
SPACK

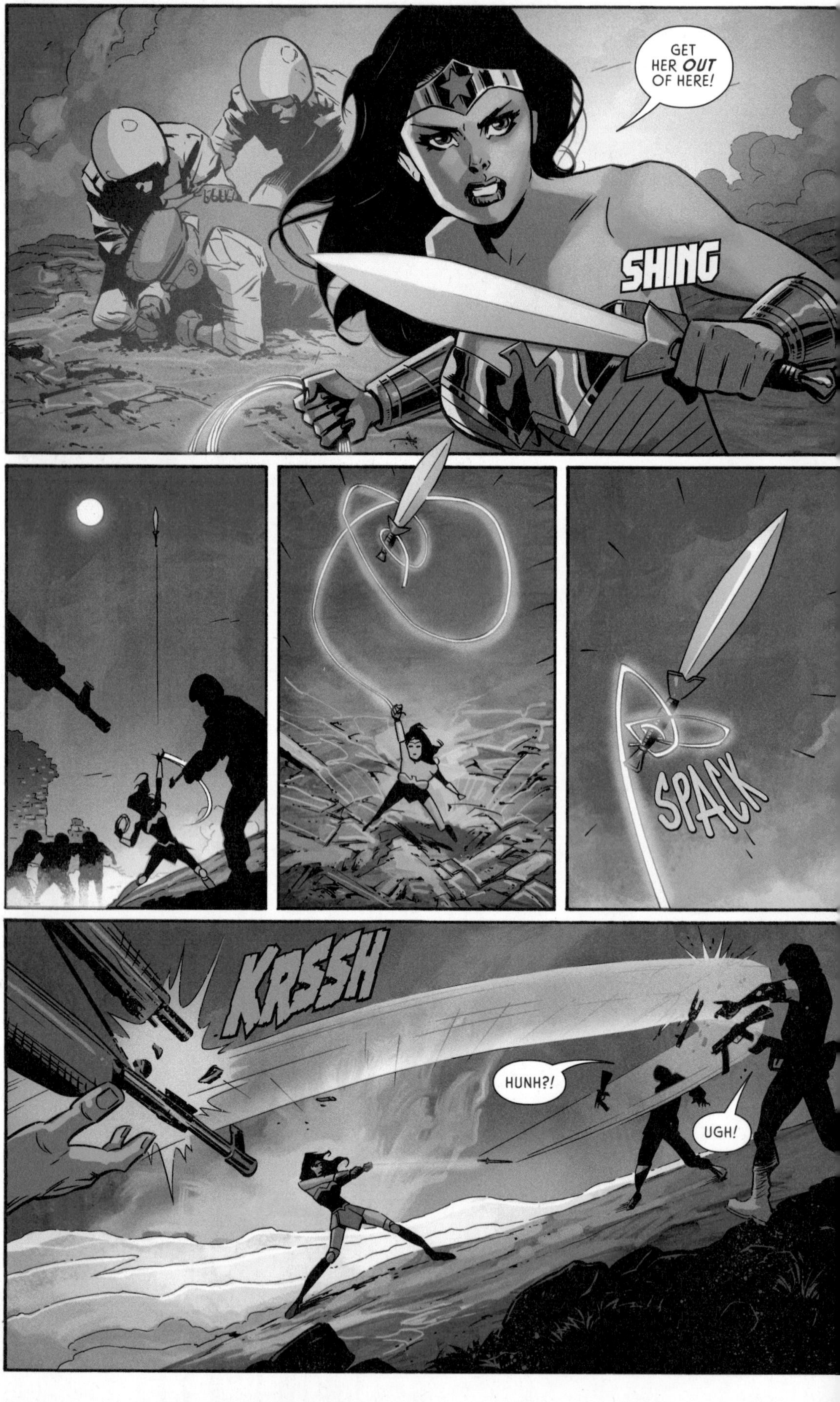
GET HER *OUT* OF HERE!
SHING
SPACK
KRSSH
HUNH?!
UGH!

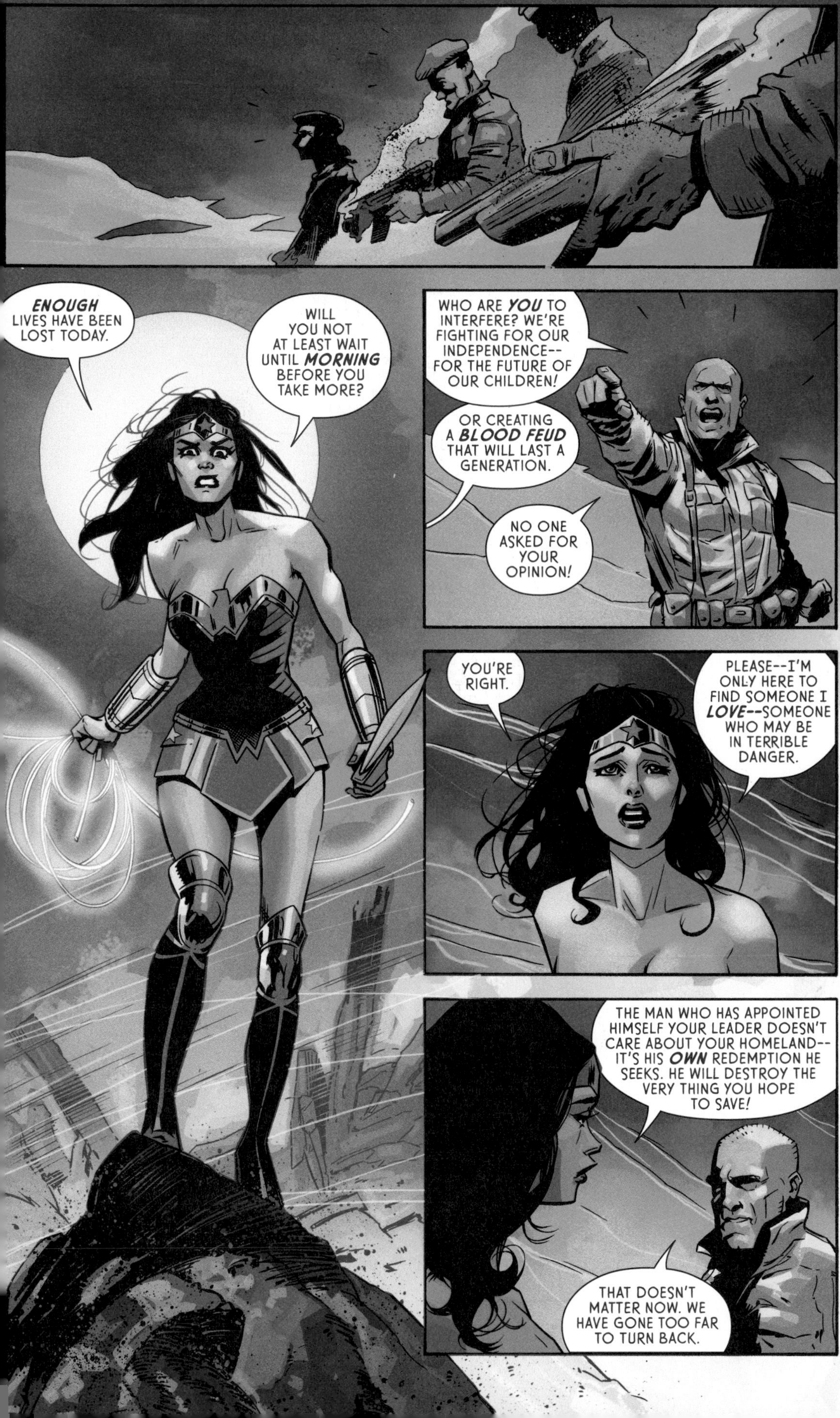
ENOUGH LIVES HAVE BEEN LOST TODAY.
WILL YOU NOT AT LEAST WAIT UNTIL MORNING BEFORE YOU TAKE MORE?
WHO ARE YOU TO INTERFERE? WE'RE FIGHTING FOR OUR INDEPENDENCE--FOR THE FUTURE OF OUR CHILDREN!
OR CREATING A BLOOD FEUD THAT WILL LAST A GENERATION.
NO ONE ASKED FOR YOUR OPINION!
YOU'RE RIGHT.
PLEASE--I'M ONLY HERE TO FIND SOMEONE I LOVE--SOMEONE WHO MAY BE IN TERRIBLE DANGER.
THE MAN WHO HAS APPOINTED HIMSELF YOUR LEADER DOESN'T CARE ABOUT YOUR HOMELAND--IT'S HIS OWN REDEMPTION HE SEEKS. HE WILL DESTROY THE VERY THING YOU HOPE TO SAVE!
THAT DOESN'T MATTER NOW. WE HAVE GONE TOO FAR TO TURN BACK.

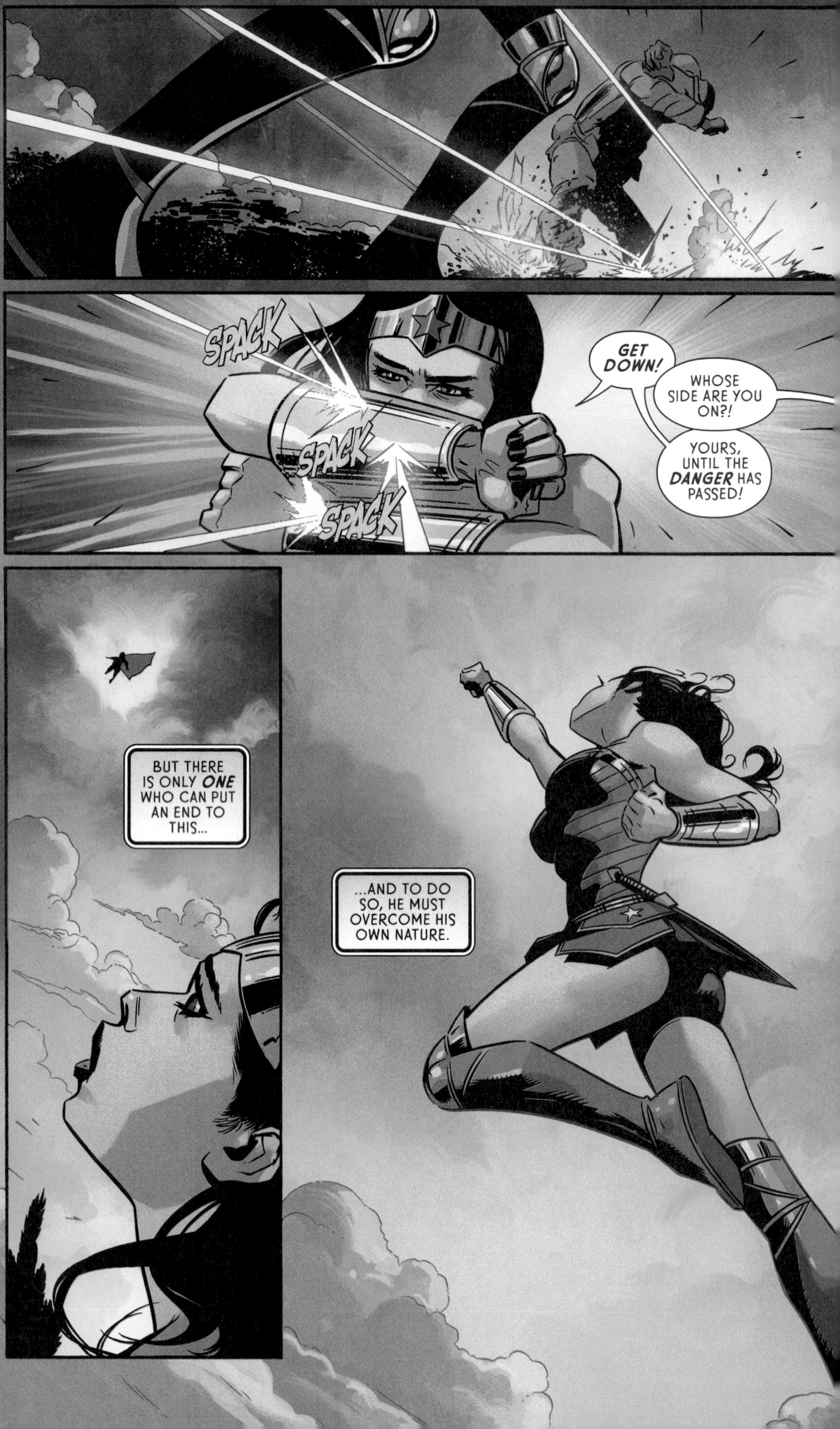

SPACK
SPACK
SPACK
GET DOWN!
WHOSE SIDE ARE YOU ON?!
YOURS, UNTIL THE DANGER HAS PASSED!
BUT THERE IS ONLY ONE WHO CAN PUT AN END TO THIS...
...AND TO DO SO, HE MUST OVERCOME HIS OWN NATURE.

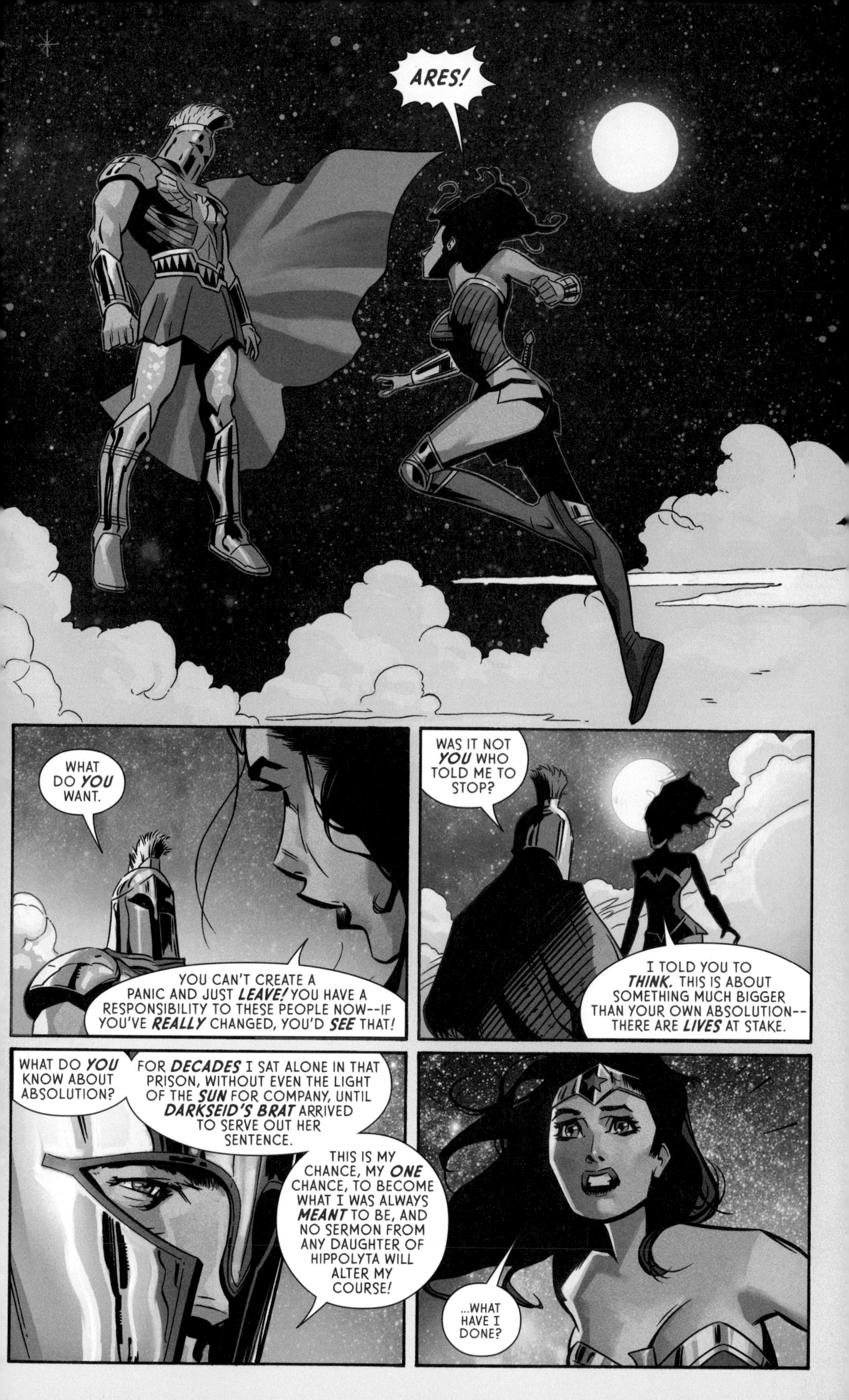

ARES!
WHAT DO YOU WANT.
YOU CAN'T CREATE A PANIC AND JUST LEAVE! YOU HAVE A RESPONSIBILITY TO THESE PEOPLE NOW--IF YOU'VE REALLY CHANGED, YOU'D SEE THAT!
WAS IT NOT YOU WHO TOLD ME TO STOP?
I TOLD YOU TO THINK. THIS IS ABOUT SOMETHING MUCH BIGGER THAN YOUR OWN ABSOLUTION--THERE ARE LIVES AT STAKE.
WHAT DO YOU KNOW ABOUT ABSOLUTION?
FOR DECADES I SAT ALONE IN THAT PRISON, WITHOUT EVEN THE LIGHT OF THE SUN FOR COMPANY, UNTIL DARKSEID'S BRAT ARRIVED TO SERVE OUT HER SENTENCE.
THIS IS MY CHANCE, MY ONE CHANCE, TO BECOME WHAT I WAS ALWAYS MEANT TO BE, AND NO SERMON FROM ANY DAUGHTER OF HIPPOLYTA WILL ALTER MY COURSE!
...WHAT HAVE I DONE?

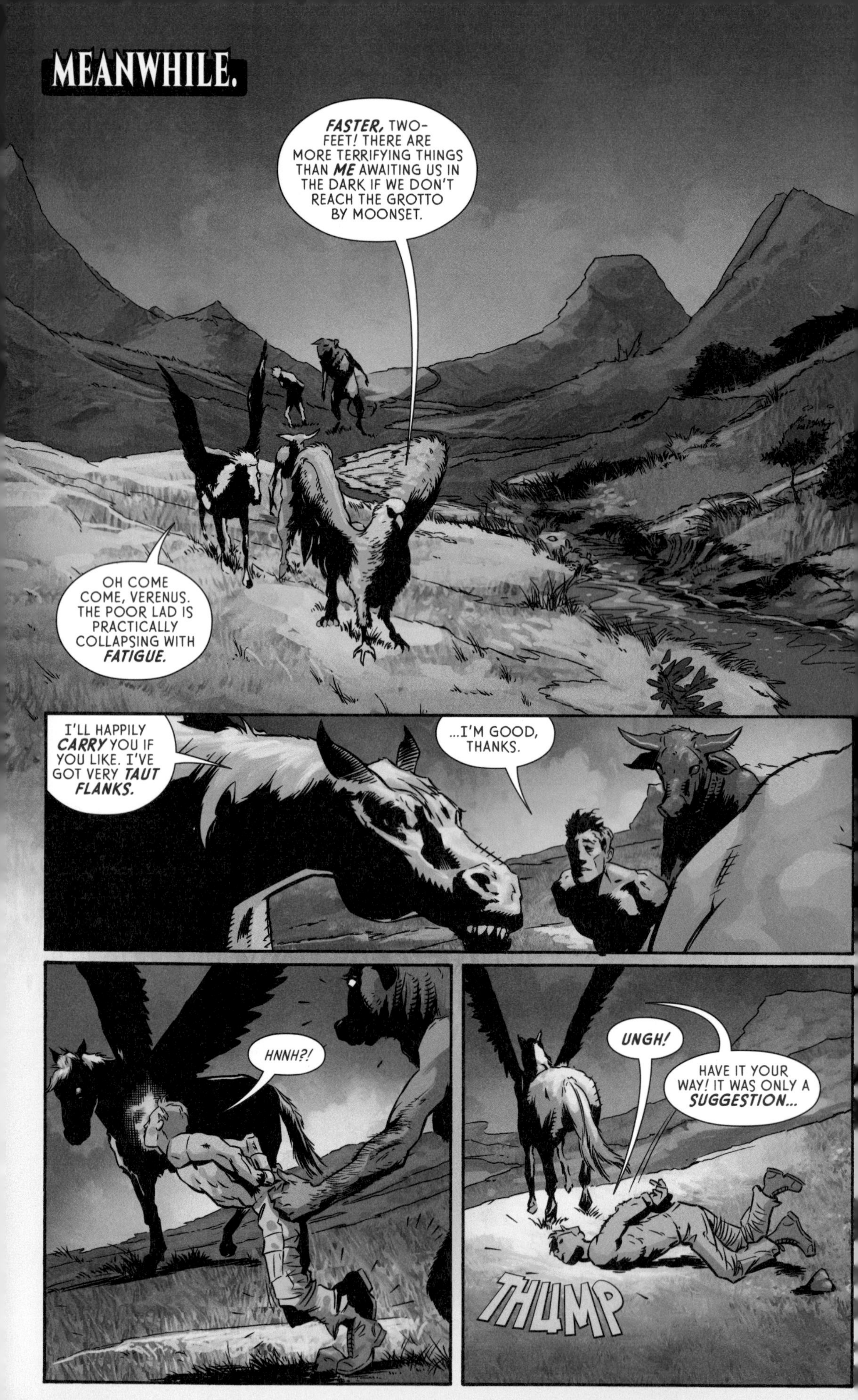
MEANWHILE.
FASTER, TWO-FEET! THERE ARE MORE TERRIFYING THINGS THAN ME AWAITING US IN THE DARK IF WE DON'T REACH THE GROTTO BY MOONSET.
OH COME COME, VERENUS. THE POOR LAD IS PRACTICALLY COLLAPSING WITH FATIGUE.
I'LL HAPPILY CARRY YOU IF YOU LIKE. I'VE GOT VERY TAUT FLANKS.
...I'M GOOD, THANKS.
HNNH?!
UNGH!
HAVE IT YOUR WAY! IT WAS ONLY A SUGGESTION...
THUMP

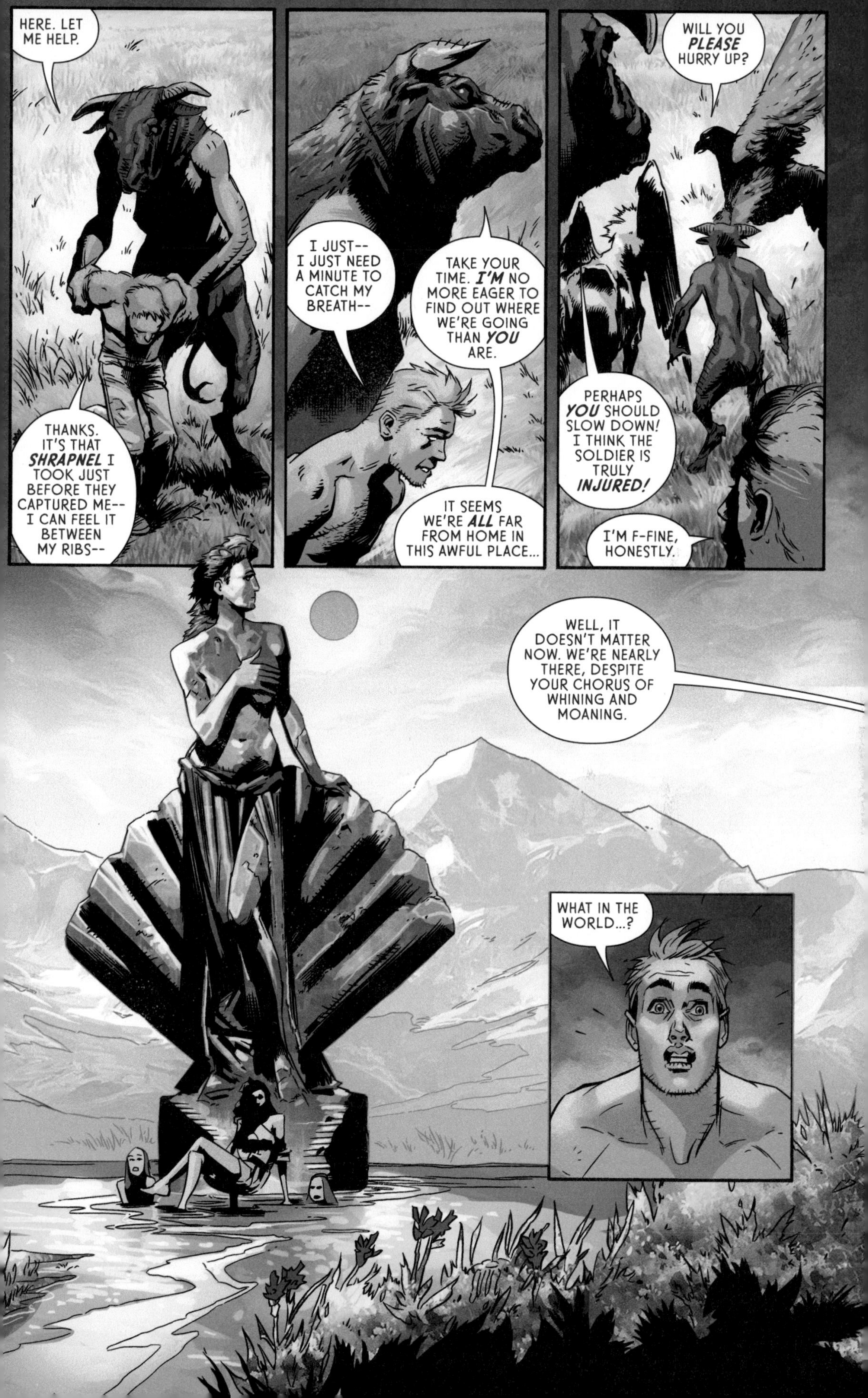
HERE. LET ME HELP.
THANKS. IT'S THAT SHRAPNEL I TOOK JUST BEFORE THEY CAPTURED ME-- I CAN FEEL IT BETWEEN MY RIBS--
I JUST-- I JUST NEED A MINUTE TO CATCH MY BREATH--
TAKE YOUR TIME. I'M NO MORE EAGER TO FIND OUT WHERE WE'RE GOING THAN YOU ARE.
IT SEEMS WE'RE ALL FAR FROM HOME IN THIS AWFUL PLACE...
WILL YOU PLEASE HURRY UP?
PERHAPS YOU SHOULD SLOW DOWN! I THINK THE SOLDIER IS TRULY INJURED!
I'M F-FINE, HONESTLY.
WELL, IT DOESN'T MATTER NOW. WE'RE NEARLY THERE, DESPITE YOUR CHORUS OF WHINING AND MOANING.
WHAT IN THE WORLD...?

WELL, WELL, WELL.
A MAN.
WELCOME, SON OF PROMETHEUS. I AM APHRODITE, AND I AM MASTER HERE.
THE JUST WAR PART III
G. WILLOW WILSON WRITER CARY NORD PENCILS MICK GRAY INKS
ROMULO FAJARDO JR. COLORS PAT BROSSEAU LETTERING
TERRY DODSON & RACHEL DODSON COVER
DAVE WIELGOSZ ASST. EDITOR
CHRIS CONROY EDITOR JAMIE S. RICH GROUP EDITOR

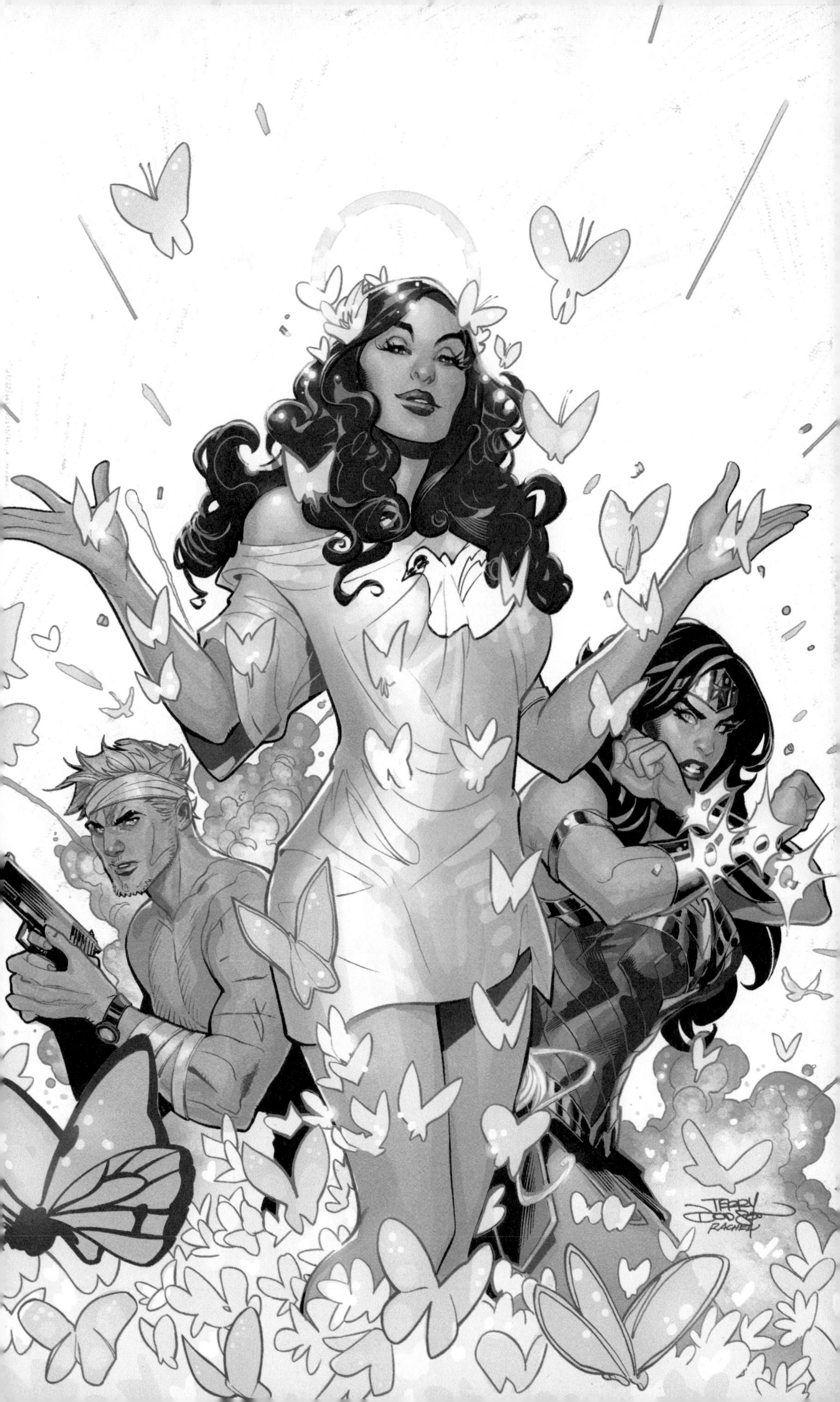

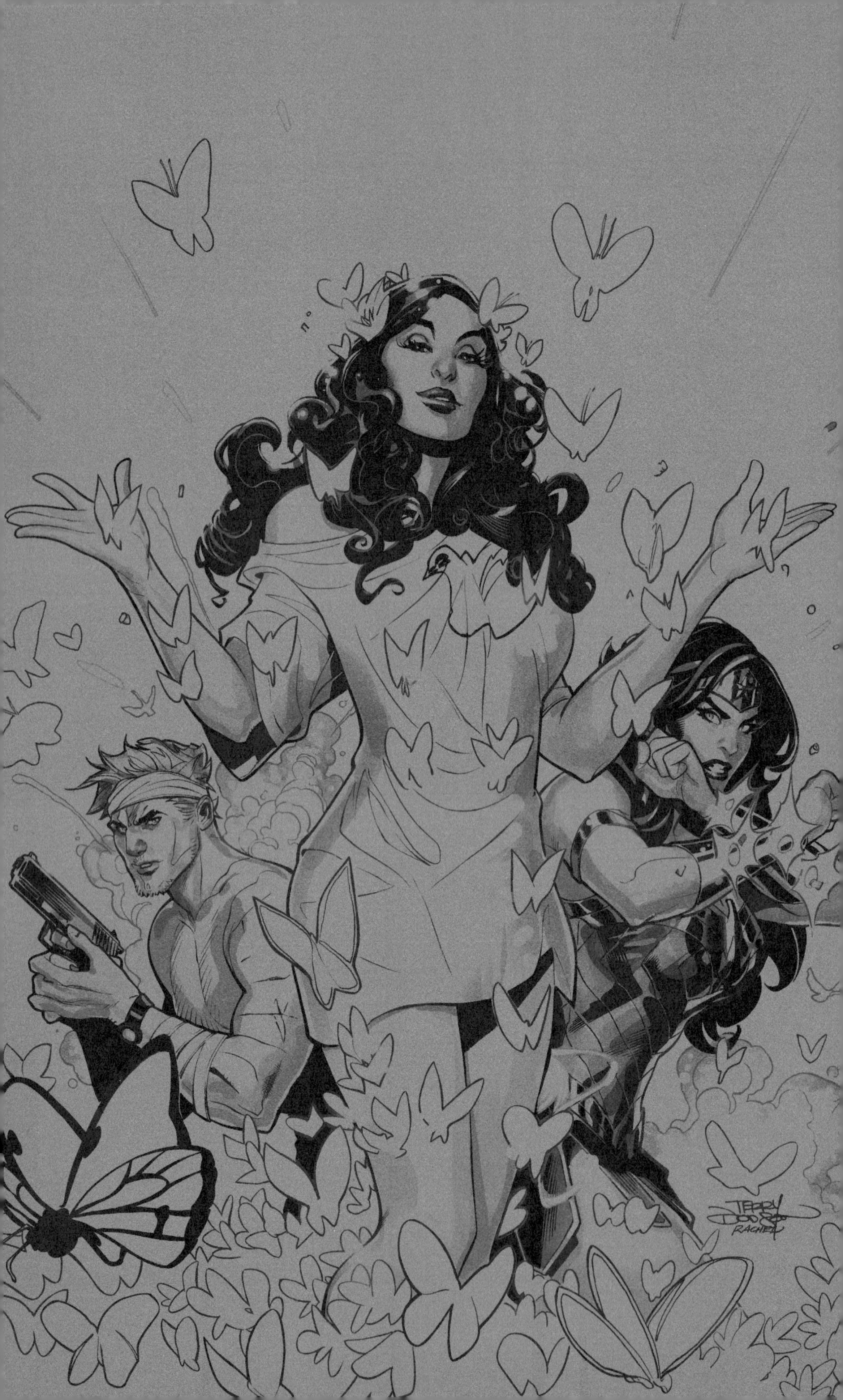

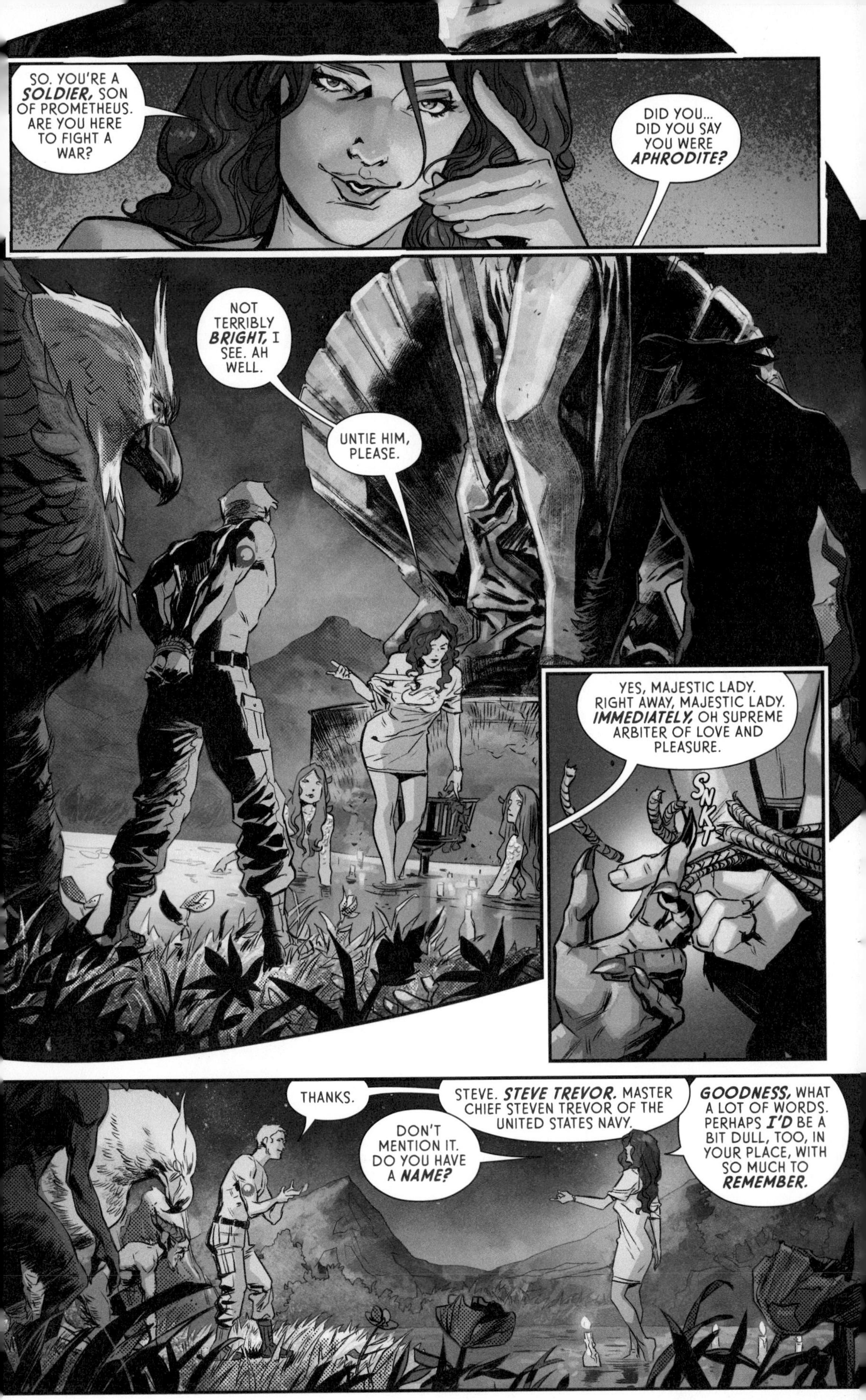

SO. YOU'RE A **SOLDIER,** SON OF PROMETHEUS. ARE YOU HERE TO FIGHT A WAR?
DID YOU... DID YOU SAY YOU WERE **APHRODITE?**
NOT TERRIBLY **BRIGHT,** I SEE. AH WELL.
UNTIE HIM, PLEASE.
YES, MAJESTIC LADY. RIGHT AWAY, MAJESTIC LADY. **IMMEDIATELY,** OH SUPREME ARBITER OF LOVE AND PLEASURE.
SNKT
THANKS.
DON'T MENTION IT. DO YOU HAVE A **NAME?**
STEVE. **STEVE TREVOR.** MASTER CHIEF STEVEN TREVOR OF THE UNITED STATES NAVY.
GOODNESS, WHAT A LOT OF WORDS. PERHAPS **I'D** BE A BIT DULL, TOO, IN YOUR PLACE, WITH SO MUCH TO **REMEMBER.**

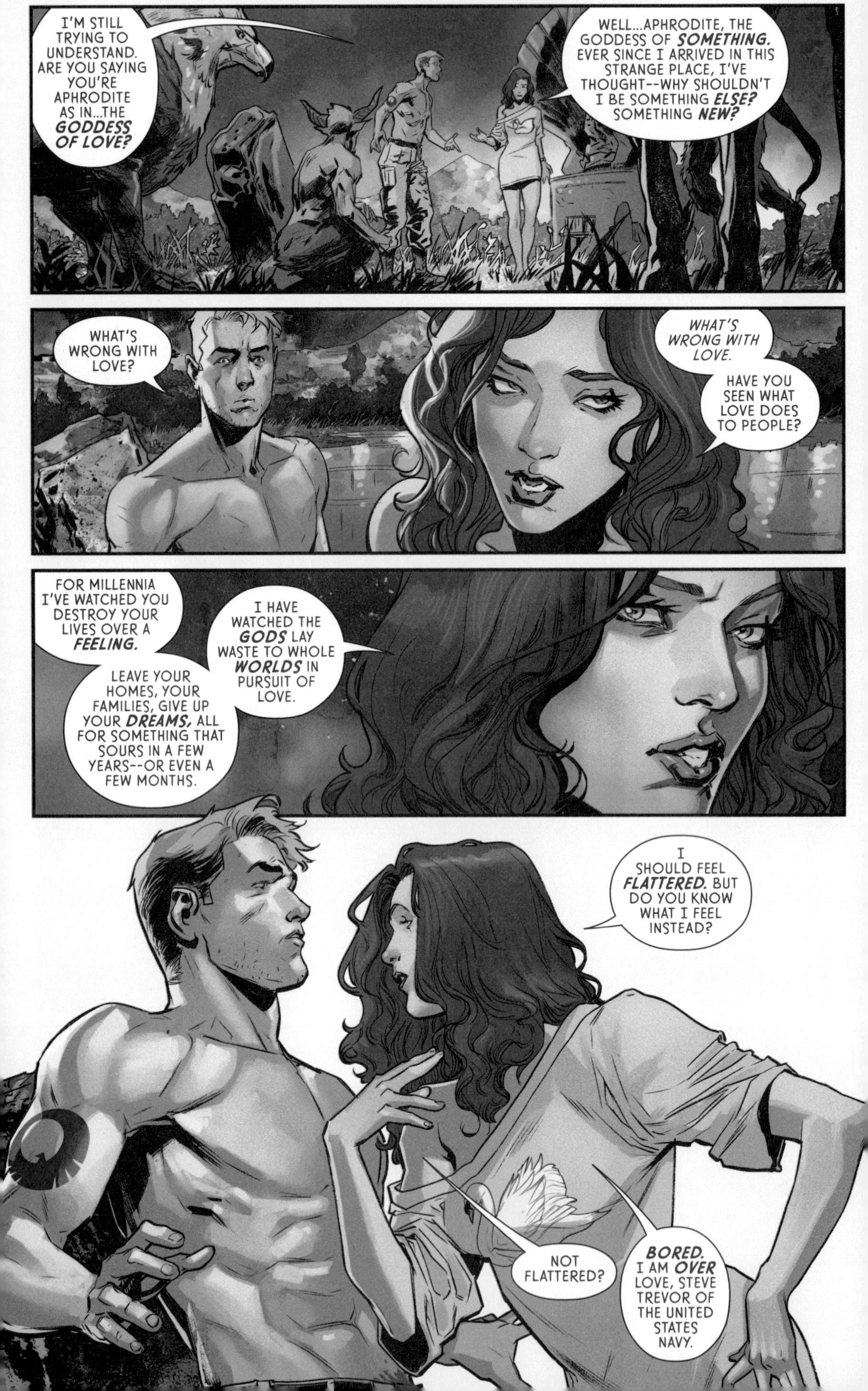
I'M STILL TRYING TO UNDERSTAND. ARE YOU SAYING YOU'RE APHRODITE AS IN...THE **GODDESS OF LOVE?**
WELL...APHRODITE, THE GODDESS OF ***SOMETHING.*** EVER SINCE I ARRIVED IN THIS STRANGE PLACE, I'VE THOUGHT--WHY SHOULDN'T I BE SOMETHING ***ELSE?*** SOMETHING ***NEW?***
WHAT'S WRONG WITH LOVE?
WHAT'S WRONG WITH LOVE.
HAVE YOU SEEN WHAT LOVE DOES TO PEOPLE?
FOR MILLENNIA I'VE WATCHED YOU DESTROY YOUR LIVES OVER A ***FEELING.***
LEAVE YOUR HOMES, YOUR FAMILIES, GIVE UP YOUR ***DREAMS,*** ALL FOR SOMETHING THAT SOURS IN A FEW YEARS--OR EVEN A FEW MONTHS.
I HAVE WATCHED THE ***GODS*** LAY WASTE TO WHOLE ***WORLDS*** IN PURSUIT OF LOVE.
I SHOULD FEEL ***FLATTERED.*** BUT DO YOU KNOW WHAT I FEEL INSTEAD?
NOT FLATTERED?
BORED. I AM ***OVER*** LOVE, STEVE TREVOR OF THE UNITED STATES NAVY.

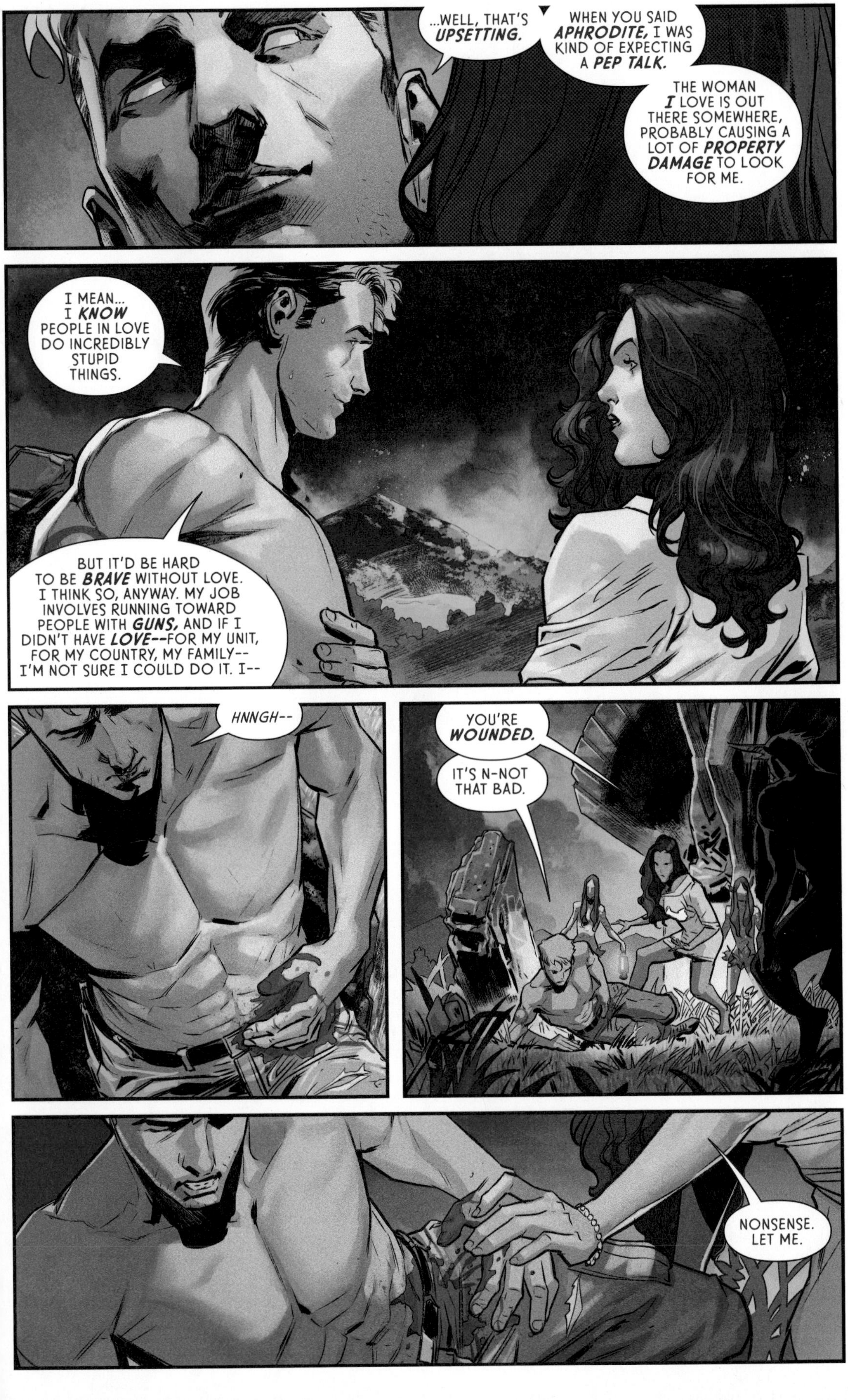
...WELL, THAT'S UPSETTING.
WHEN YOU SAID APHRODITE, I WAS KIND OF EXPECTING A PEP TALK.
THE WOMAN I LOVE IS OUT THERE SOMEWHERE, PROBABLY CAUSING A LOT OF PROPERTY DAMAGE TO LOOK FOR ME.
I MEAN... I KNOW PEOPLE IN LOVE DO INCREDIBLY STUPID THINGS.
BUT IT'D BE HARD TO BE BRAVE WITHOUT LOVE. I THINK SO, ANYWAY. MY JOB INVOLVES RUNNING TOWARD PEOPLE WITH GUNS, AND IF I DIDN'T HAVE LOVE--FOR MY UNIT, FOR MY COUNTRY, MY FAMILY-- I'M NOT SURE I COULD DO IT. I--
HNNGH--
YOU'RE WOUNDED.
IT'S N-NOT THAT BAD.
NONSENSE. LET ME.

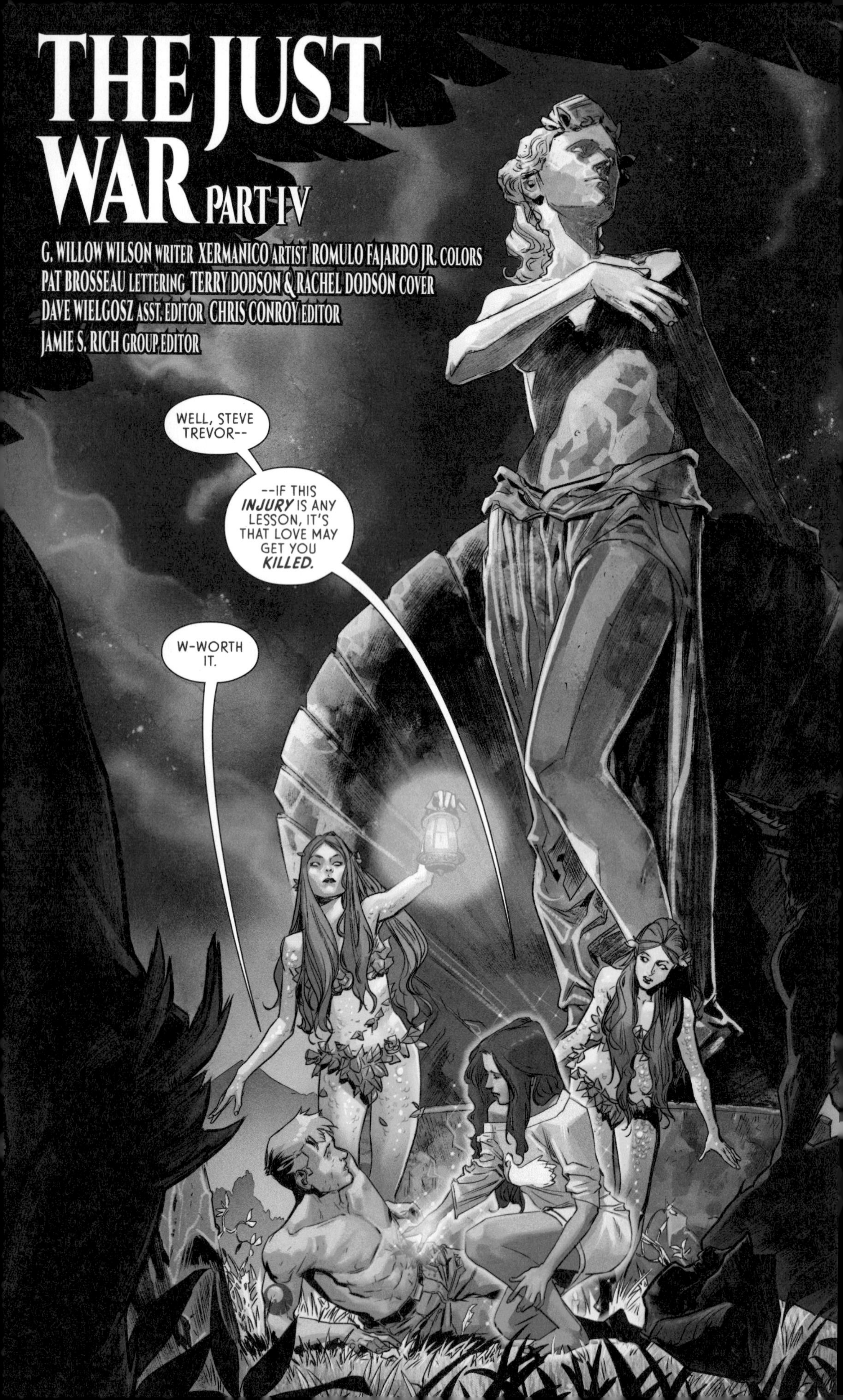
THE JUST WAR PART IV
G. WILLOW WILSON WRITER XERMANICO ARTIST ROMULO FAJARDO JR. COLORS
PAT BROSSEAU LETTERING TERRY DODSON & RACHEL DODSON COVER
DAVE WIELGOSZ ASST. EDITOR CHRIS CONROY EDITOR
JAMIE S. RICH GROUP EDITOR
WELL, STEVE TREVOR--
--IF THIS *INJURY* IS ANY LESSON, IT'S THAT LOVE MAY GET YOU *KILLED.*
W-WORTH IT.

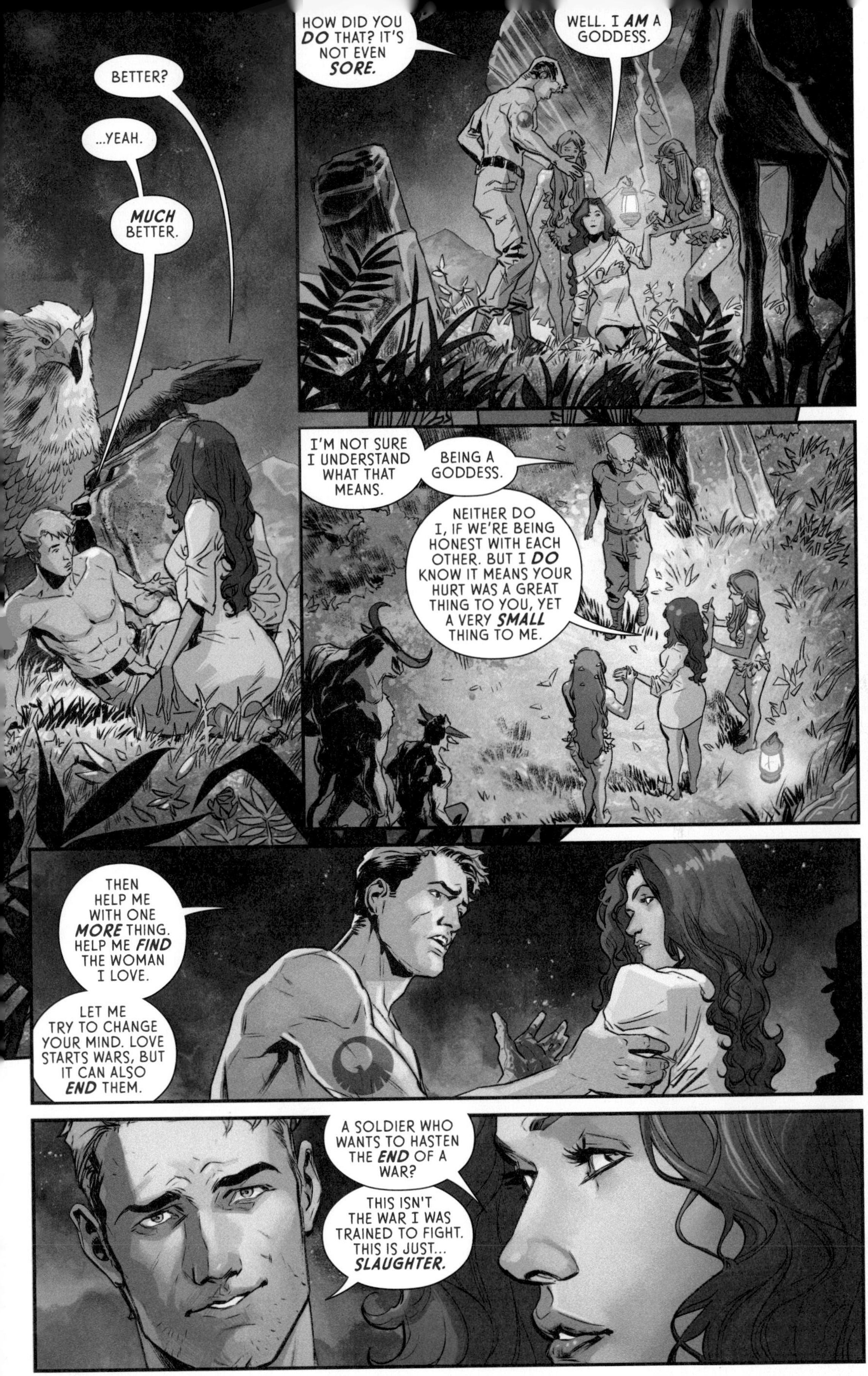
BETTER?
...YEAH.
MUCH BETTER.
HOW DID YOU DO THAT? IT'S NOT EVEN SORE.
WELL. I AM A GODDESS.
I'M NOT SURE I UNDERSTAND WHAT THAT MEANS.
BEING A GODDESS.
NEITHER DO I, IF WE'RE BEING HONEST WITH EACH OTHER. BUT I DO KNOW IT MEANS YOUR HURT WAS A GREAT THING TO YOU, YET A VERY SMALL THING TO ME.
THEN HELP ME WITH ONE MORE THING. HELP ME FIND THE WOMAN I LOVE.
LET ME TRY TO CHANGE YOUR MIND. LOVE STARTS WARS, BUT IT CAN ALSO END THEM.
A SOLDIER WHO WANTS TO HASTEN THE END OF A WAR?
THIS ISN'T THE WAR I WAS TRAINED TO FIGHT. THIS IS JUST... SLAUGHTER.

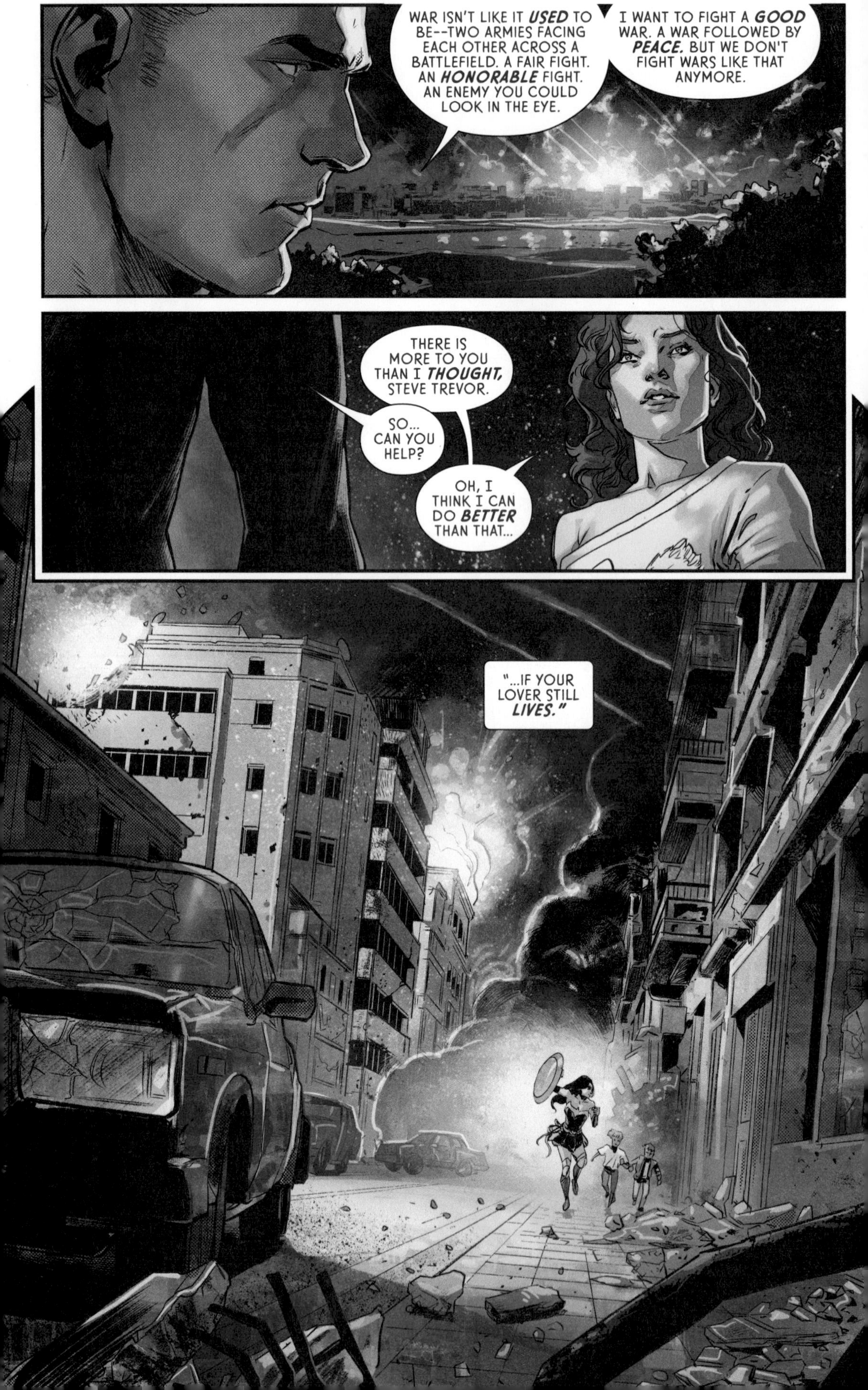

WAR ISN'T LIKE IT USED TO BE--TWO ARMIES FACING EACH OTHER ACROSS A BATTLEFIELD. A FAIR FIGHT. AN HONORABLE FIGHT. AN ENEMY YOU COULD LOOK IN THE EYE.
I WANT TO FIGHT A GOOD WAR. A WAR FOLLOWED BY PEACE. BUT WE DON'T FIGHT WARS LIKE THAT ANYMORE.
THERE IS MORE TO YOU THAN I THOUGHT, STEVE TREVOR.
SO... CAN YOU HELP?
OH, I THINK I CAN DO BETTER THAN THAT...
"...IF YOUR LOVER STILL LIVES."

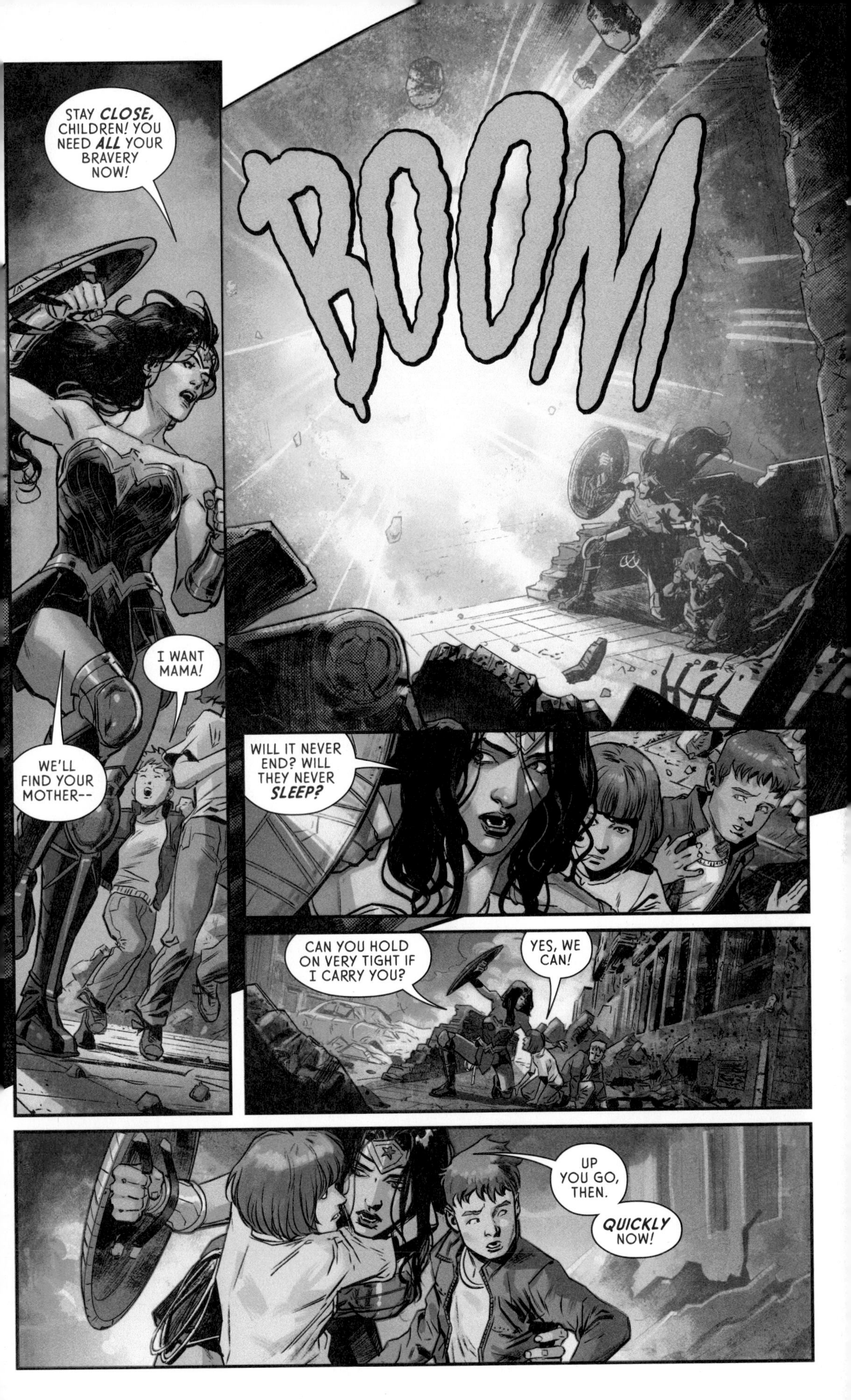

STAY CLOSE, CHILDREN! YOU NEED ALL YOUR BRAVERY NOW!
BOOM
I WANT MAMA!
WE'LL FIND YOUR MOTHER--
WILL IT NEVER END? WILL THEY NEVER SLEEP?
CAN YOU HOLD ON VERY TIGHT IF I CARRY YOU?
YES, WE CAN!
UP YOU GO, THEN.
QUICKLY NOW!

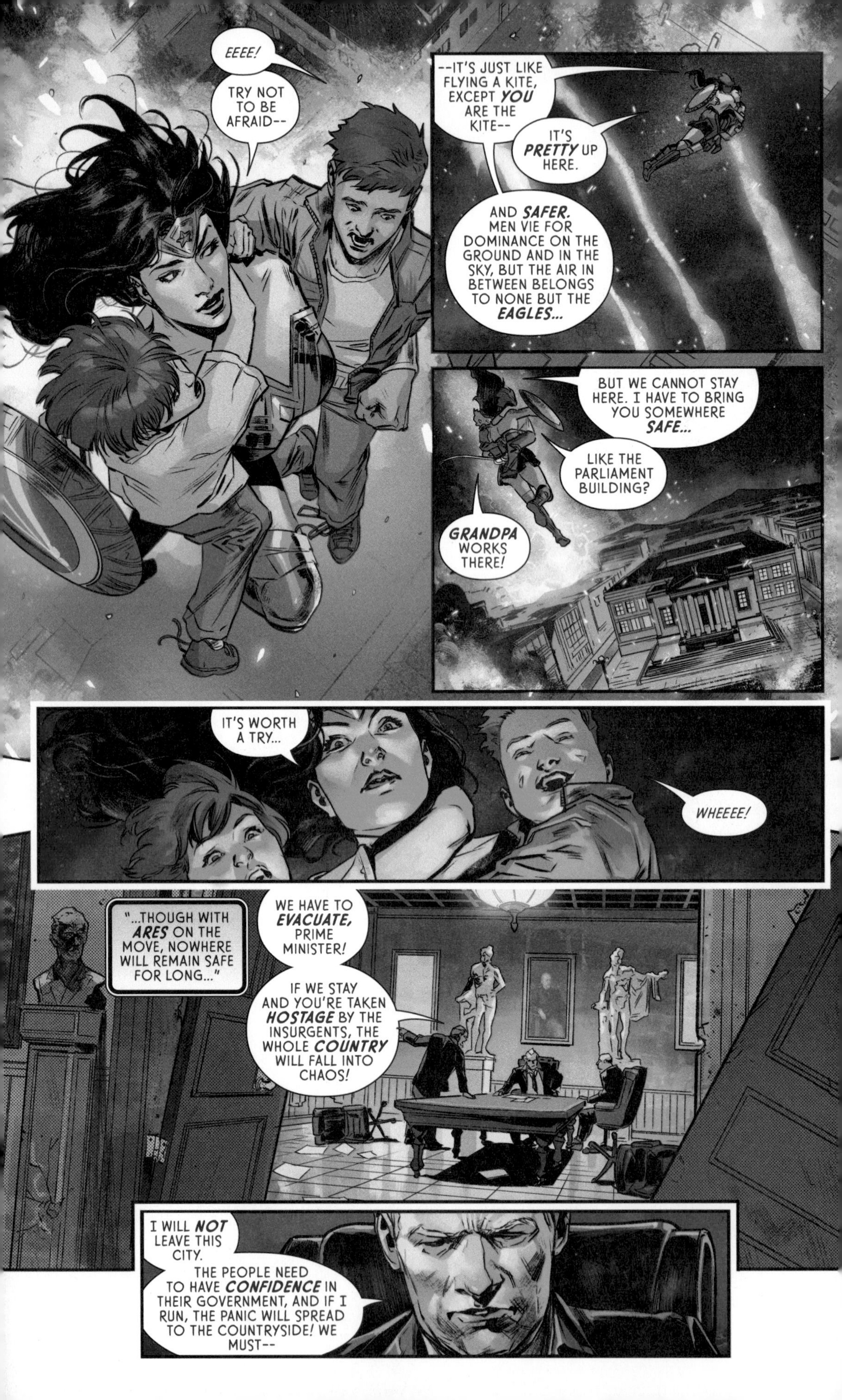
EEEE!
TRY NOT TO BE AFRAID--
--IT'S JUST LIKE FLYING A KITE, EXCEPT YOU ARE THE KITE--
IT'S PRETTY UP HERE.
AND SAFER. MEN VIE FOR DOMINANCE ON THE GROUND AND IN THE SKY, BUT THE AIR IN BETWEEN BELONGS TO NONE BUT THE EAGLES...
BUT WE CANNOT STAY HERE. I HAVE TO BRING YOU SOMEWHERE SAFE...
LIKE THE PARLIAMENT BUILDING?
GRANDPA WORKS THERE!
IT'S WORTH A TRY...
WHEEEE!
"...THOUGH WITH ARES ON THE MOVE, NOWHERE WILL REMAIN SAFE FOR LONG..."
WE HAVE TO EVACUATE, PRIME MINISTER!
IF WE STAY AND YOU'RE TAKEN HOSTAGE BY THE INSURGENTS, THE WHOLE COUNTRY WILL FALL INTO CHAOS!
I WILL NOT LEAVE THIS CITY.
THE PEOPLE NEED TO HAVE CONFIDENCE IN THEIR GOVERNMENT, AND IF I RUN, THE PANIC WILL SPREAD TO THE COUNTRYSIDE! WE MUST--

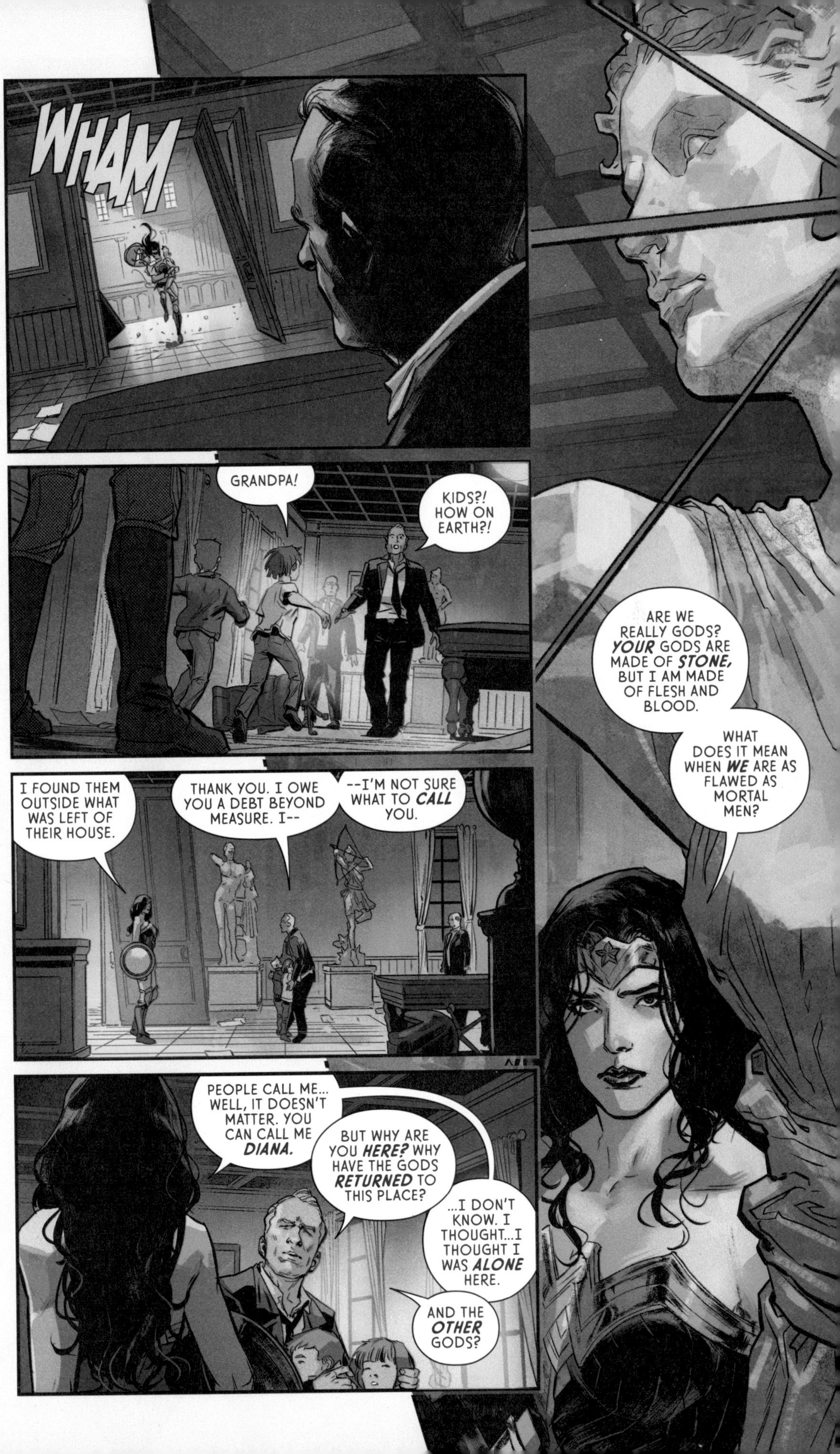

WHAM
GRANDPA!
KIDS?! HOW ON EARTH?!
I FOUND THEM OUTSIDE WHAT WAS LEFT OF THEIR HOUSE.
THANK YOU. I OWE YOU A DEBT BEYOND MEASURE. I--
--I'M NOT SURE WHAT TO CALL YOU.
PEOPLE CALL ME... WELL, IT DOESN'T MATTER. YOU CAN CALL ME DIANA.
BUT WHY ARE YOU HERE? WHY HAVE THE GODS RETURNED TO THIS PLACE?
...I DON'T KNOW. I THOUGHT...I THOUGHT I WAS ALONE HERE.
AND THE OTHER GODS?
ARE WE REALLY GODS? YOUR GODS ARE MADE OF STONE, BUT I AM MADE OF FLESH AND BLOOD.
WHAT DOES IT MEAN WHEN WE ARE AS FLAWED AS MORTAL MEN?

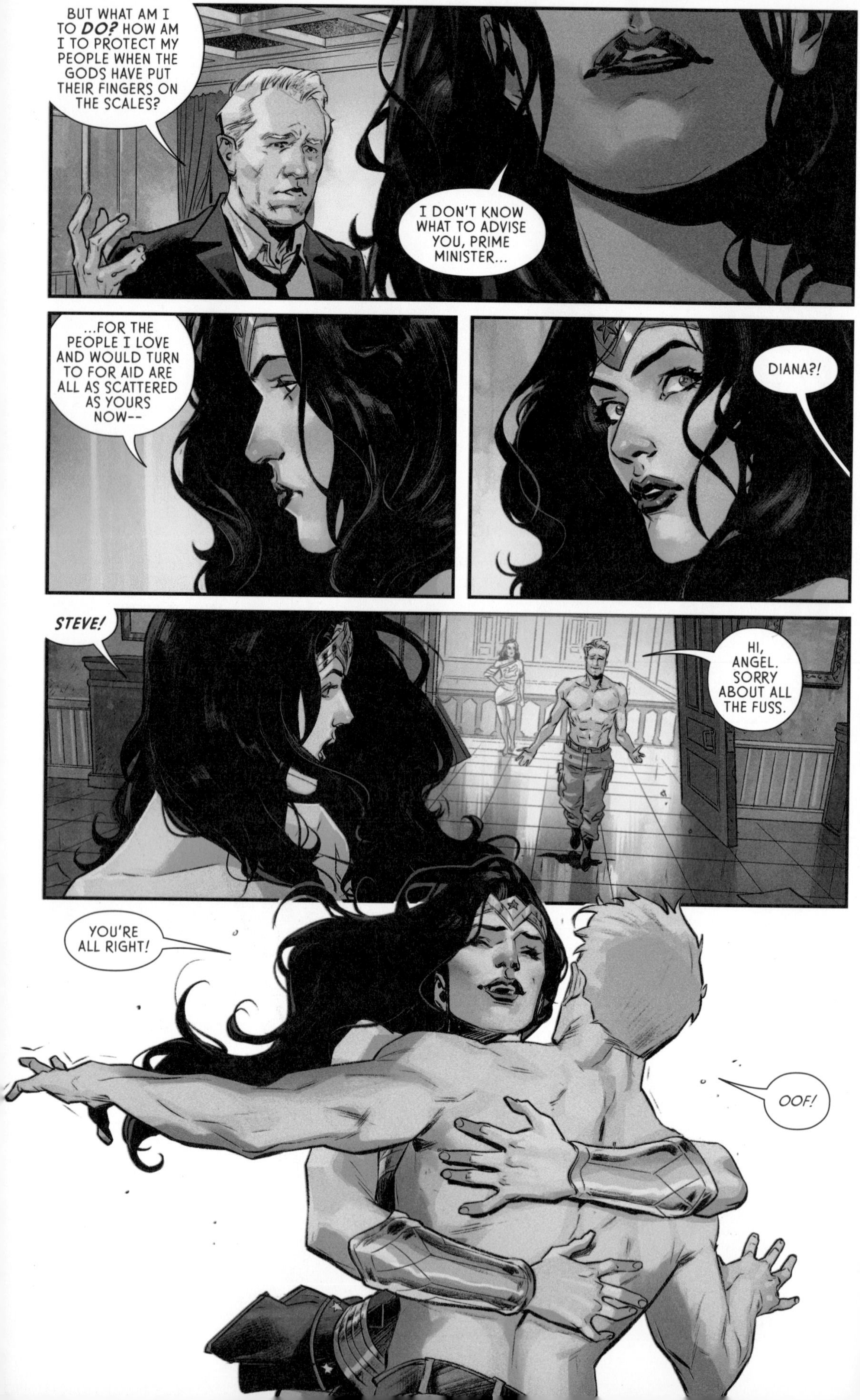
BUT WHAT AM I TO *DO?* HOW AM I TO PROTECT MY PEOPLE WHEN THE GODS HAVE PUT THEIR FINGERS ON THE SCALES?
I DON'T KNOW WHAT TO ADVISE YOU, PRIME MINISTER...
...FOR THE PEOPLE I LOVE AND WOULD TURN TO FOR AID ARE ALL AS SCATTERED AS YOURS NOW--
DIANA?!
STEVE!
HI, ANGEL. SORRY ABOUT ALL THE FUSS.
YOU'RE ALL RIGHT!
OOF!

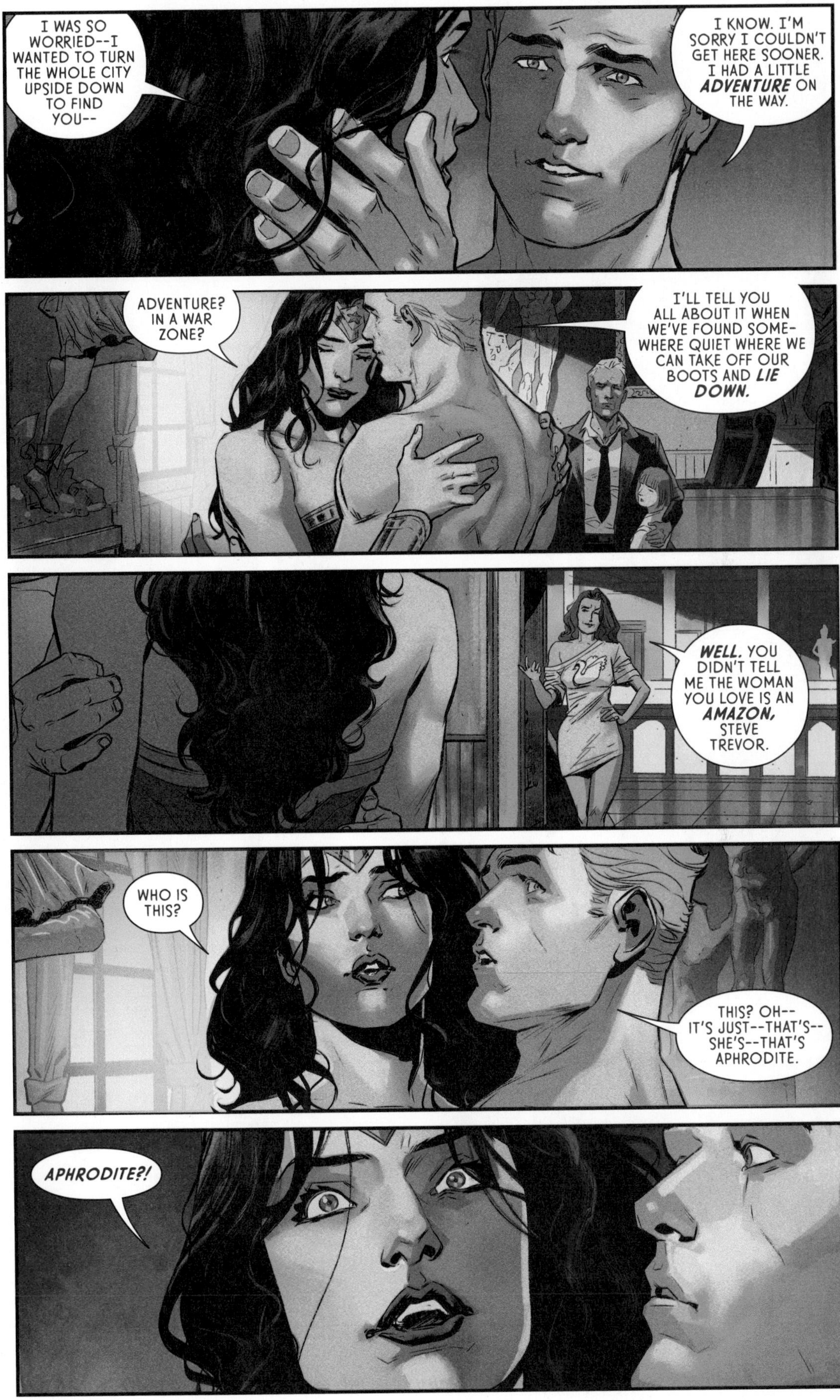
I WAS SO WORRIED--I WANTED TO TURN THE WHOLE CITY UPSIDE DOWN TO FIND YOU--
I KNOW. I'M SORRY I COULDN'T GET HERE SOONER. I HAD A LITTLE ***ADVENTURE*** ON THE WAY.
ADVENTURE? IN A WAR ZONE?
I'LL TELL YOU ALL ABOUT IT WHEN WE'VE FOUND SOME-WHERE QUIET WHERE WE CAN TAKE OFF OUR BOOTS AND ***LIE DOWN.***
WELL. YOU DIDN'T TELL ME THE WOMAN YOU LOVE IS AN ***AMAZON,*** STEVE TREVOR.
WHO IS THIS?
THIS? OH--IT'S JUST--THAT'S--SHE'S--THAT'S APHRODITE.
APHRODITE?!

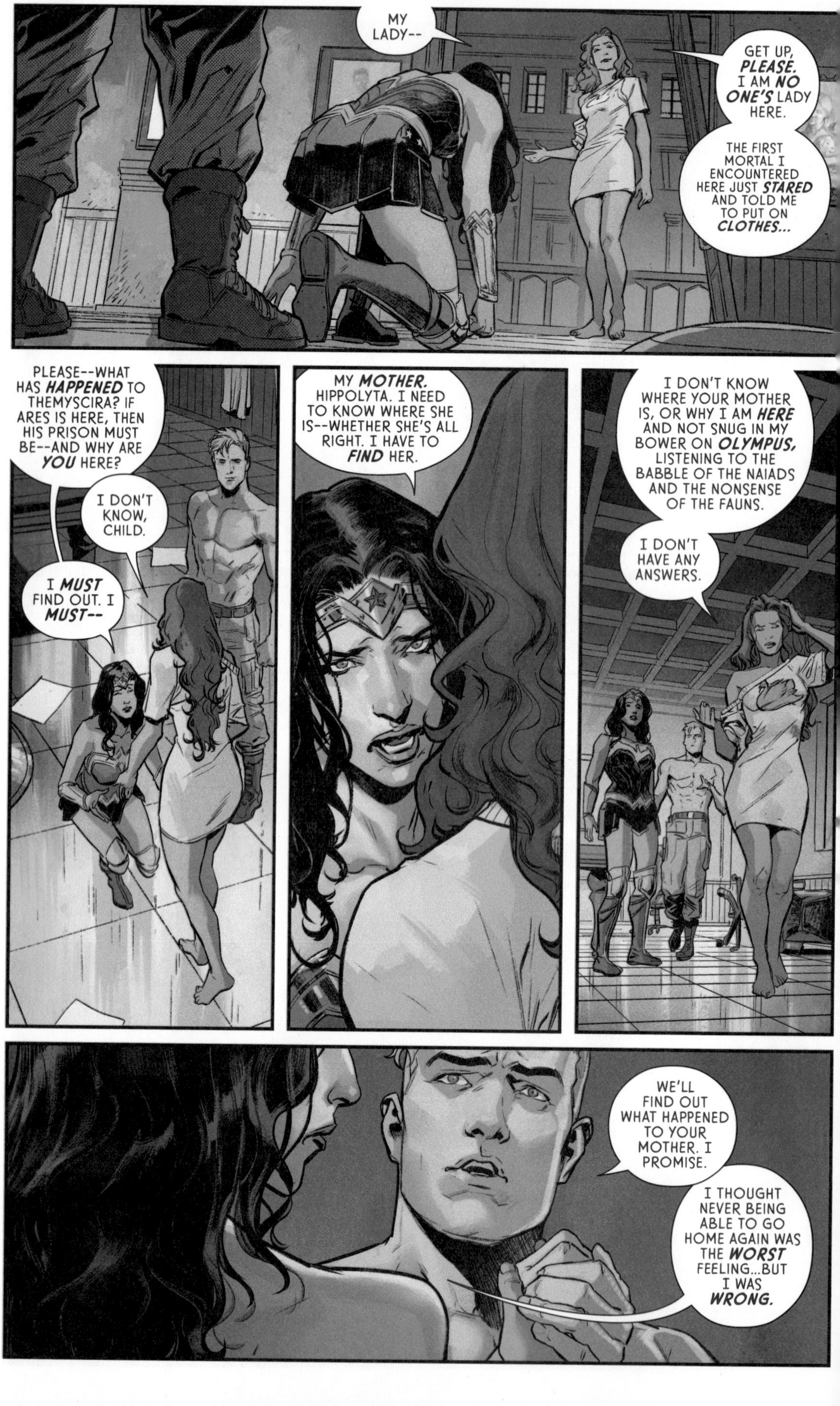

MY LADY--
GET UP, PLEASE. I AM NO ONE'S LADY HERE.
THE FIRST MORTAL I ENCOUNTERED HERE JUST STARED AND TOLD ME TO PUT ON CLOTHES...
PLEASE--WHAT HAS HAPPENED TO THEMYSCIRA? IF ARES IS HERE, THEN HIS PRISON MUST BE--AND WHY ARE YOU HERE?
I DON'T KNOW, CHILD.
I MUST FIND OUT. I MUST--
MY MOTHER. HIPPOLYTA. I NEED TO KNOW WHERE SHE IS--WHETHER SHE'S ALL RIGHT. I HAVE TO FIND HER.
I DON'T KNOW WHERE YOUR MOTHER IS, OR WHY I AM HERE AND NOT SNUG IN MY BOWER ON OLYMPUS, LISTENING TO THE BABBLE OF THE NAIADS AND THE NONSENSE OF THE FAUNS.
I DON'T HAVE ANY ANSWERS.
WE'LL FIND OUT WHAT HAPPENED TO YOUR MOTHER. I PROMISE.
I THOUGHT NEVER BEING ABLE TO GO HOME AGAIN WAS THE WORST FEELING...BUT I WAS WRONG.

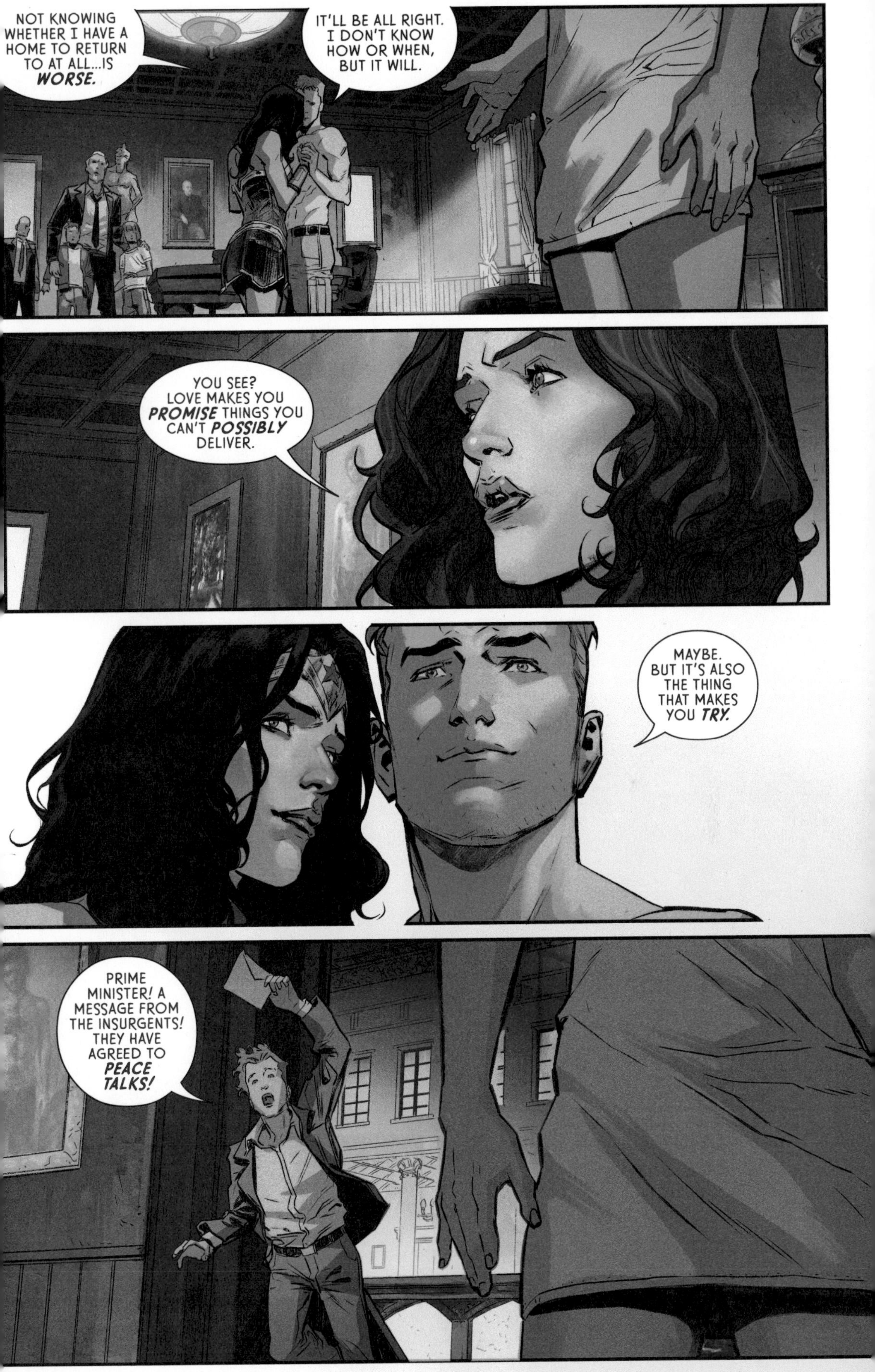
NOT KNOWING WHETHER I HAVE A HOME TO RETURN TO AT ALL...IS **WORSE.**
IT'LL BE ALL RIGHT. I DON'T KNOW HOW OR WHEN, BUT IT WILL.
YOU SEE? LOVE MAKES YOU **PROMISE** THINGS YOU CAN'T **POSSIBLY** DELIVER.
MAYBE. BUT IT'S ALSO THE THING THAT MAKES YOU **TRY.**
PRIME MINISTER! A MESSAGE FROM THE INSURGENTS! THEY HAVE AGREED TO **PEACE TALKS!**

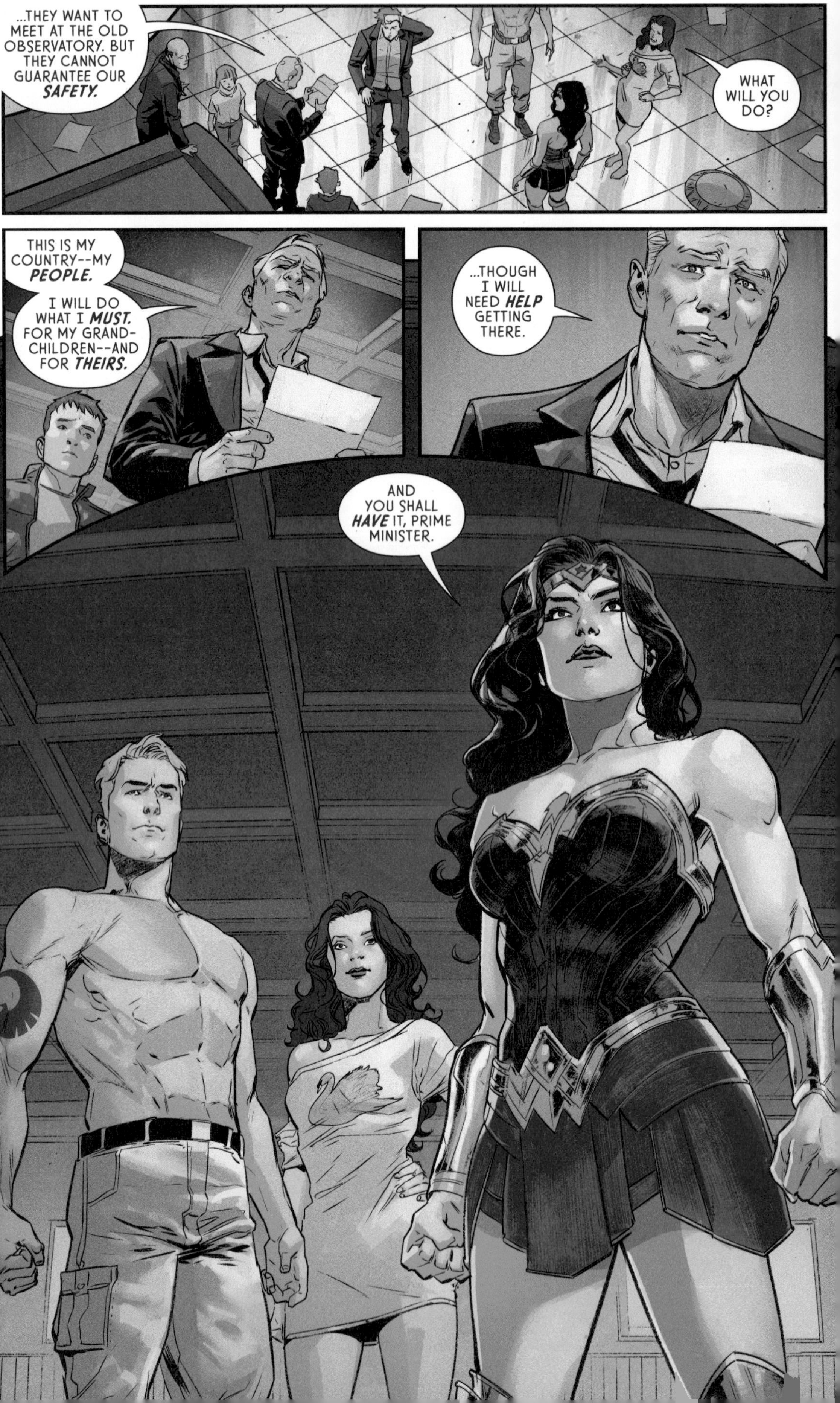
...THEY WANT TO MEET AT THE OLD OBSERVATORY. BUT THEY CANNOT GUARANTEE OUR *SAFETY.*
WHAT WILL YOU DO?
THIS IS MY COUNTRY--MY *PEOPLE.*
I WILL DO WHAT I *MUST.* FOR MY GRAND-CHILDREN--AND FOR *THEIRS.*
...THOUGH I WILL NEED *HELP* GETTING THERE.
AND YOU SHALL *HAVE* IT, PRIME MINISTER.

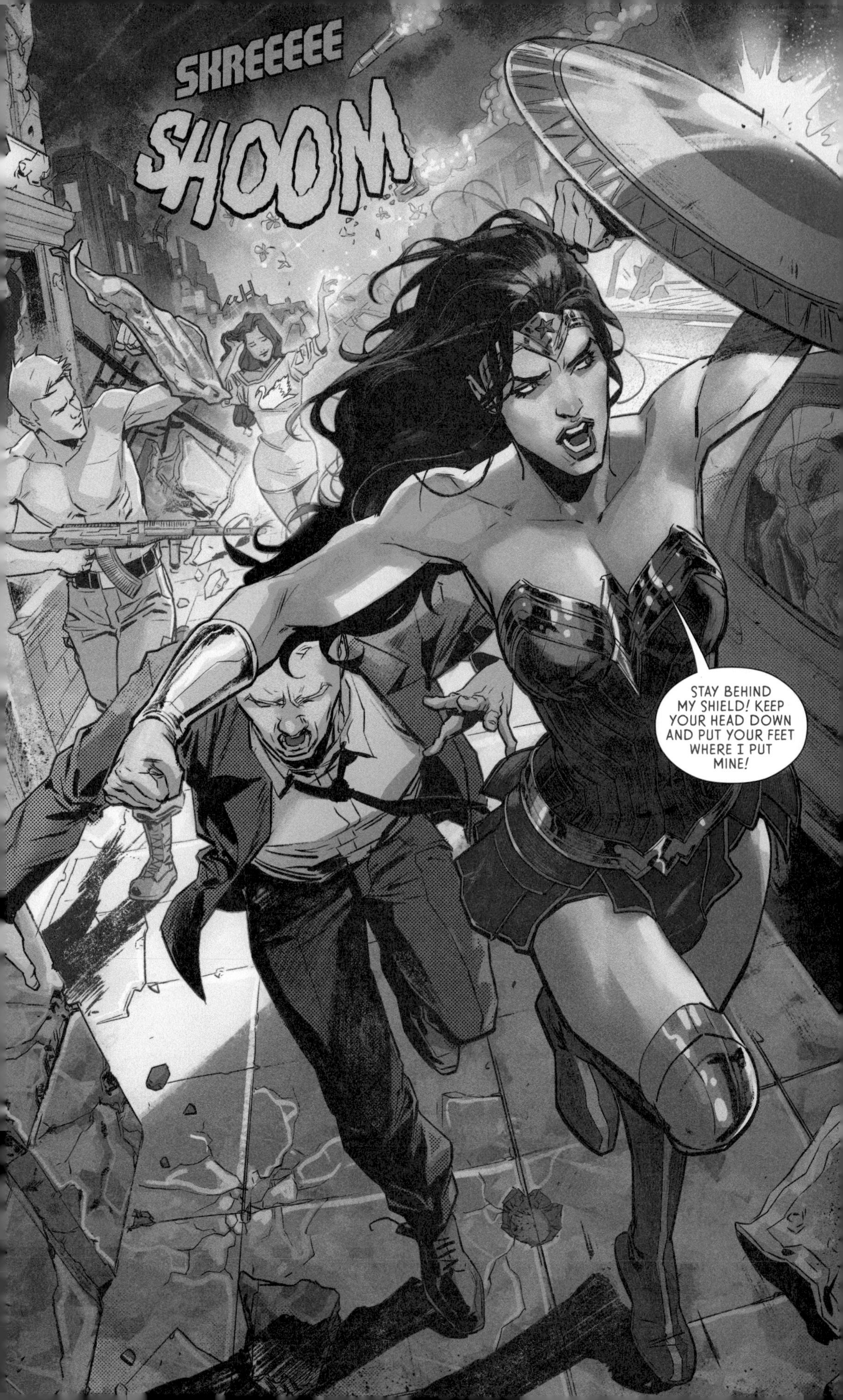
SKREEEEE
SHOOM
STAY BEHIND MY SHIELD! KEEP YOUR HEAD DOWN AND PUT YOUR FEET WHERE I PUT MINE!

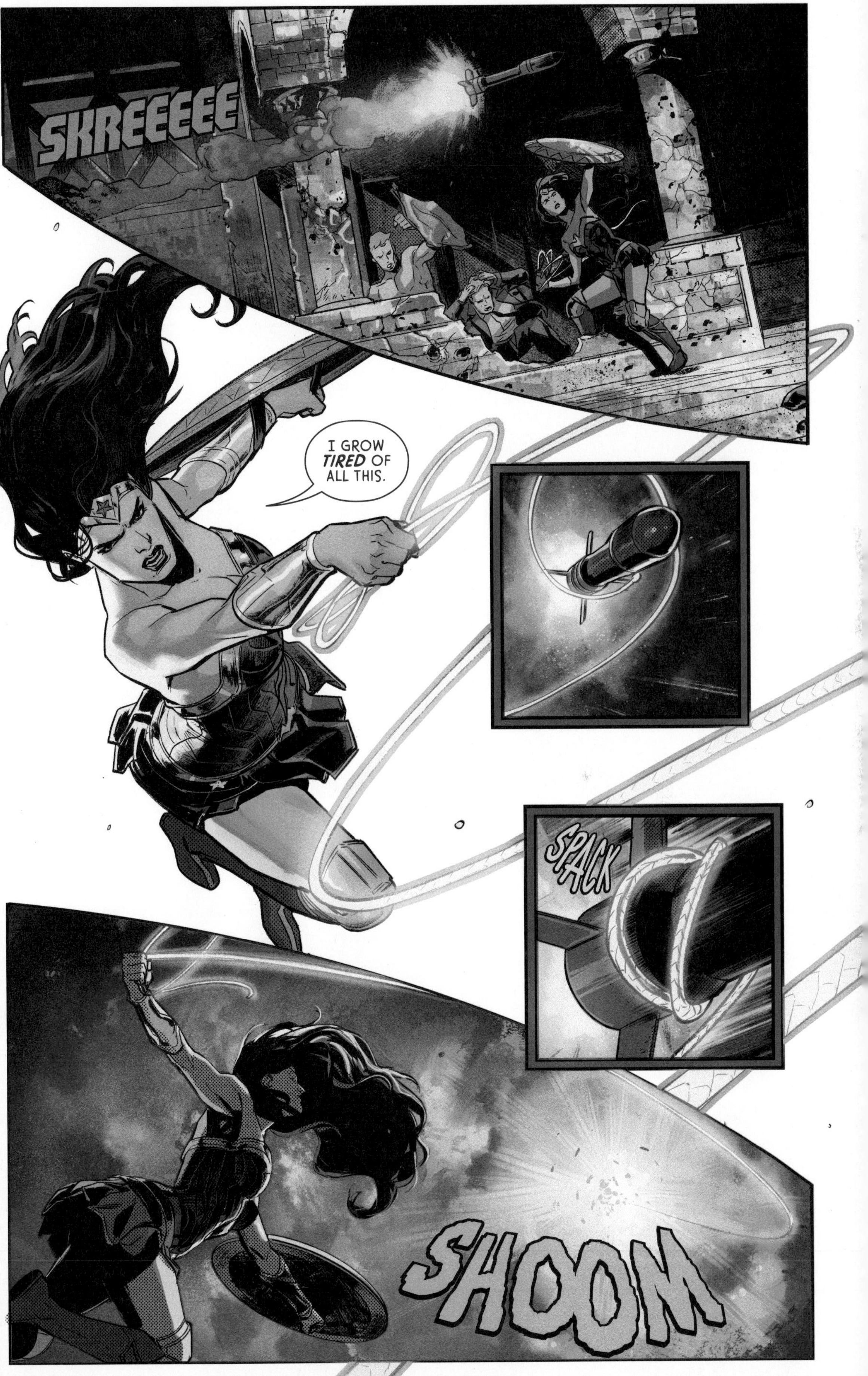
SKREEEEE
I GROW *TIRED* OF ALL THIS.
SPACK
SHOOM

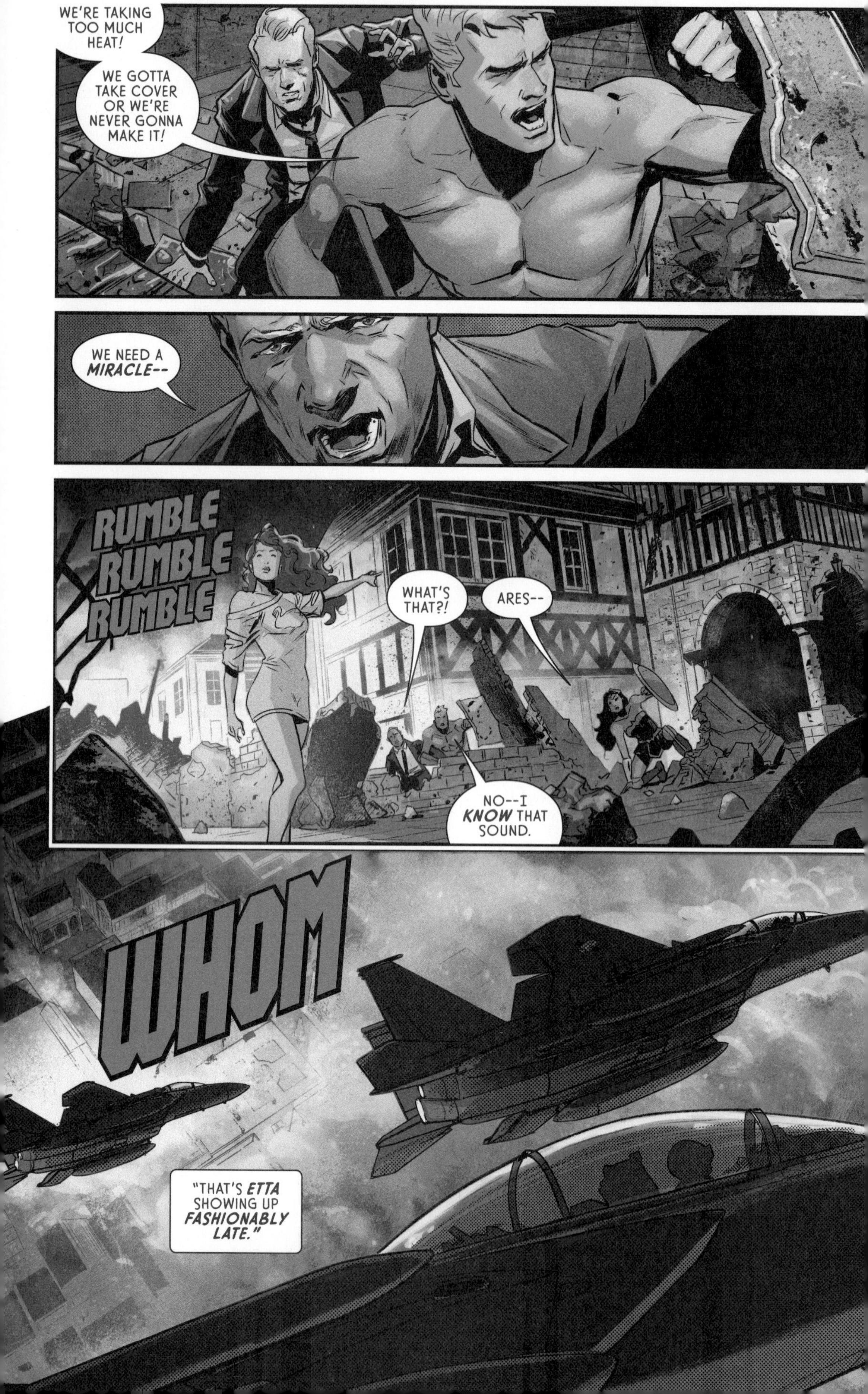

WE'RE TAKING TOO MUCH HEAT!
WE GOTTA TAKE COVER OR WE'RE NEVER GONNA MAKE IT!
WE NEED A *MIRACLE--*
RUMBLE RUMBLE RUMBLE
WHAT'S THAT?!
ARES--
NO--I *KNOW* THAT SOUND.
WHOM
"THAT'S *ETTA* SHOWING UP *FASHIONABLY LATE.*"

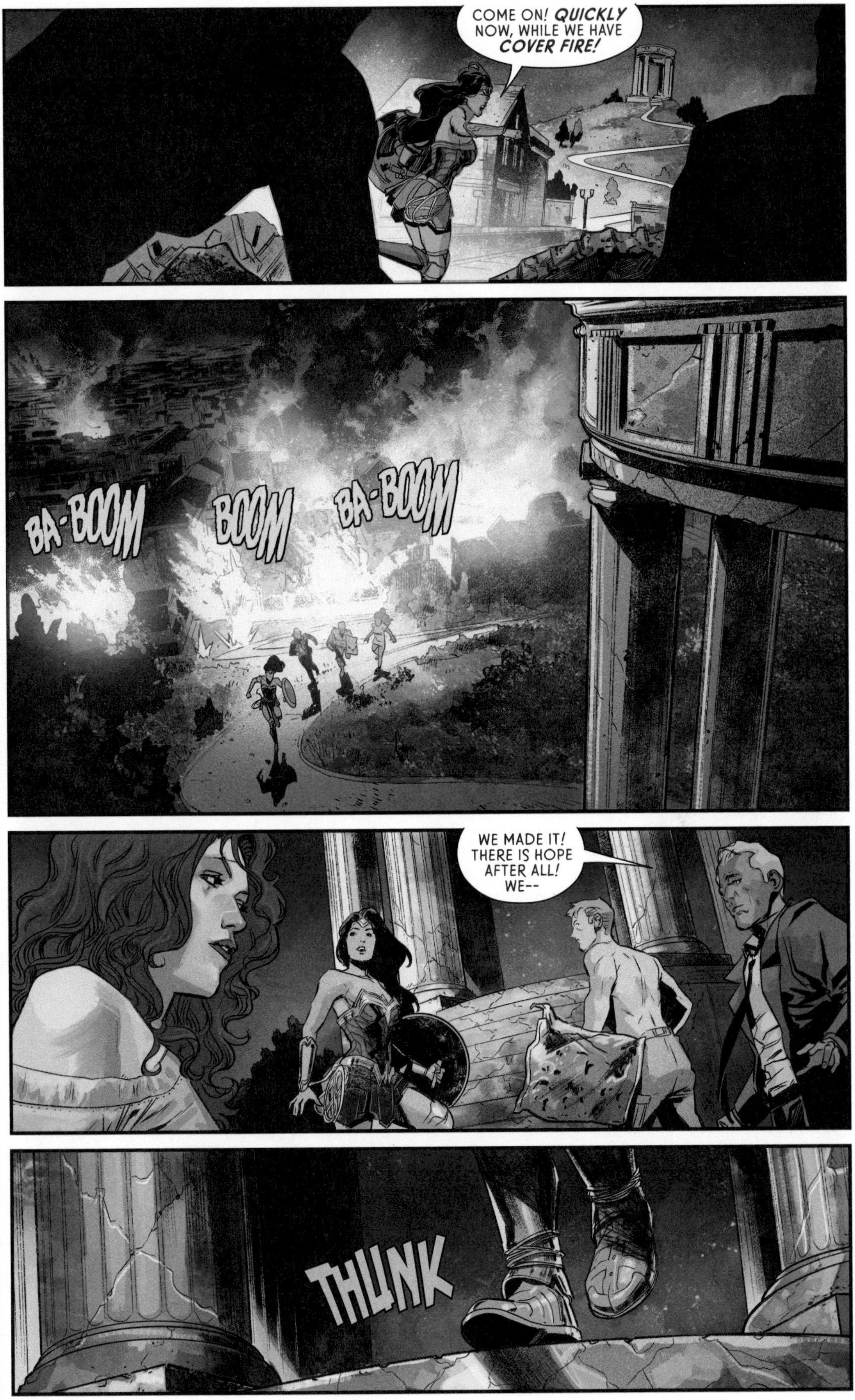
COME ON! QUICKLY NOW, WHILE WE HAVE COVER FIRE!
BA-BOOM
BOOM
BA-BOOM
WE MADE IT! THERE IS HOPE AFTER ALL! WE--
THUNK

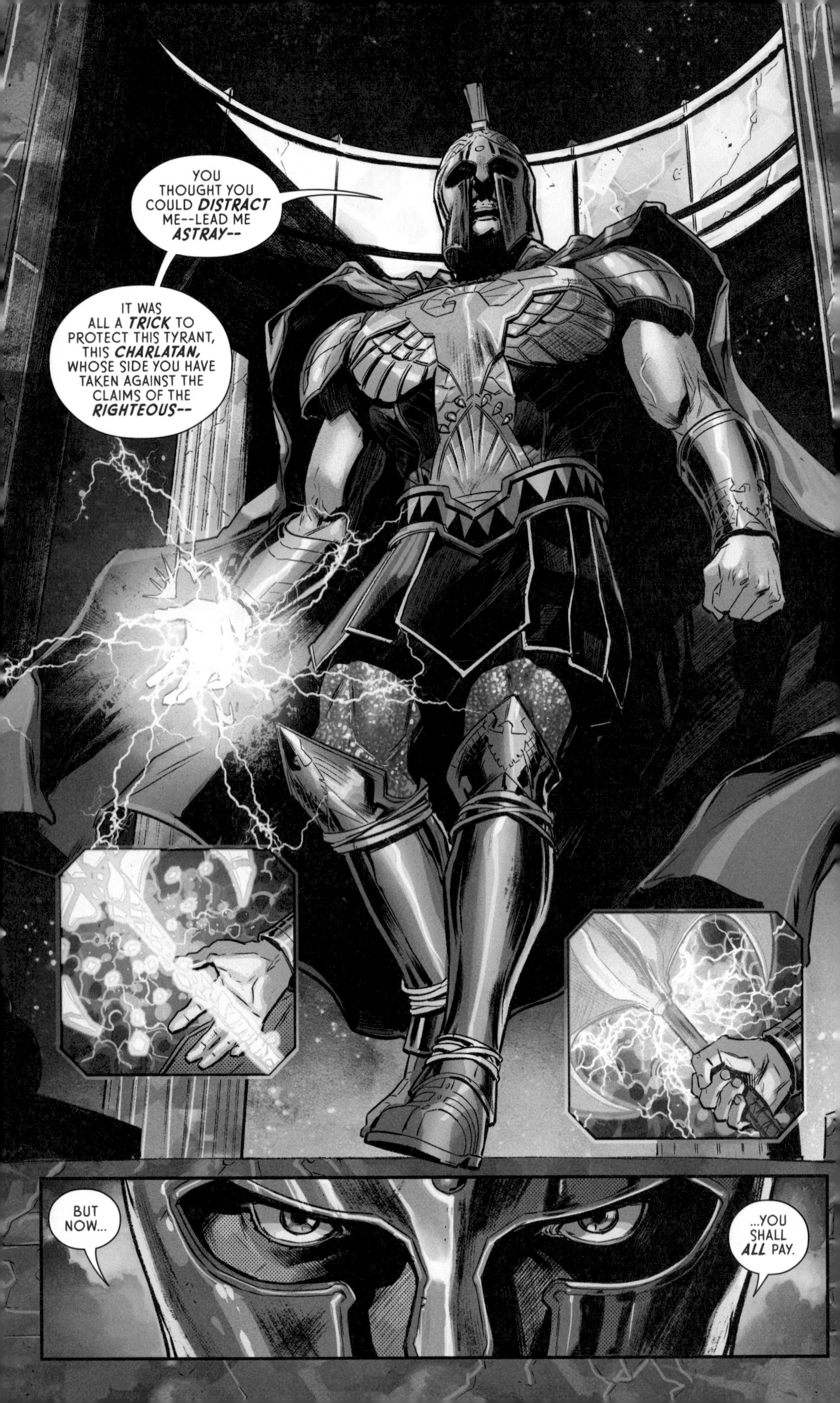
YOU THOUGHT YOU COULD DISTRACT ME--LEAD ME ASTRAY--
IT WAS ALL A TRICK TO PROTECT THIS TYRANT, THIS CHARLATAN, WHOSE SIDE YOU HAVE TAKEN AGAINST THE CLAIMS OF THE RIGHTEOUS--
BUT NOW...
...YOU SHALL ALL PAY.

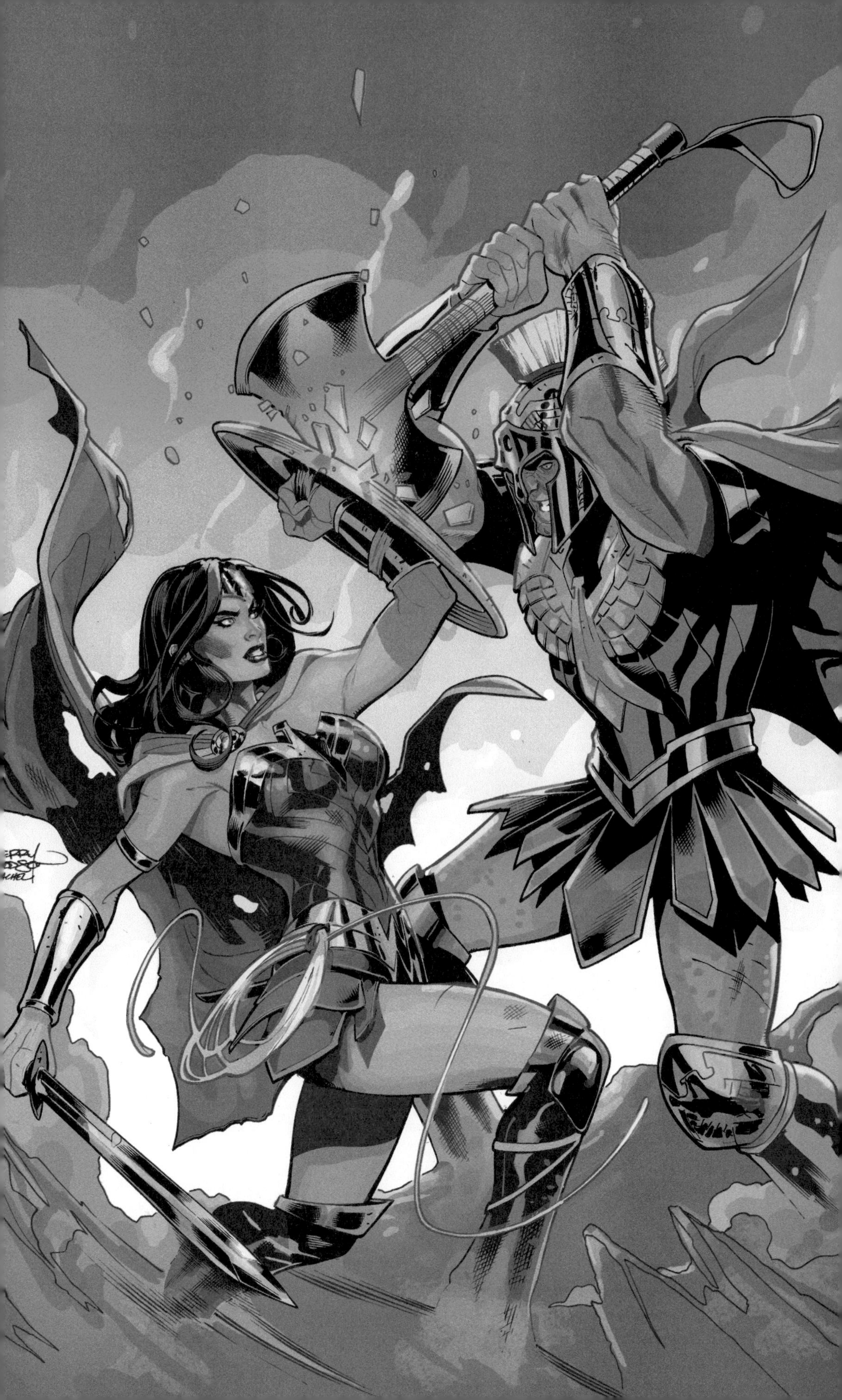

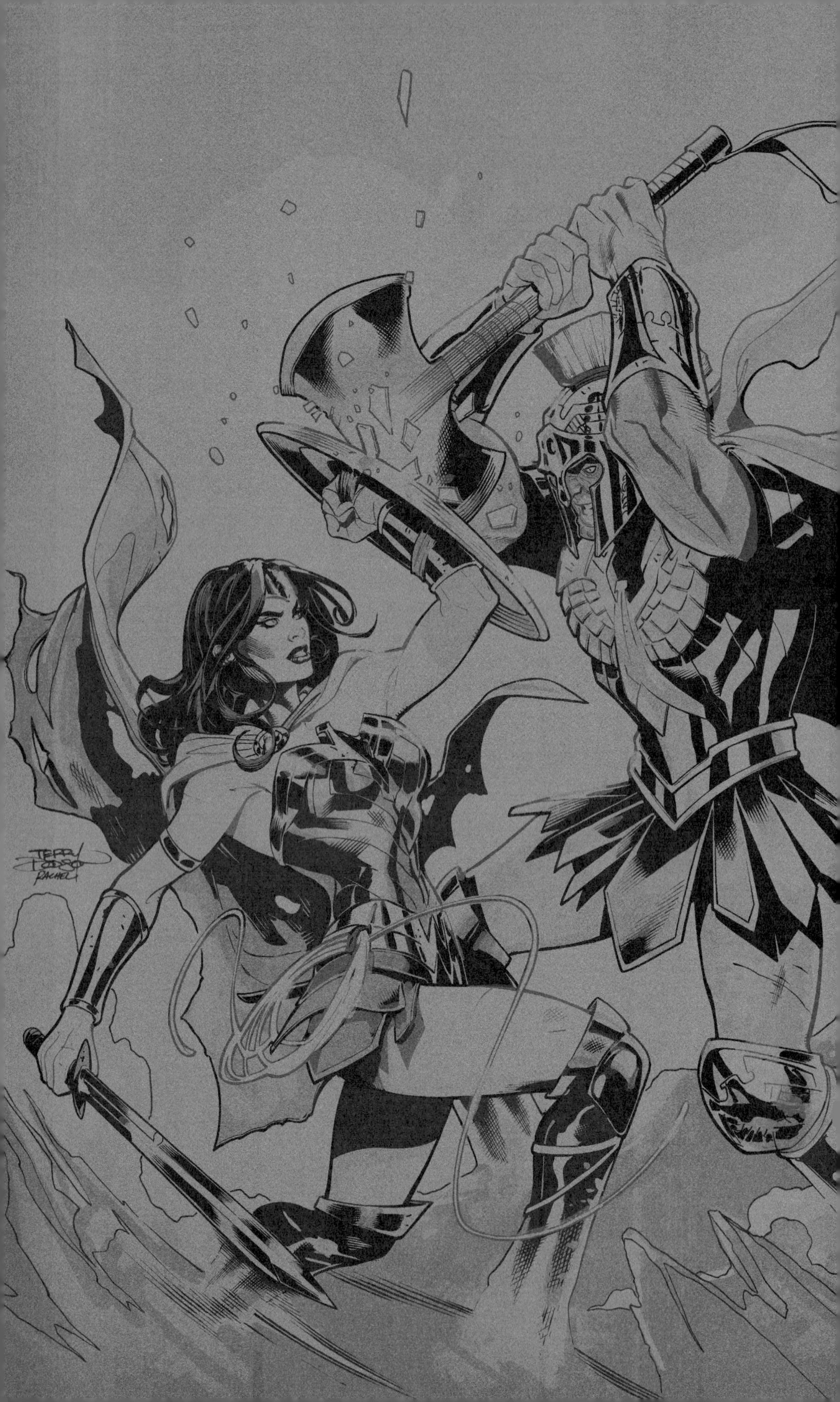
TERRY DODSON
RACHEL

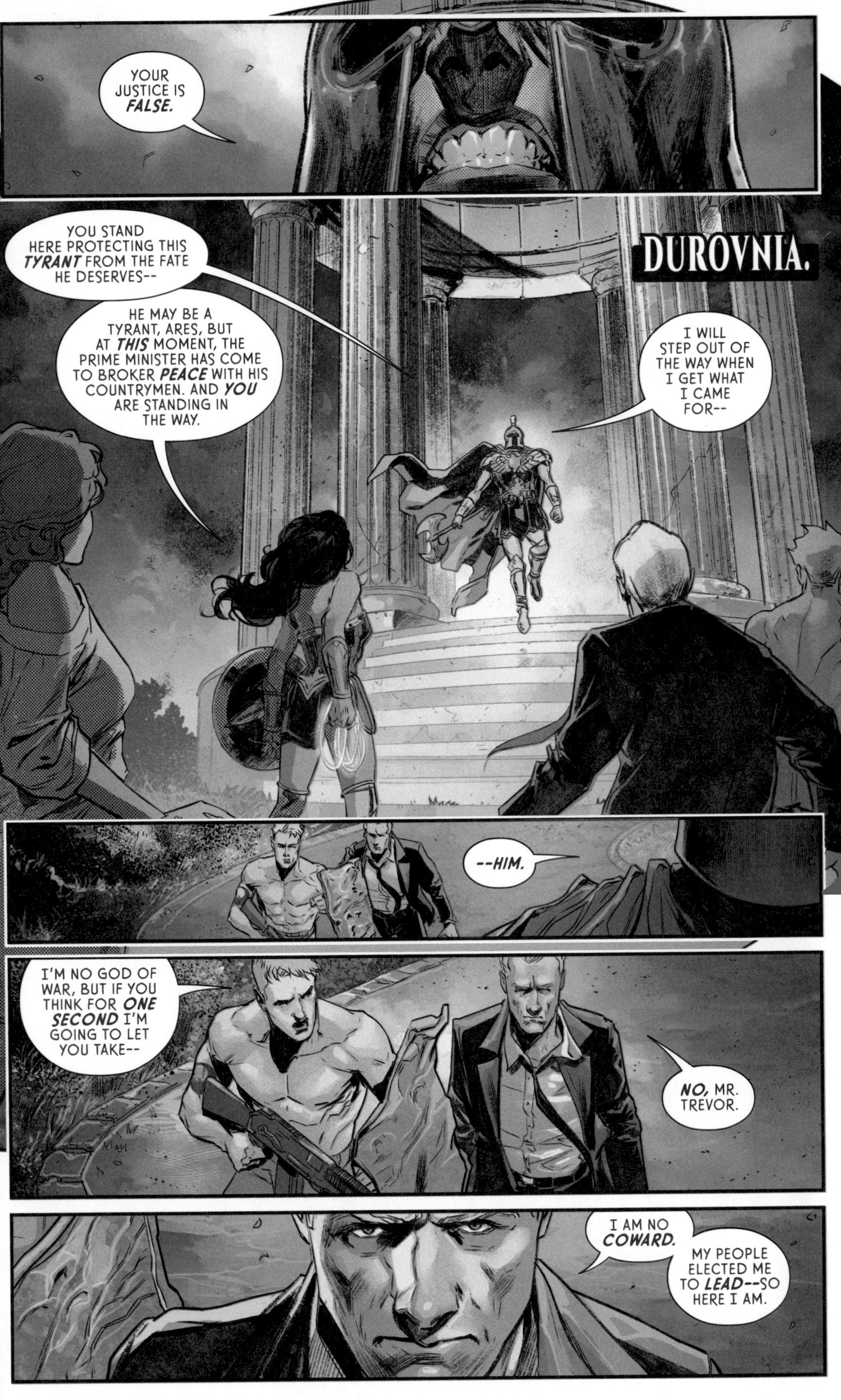
YOUR JUSTICE IS FALSE.
DUROVNIA.
YOU STAND HERE PROTECTING THIS TYRANT FROM THE FATE HE DESERVES--
HE MAY BE A TYRANT, ARES, BUT AT THIS MOMENT, THE PRIME MINISTER HAS COME TO BROKER PEACE WITH HIS COUNTRYMEN. AND YOU ARE STANDING IN THE WAY.
I WILL STEP OUT OF THE WAY WHEN I GET WHAT I CAME FOR--
--HIM.
I'M NO GOD OF WAR, BUT IF YOU THINK FOR ONE SECOND I'M GOING TO LET YOU TAKE--
NO, MR. TREVOR.
I AM NO COWARD.
MY PEOPLE ELECTED ME TO LEAD--SO HERE I AM.

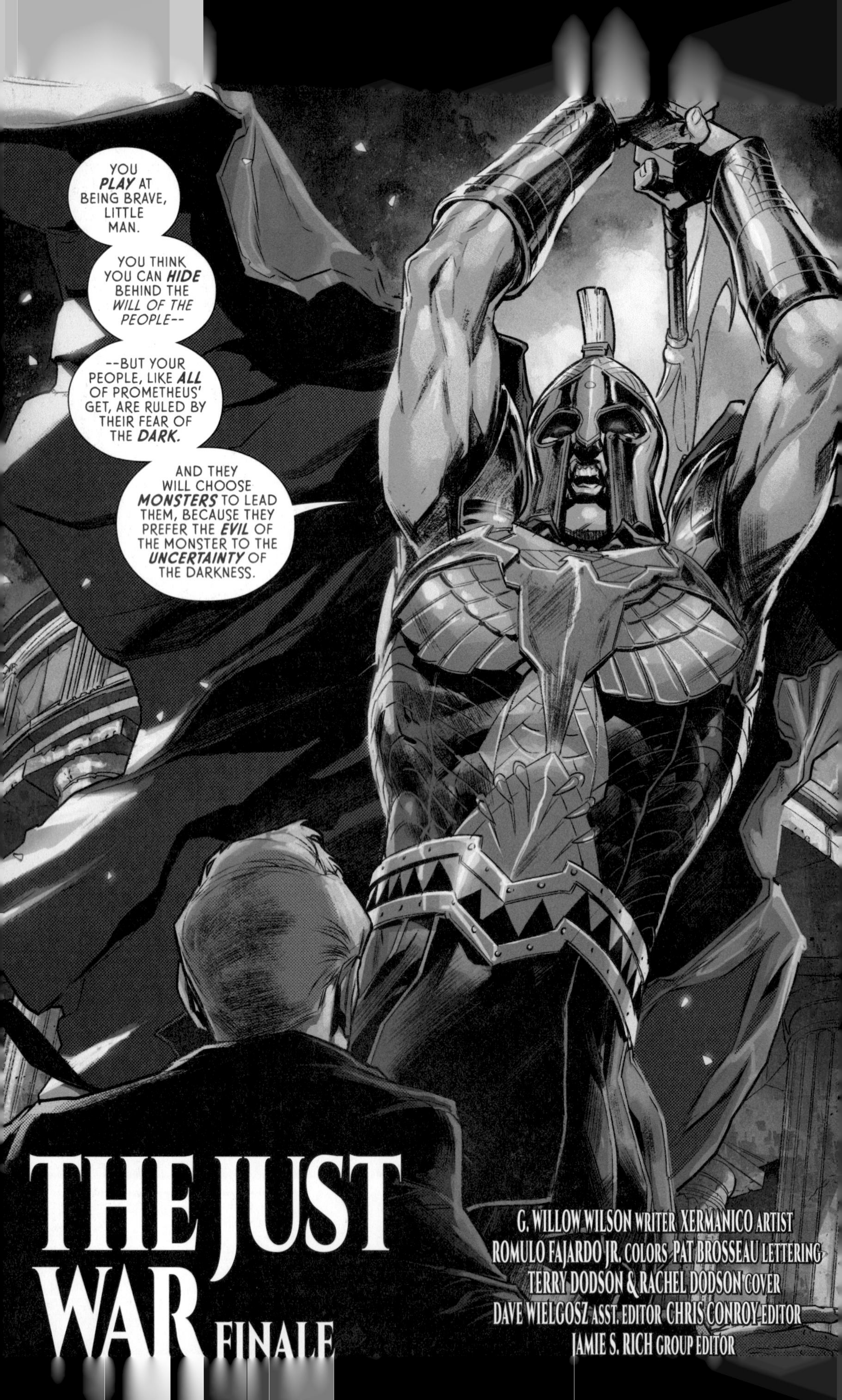
YOU PLAY AT BEING BRAVE, LITTLE MAN.
YOU THINK YOU CAN HIDE BEHIND THE WILL OF THE PEOPLE--
--BUT YOUR PEOPLE, LIKE ALL OF PROMETHEUS' GET, ARE RULED BY THEIR FEAR OF THE DARK.
AND THEY WILL CHOOSE MONSTERS TO LEAD THEM, BECAUSE THEY PREFER THE EVIL OF THE MONSTER TO THE UNCERTAINTY OF THE DARKNESS.
THE JUST WAR FINALE
G. WILLOW WILSON WRITER XERMANICO ARTIST
ROMULO FAJARDO JR. COLORS PAT BROSSEAU LETTERING
TERRY DODSON & RACHEL DODSON COVER
DAVE WIELGOSZ ASST. EDITOR CHRIS CONROY EDITOR
JAMIE S. RICH GROUP EDITOR

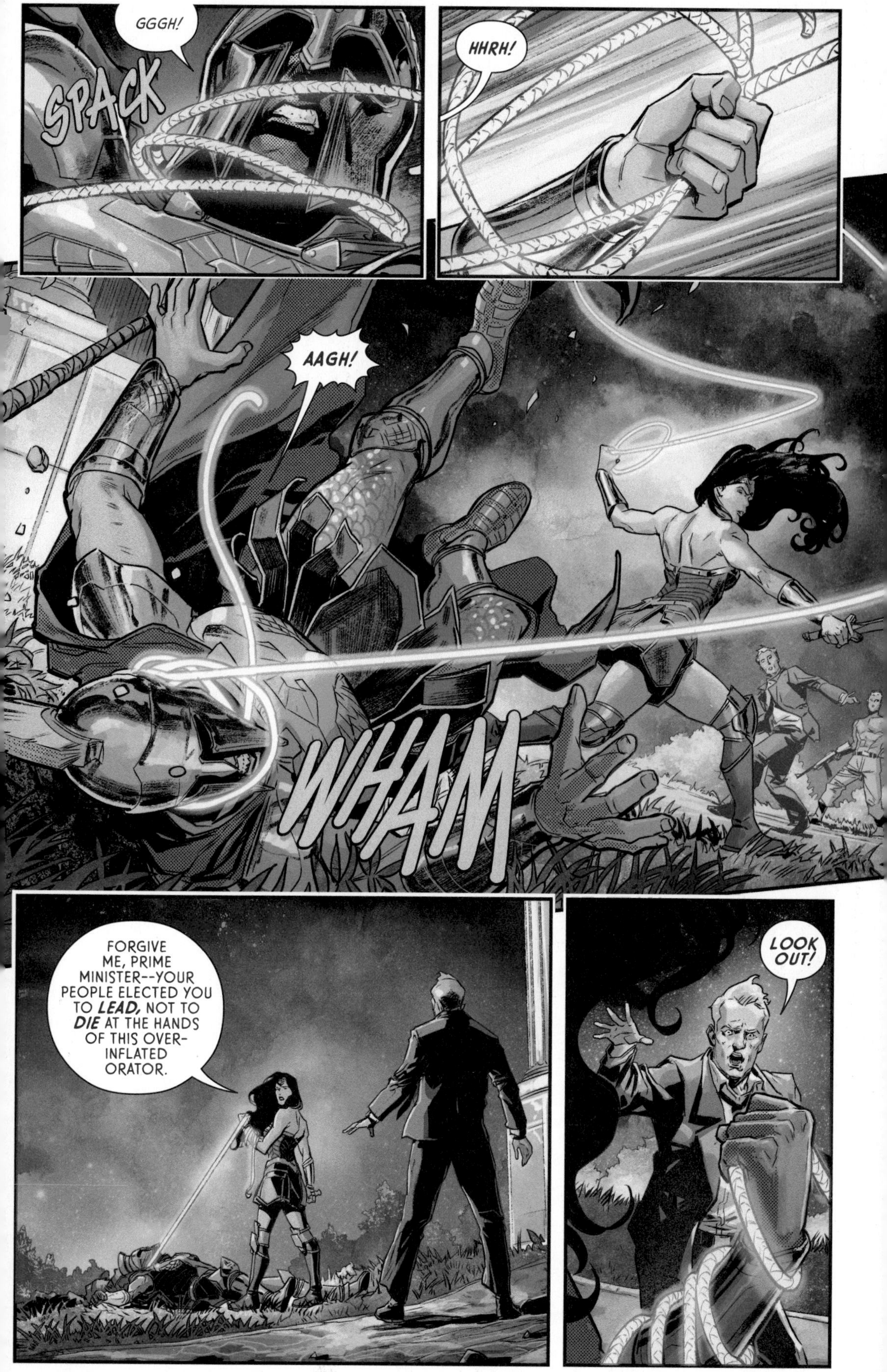
GGGH!
SPACK
HHRH!
AAGH!
WHAM
FORGIVE ME, PRIME MINISTER--YOUR PEOPLE ELECTED YOU TO **LEAD,** NOT TO **DIE** AT THE HANDS OF THIS OVER-INFLATED ORATOR.
LOOK OUT!

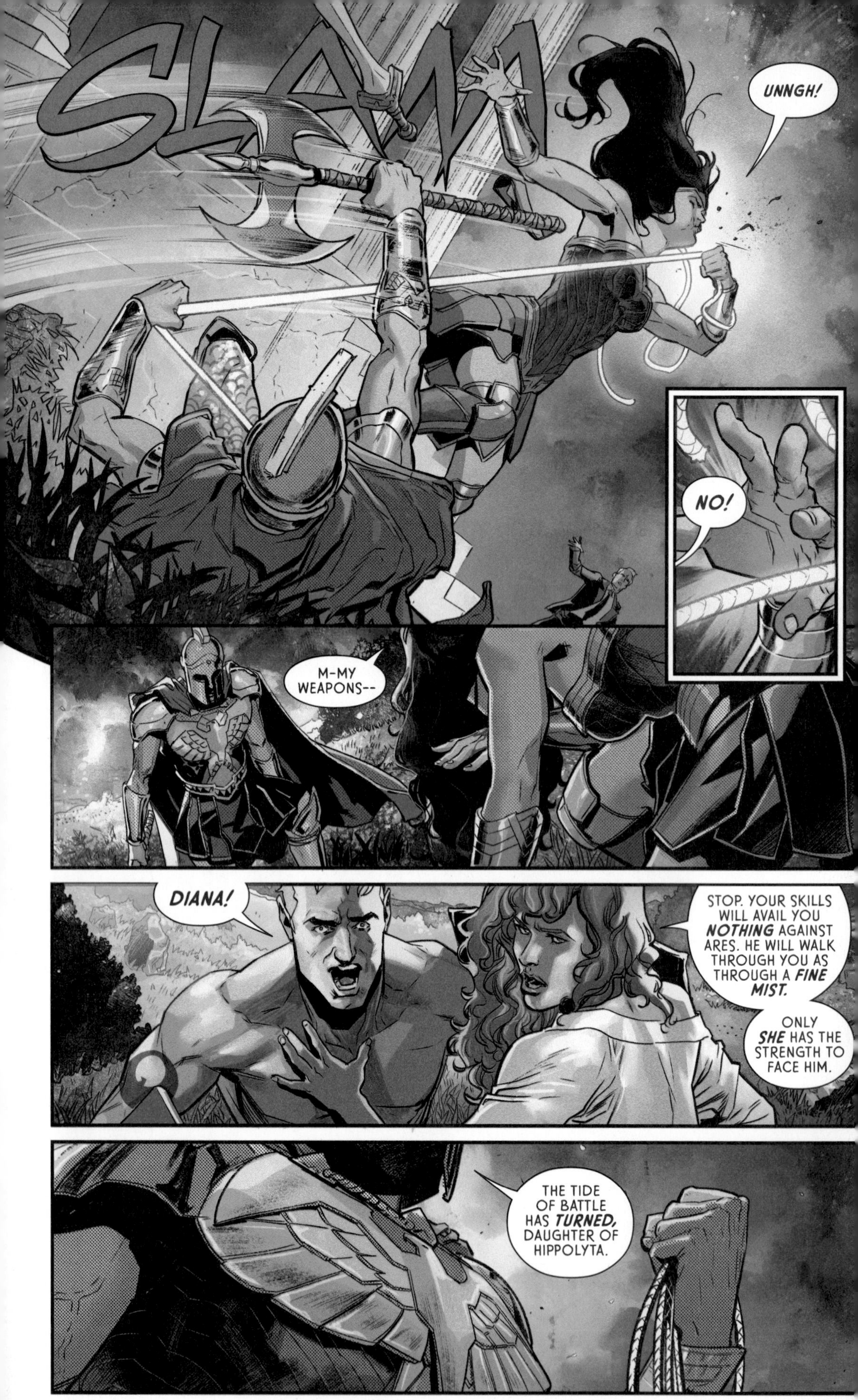
SLAM
UNNGH!
NO!
M-MY WEAPONS--
DIANA!
STOP. YOUR SKILLS WILL AVAIL YOU NOTHING AGAINST ARES. HE WILL WALK THROUGH YOU AS THROUGH A FINE MIST.
ONLY SHE HAS THE STRENGTH TO FACE HIM.
THE TIDE OF BATTLE HAS TURNED, DAUGHTER OF HIPPOLYTA.

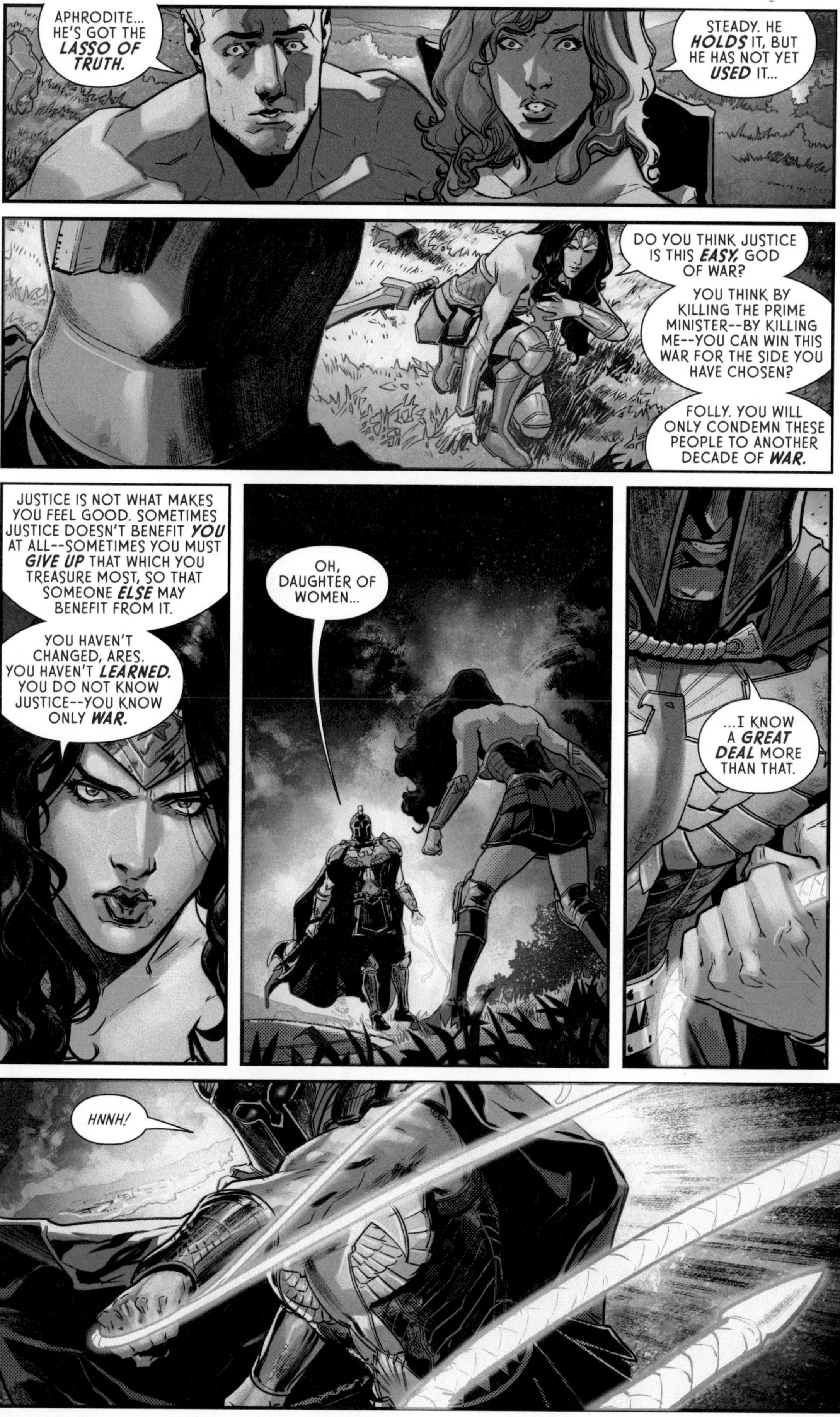

APHRODITE... HE'S GOT THE **LASSO OF TRUTH.**
STEADY. HE **HOLDS** IT, BUT HE HAS NOT YET **USED** IT...
DO YOU THINK JUSTICE IS THIS **EASY,** GOD OF WAR?
YOU THINK BY KILLING THE PRIME MINISTER--BY KILLING ME--YOU CAN WIN THIS WAR FOR THE SIDE YOU HAVE CHOSEN?
FOLLY. YOU WILL ONLY CONDEMN THESE PEOPLE TO ANOTHER DECADE OF **WAR.**
JUSTICE IS NOT WHAT MAKES YOU FEEL GOOD. SOMETIMES JUSTICE DOESN'T BENEFIT **YOU** AT ALL--SOMETIMES YOU MUST **GIVE UP** THAT WHICH YOU TREASURE MOST, SO THAT SOMEONE **ELSE** MAY BENEFIT FROM IT.
YOU HAVEN'T CHANGED, ARES. YOU HAVEN'T **LEARNED.** YOU DO NOT KNOW JUSTICE--YOU KNOW ONLY **WAR.**
OH, DAUGHTER OF WOMEN...
...I KNOW A **GREAT DEAL** MORE THAN THAT.
HNNH!

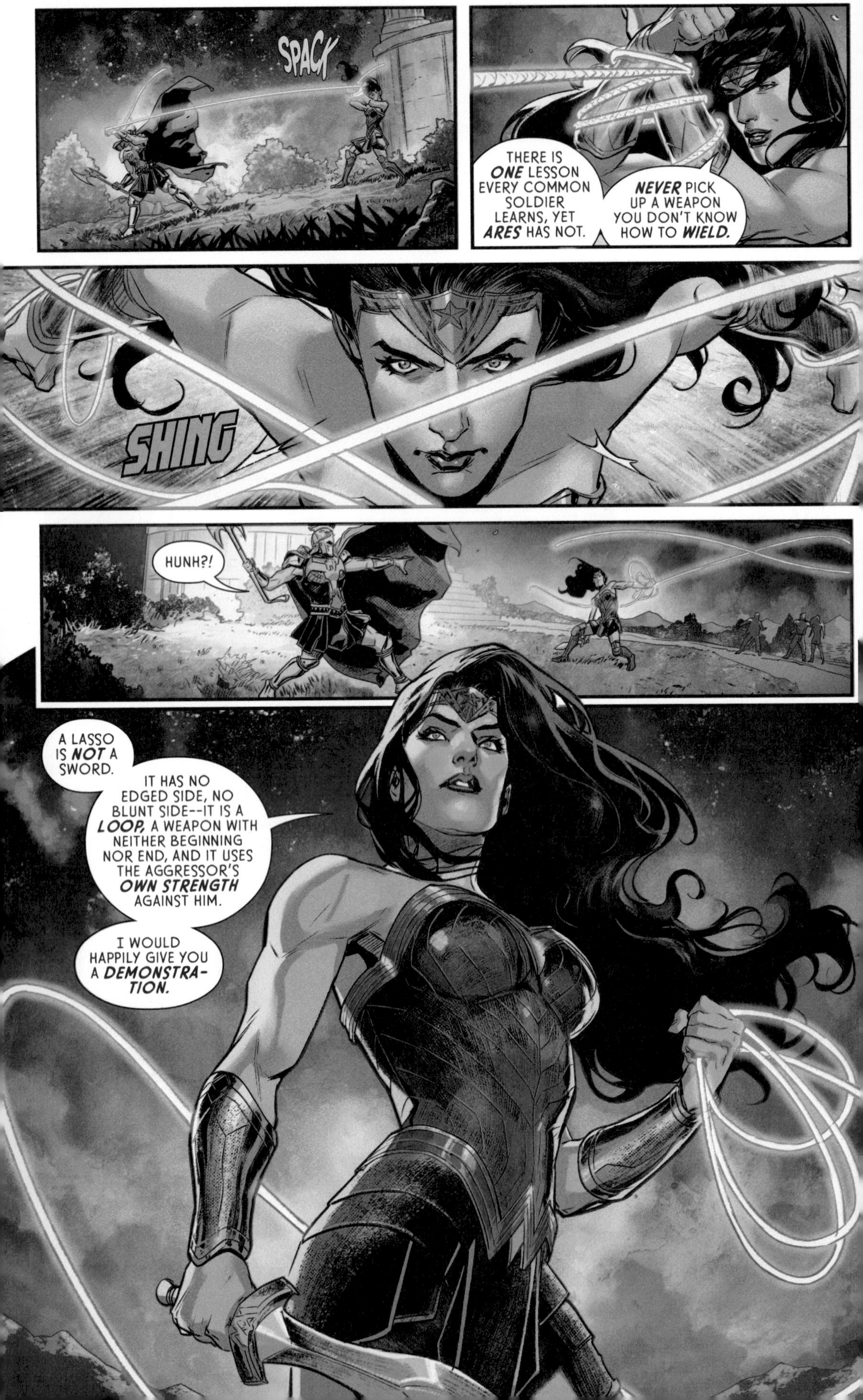
SPACK
THERE IS ONE LESSON EVERY COMMON SOLDIER LEARNS, YET ARES HAS NOT.
NEVER PICK UP A WEAPON YOU DON'T KNOW HOW TO WIELD.
SHING
HUNH?!
A LASSO IS NOT A SWORD.
IT HAS NO EDGED SIDE, NO BLUNT SIDE--IT IS A LOOP, A WEAPON WITH NEITHER BEGINNING NOR END, AND IT USES THE AGGRESSOR'S OWN STRENGTH AGAINST HIM.
I WOULD HAPPILY GIVE YOU A DEMONSTRATION.

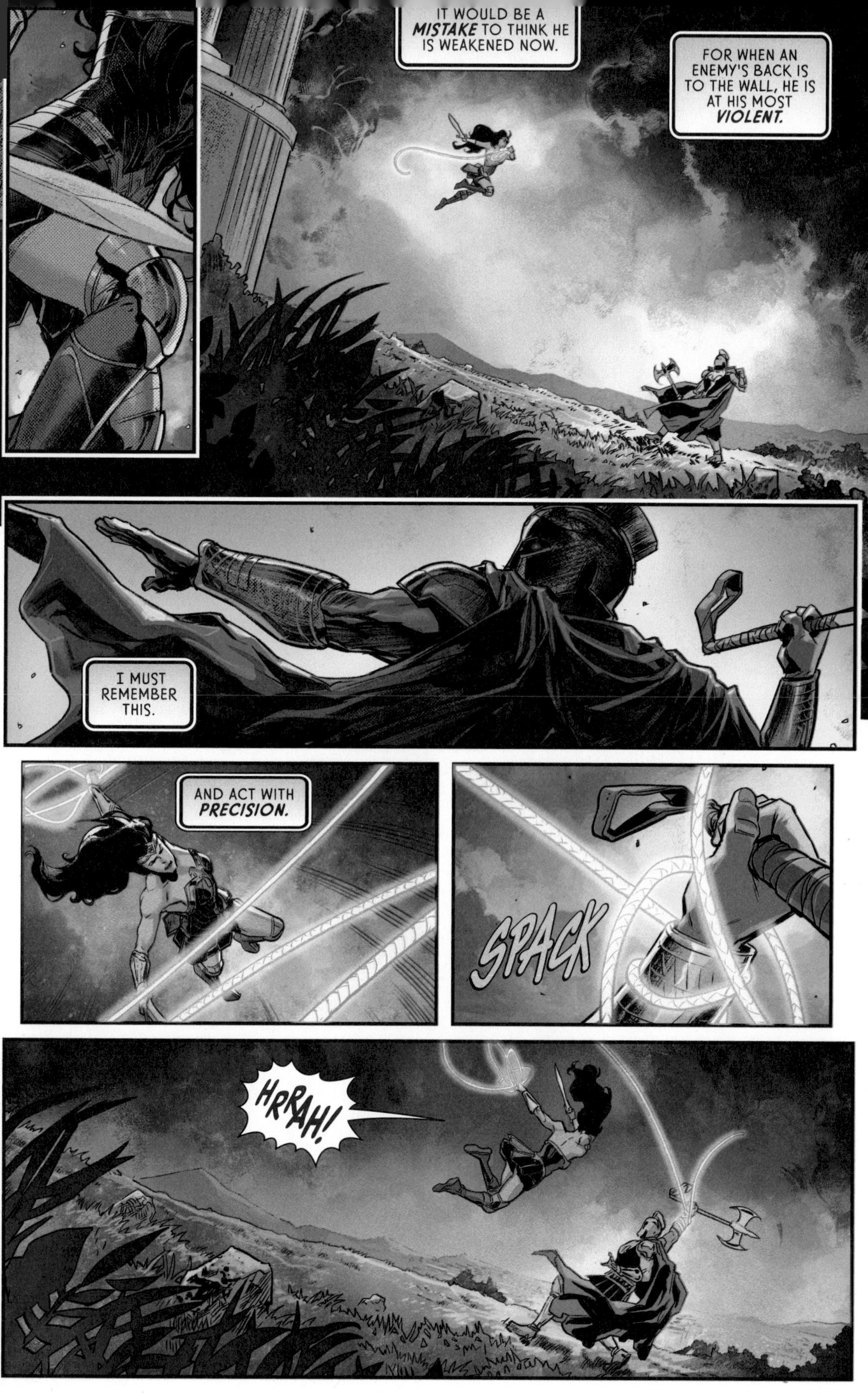

IT WOULD BE A MISTAKE TO THINK HE IS WEAKENED NOW.
FOR WHEN AN ENEMY'S BACK IS TO THE WALL, HE IS AT HIS MOST VIOLENT.
I MUST REMEMBER THIS.
AND ACT WITH PRECISION.
SPACK
HRRAH!

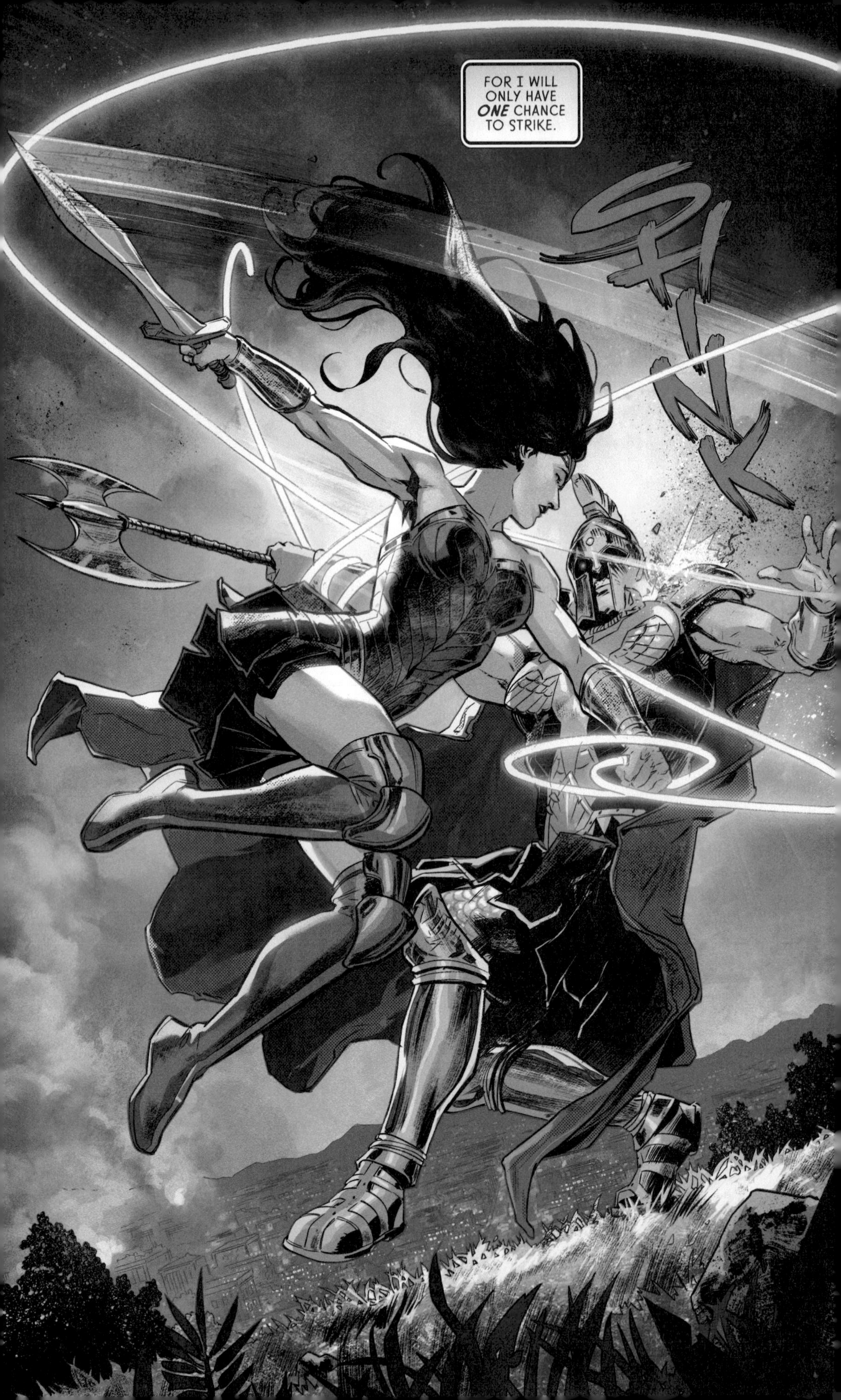

FOR I WILL ONLY HAVE *ONE* CHANCE TO STRIKE.
SHINK

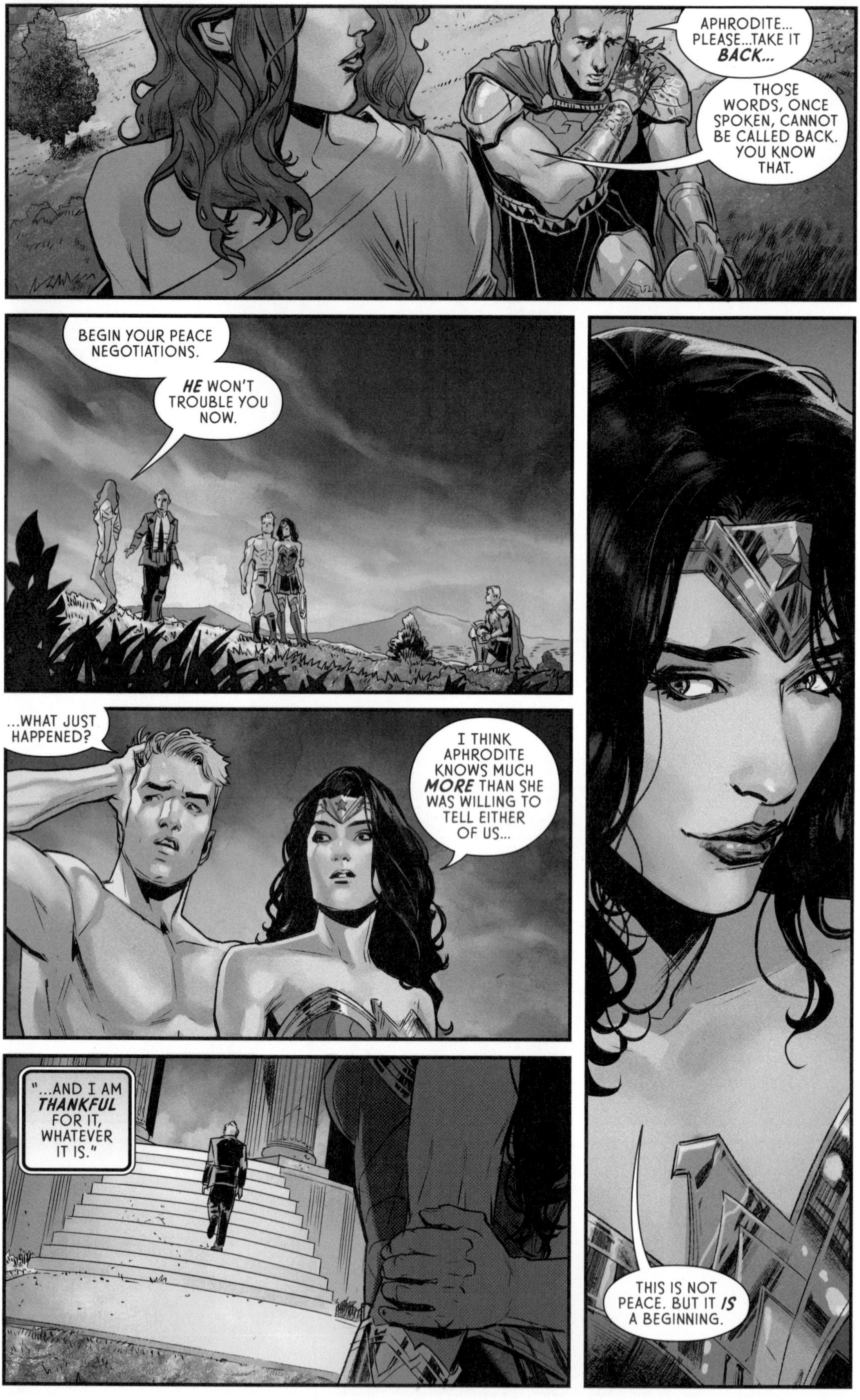
APHRODITE... PLEASE...TAKE IT **BACK...**
THOSE WORDS, ONCE SPOKEN, CANNOT BE CALLED BACK. YOU KNOW THAT.
BEGIN YOUR PEACE NEGOTIATIONS.
HE WON'T TROUBLE YOU NOW.
...WHAT JUST HAPPENED?
I THINK APHRODITE KNOWS MUCH ***MORE*** THAN SHE WAS WILLING TO TELL EITHER OF US...
"...AND I AM ***THANKFUL*** FOR IT, WHATEVER IT IS."
THIS IS NOT PEACE. BUT IT ***IS*** A BEGINNING.

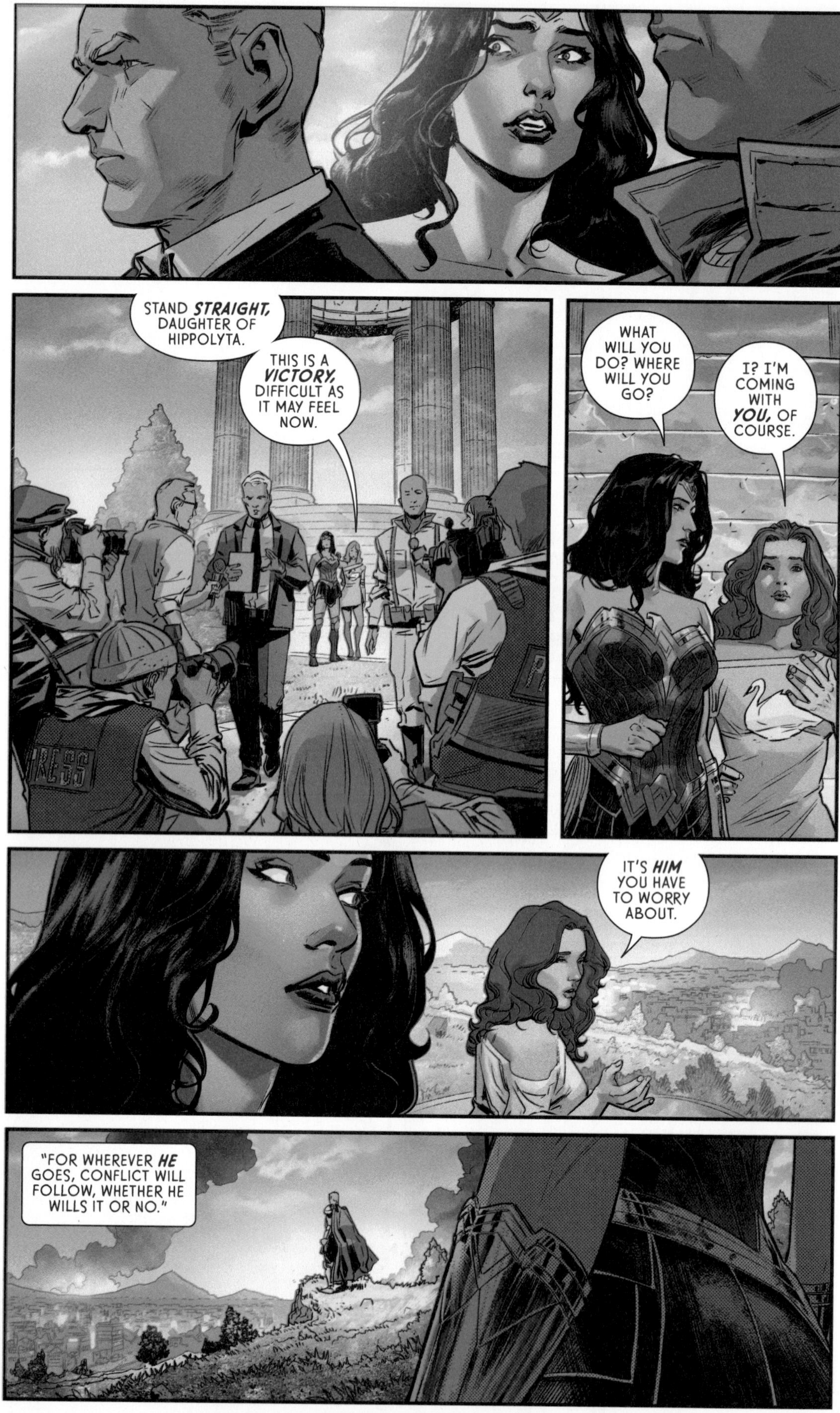

STAND **STRAIGHT,** DAUGHTER OF HIPPOLYTA.
THIS IS A **VICTORY,** DIFFICULT AS IT MAY FEEL NOW.
PRESS
WHAT WILL YOU DO? WHERE WILL YOU GO?
I? I'M COMING WITH **YOU,** OF COURSE.
IT'S **HIM** YOU HAVE TO WORRY ABOUT.
"FOR WHEREVER **HE** GOES, CONFLICT WILL FOLLOW, WHETHER HE WILLS IT OR NO."

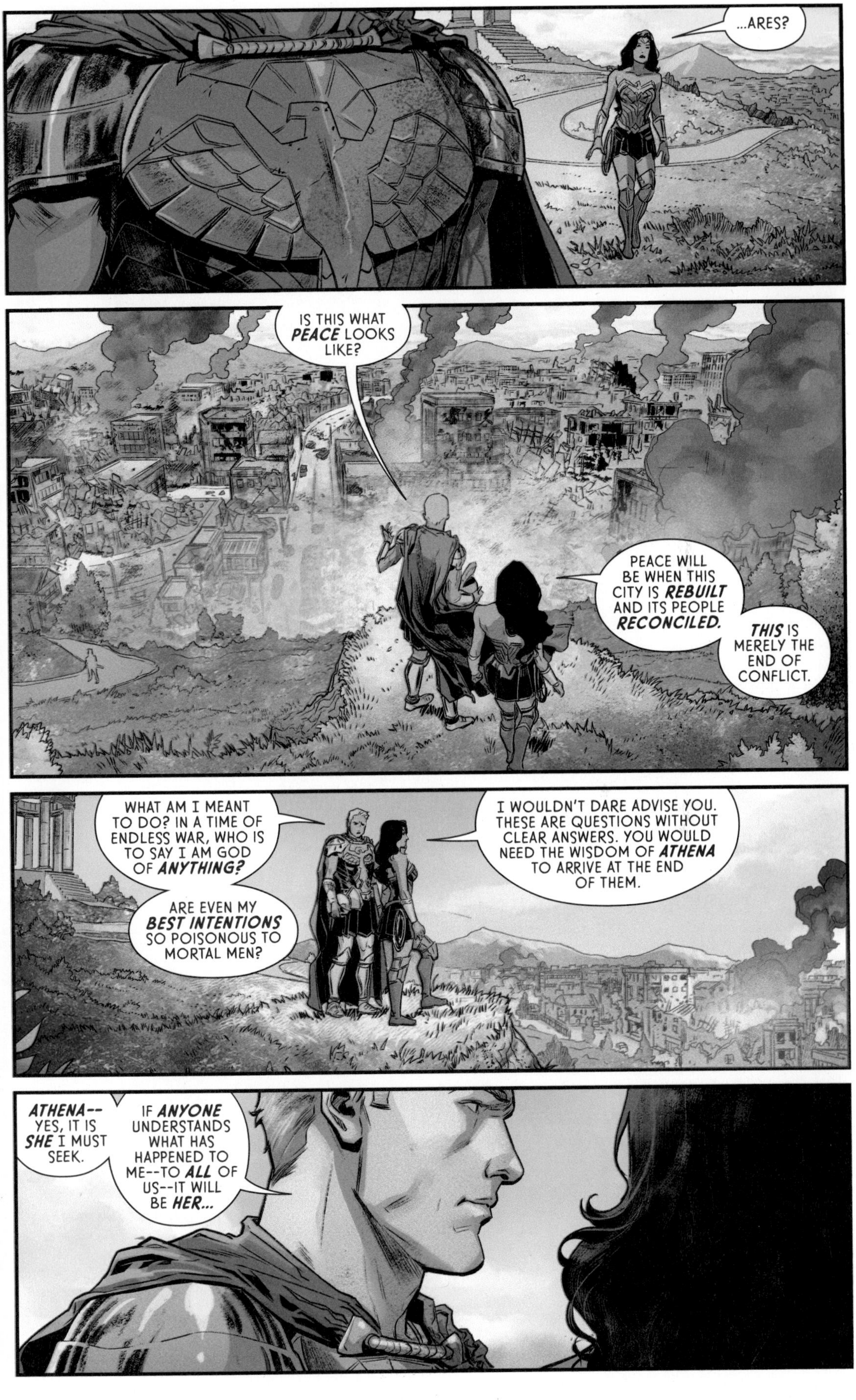
...ARES?
IS THIS WHAT PEACE LOOKS LIKE?
PEACE WILL BE WHEN THIS CITY IS REBUILT AND ITS PEOPLE RECONCILED.
THIS IS MERELY THE END OF CONFLICT.
WHAT AM I MEANT TO DO? IN A TIME OF ENDLESS WAR, WHO IS TO SAY I AM GOD OF ANYTHING?
ARE EVEN MY BEST INTENTIONS SO POISONOUS TO MORTAL MEN?
I WOULDN'T DARE ADVISE YOU. THESE ARE QUESTIONS WITHOUT CLEAR ANSWERS. YOU WOULD NEED THE WISDOM OF ATHENA TO ARRIVE AT THE END OF THEM.
ATHENA-- YES, IT IS SHE I MUST SEEK.
IF ANYONE UNDERSTANDS WHAT HAS HAPPENED TO ME--TO ALL OF US--IT WILL BE HER...

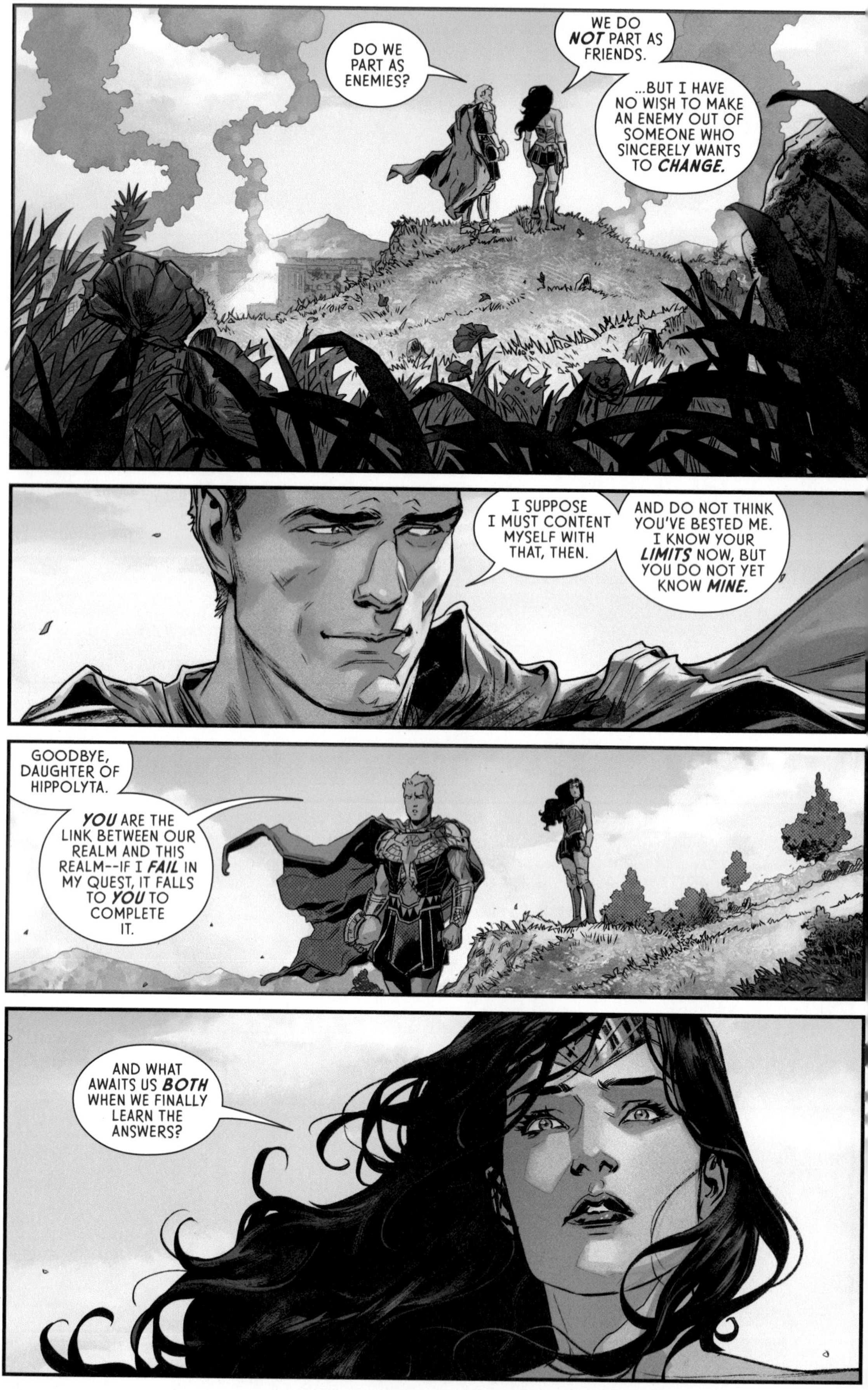
DO WE PART AS ENEMIES?
WE DO *NOT* PART AS FRIENDS.
...BUT I HAVE NO WISH TO MAKE AN ENEMY OUT OF SOMEONE WHO SINCERELY WANTS TO *CHANGE.*
I SUPPOSE I MUST CONTENT MYSELF WITH THAT, THEN.
AND DO NOT THINK YOU'VE BESTED ME. I KNOW YOUR *LIMITS* NOW, BUT YOU DO NOT YET KNOW *MINE.*
GOODBYE, DAUGHTER OF HIPPOLYTA.
YOU ARE THE LINK BETWEEN OUR REALM AND THIS REALM--IF I *FAIL* IN MY QUEST, IT FALLS TO *YOU* TO COMPLETE IT.
AND WHAT AWAITS US *BOTH* WHEN WE FINALLY LEARN THE ANSWERS?

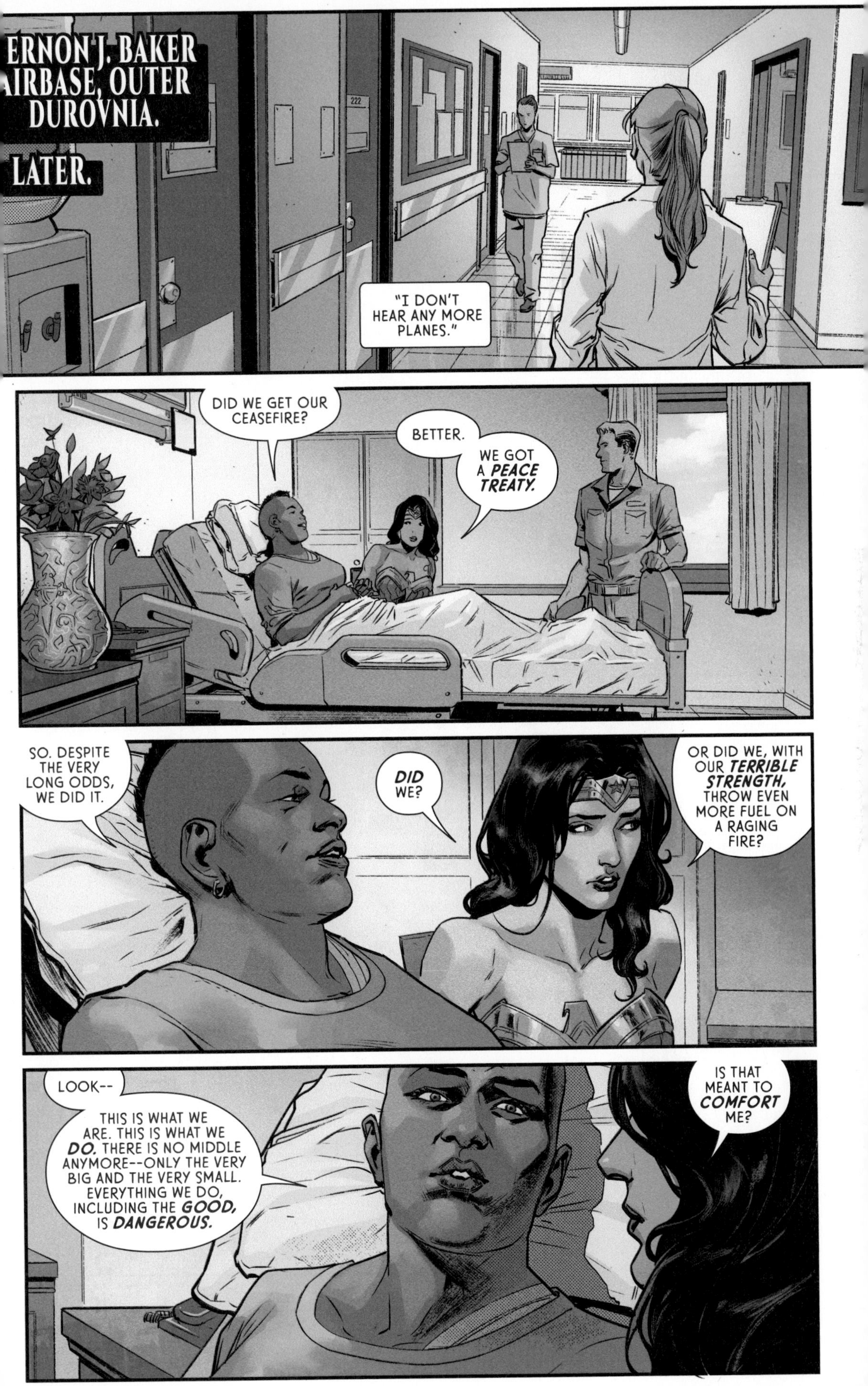

ERNON J. BAKER AIRBASE, OUTER DUROVNIA.
LATER.
"I DON'T HEAR ANY MORE PLANES."
DID WE GET OUR CEASEFIRE?
BETTER.
WE GOT A PEACE TREATY.
SO. DESPITE THE VERY LONG ODDS, WE DID IT.
DID WE?
OR DID WE, WITH OUR TERRIBLE STRENGTH, THROW EVEN MORE FUEL ON A RAGING FIRE?
LOOK--
THIS IS WHAT WE ARE. THIS IS WHAT WE DO. THERE IS NO MIDDLE ANYMORE--ONLY THE VERY BIG AND THE VERY SMALL. EVERYTHING WE DO, INCLUDING THE GOOD, IS DANGEROUS.
IS THAT MEANT TO COMFORT ME?

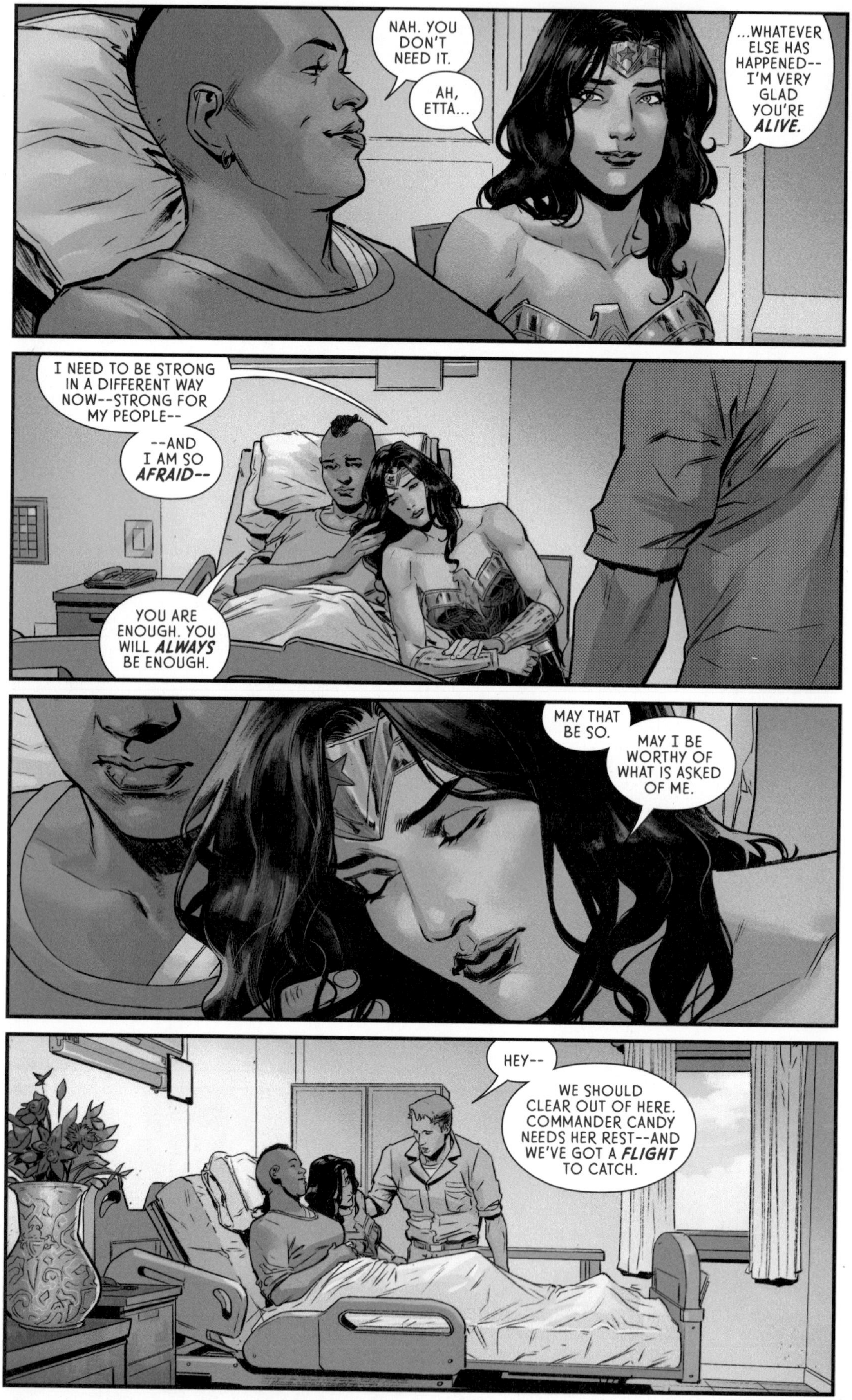
NAH. YOU DON'T NEED IT.
AH, ETTA...
...WHATEVER ELSE HAS HAPPENED--I'M VERY GLAD YOU'RE ALIVE.
I NEED TO BE STRONG IN A DIFFERENT WAY NOW--STRONG FOR MY PEOPLE--
--AND I AM SO AFRAID--
YOU ARE ENOUGH. YOU WILL ALWAYS BE ENOUGH.
MAY THAT BE SO.
MAY I BE WORTHY OF WHAT IS ASKED OF ME.
HEY--
WE SHOULD CLEAR OUT OF HERE. COMMANDER CANDY NEEDS HER REST--AND WE'VE GOT A FLIGHT TO CATCH.

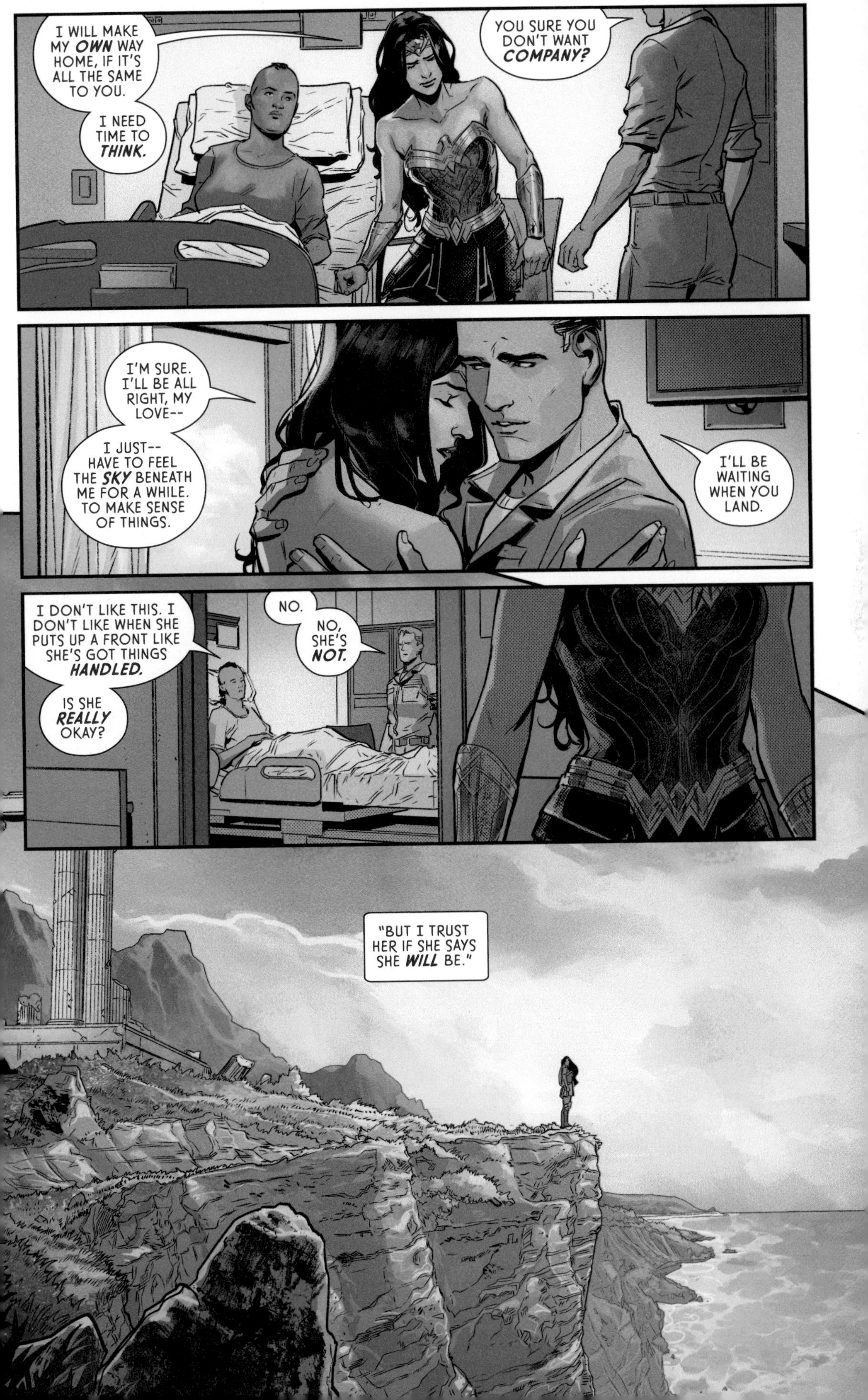
I WILL MAKE MY OWN WAY HOME, IF IT'S ALL THE SAME TO YOU.
I NEED TIME TO THINK.
YOU SURE YOU DON'T WANT COMPANY?
I'M SURE. I'LL BE ALL RIGHT, MY LOVE--
I JUST-- HAVE TO FEEL THE SKY BENEATH ME FOR A WHILE. TO MAKE SENSE OF THINGS.
I'LL BE WAITING WHEN YOU LAND.
I DON'T LIKE THIS. I DON'T LIKE WHEN SHE PUTS UP A FRONT LIKE SHE'S GOT THINGS HANDLED.
IS SHE REALLY OKAY?
NO.
NO, SHE'S NOT.
"BUT I TRUST HER IF SHE SAYS SHE WILL BE."

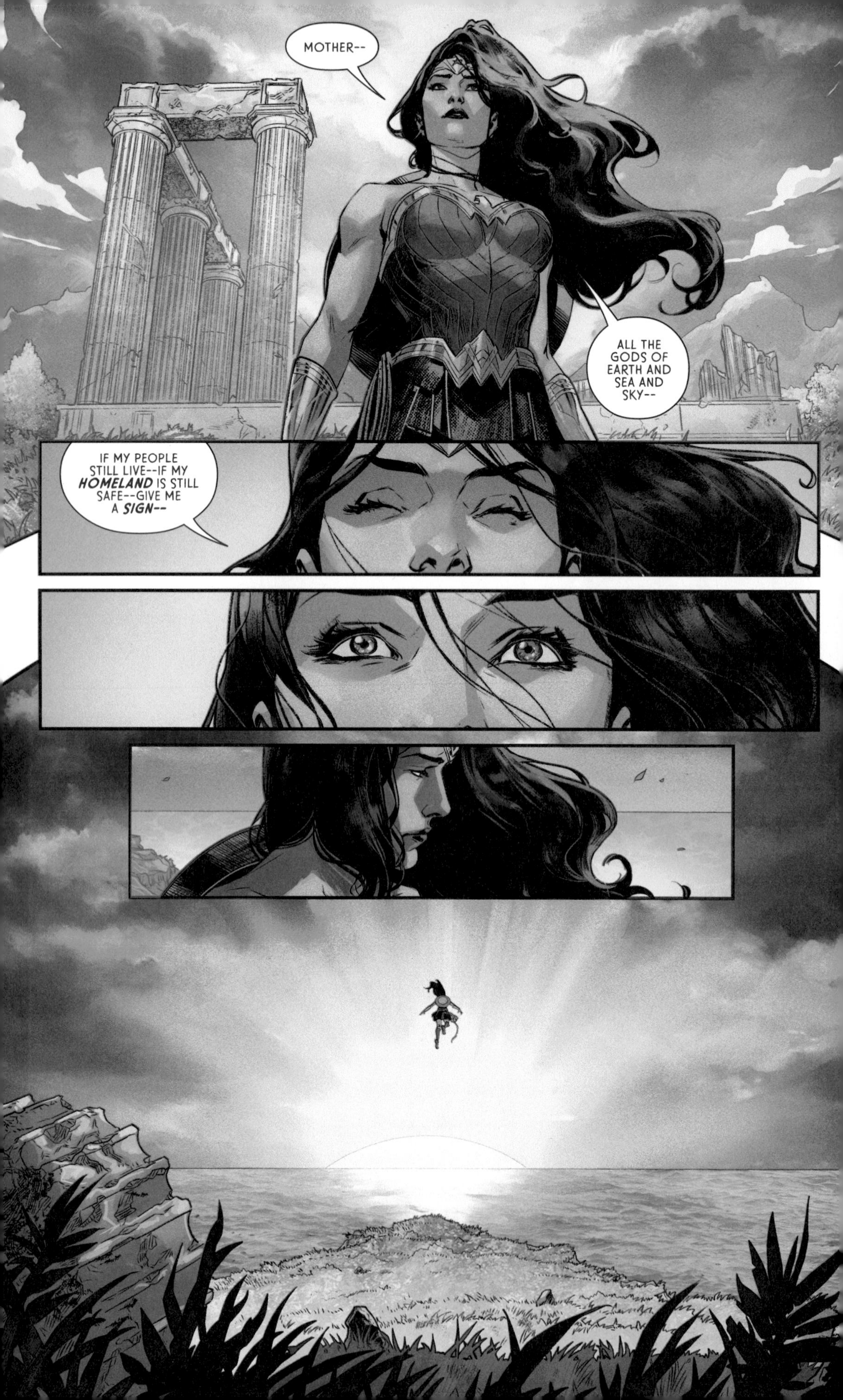
MOTHER--
ALL THE GODS OF EARTH AND SEA AND SKY--
IF MY PEOPLE STILL LIVE--IF MY **HOMELAND** IS STILL SAFE--GIVE ME A **SIGN--**

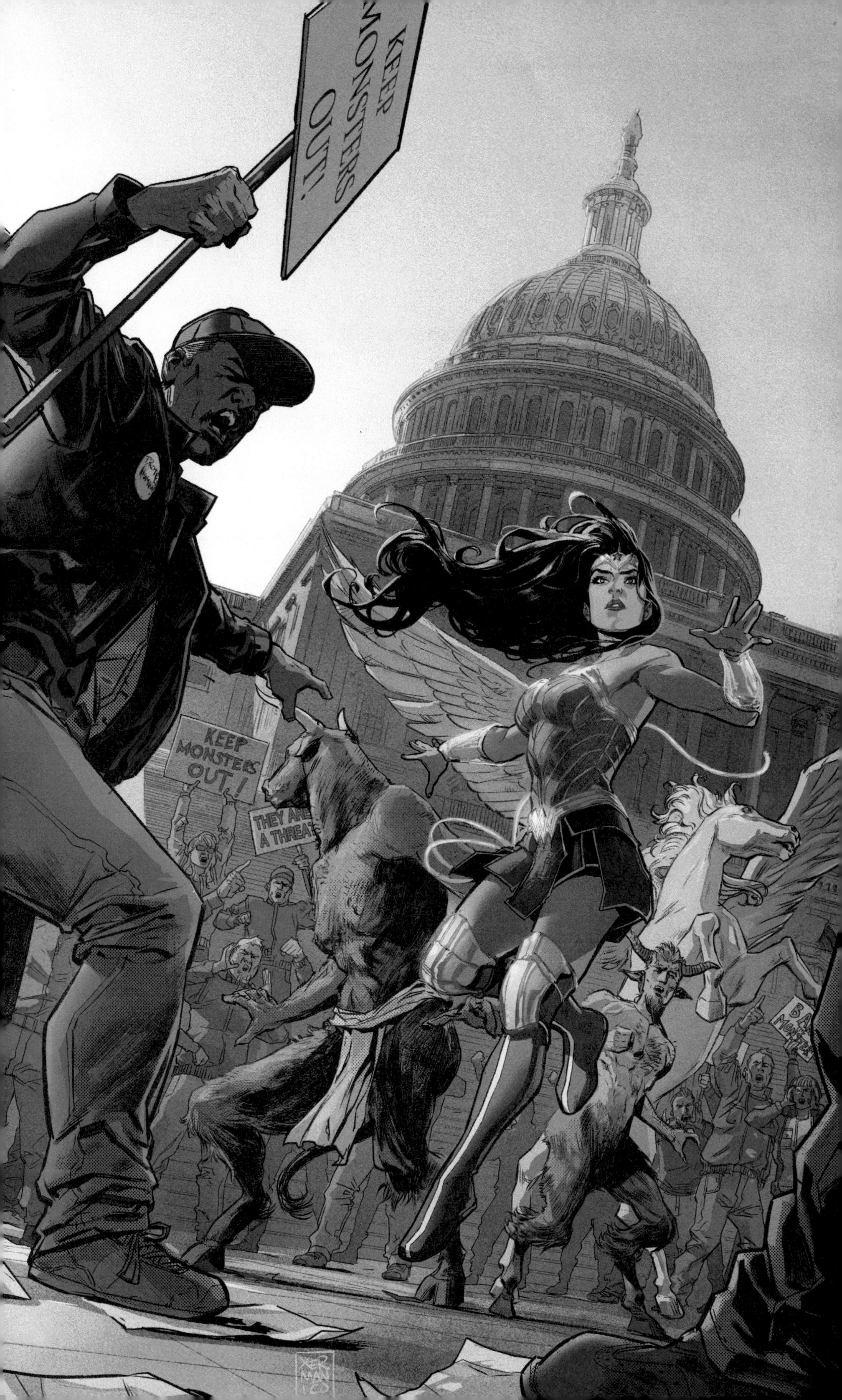
KEEP MONSTERS OUT!
KEEP MONSTERS OUT!
THEY ARE A THREAT

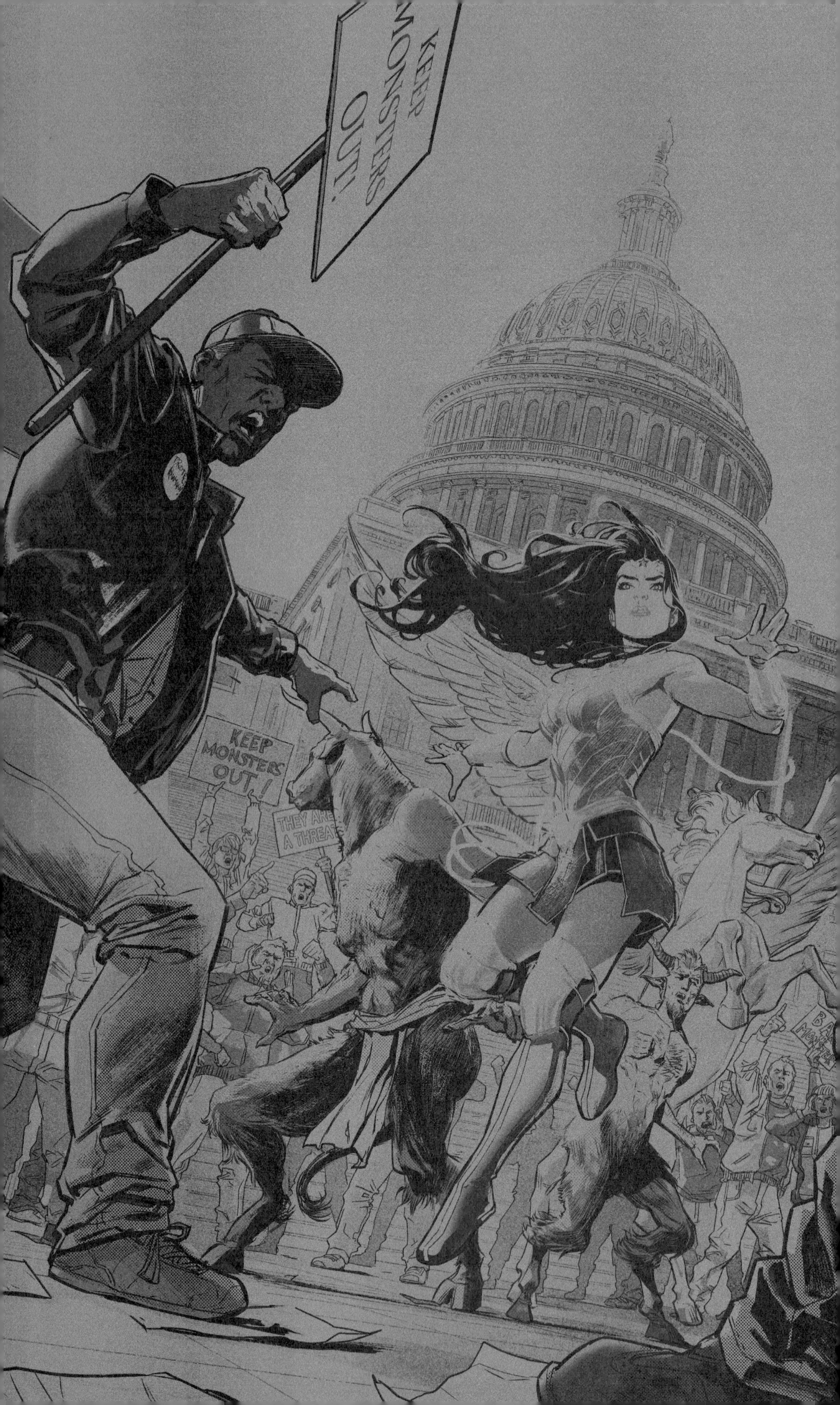
KEEP MONSTERS OUT!
KEEP MONSTERS' OUT!
THEY ARE A THREA

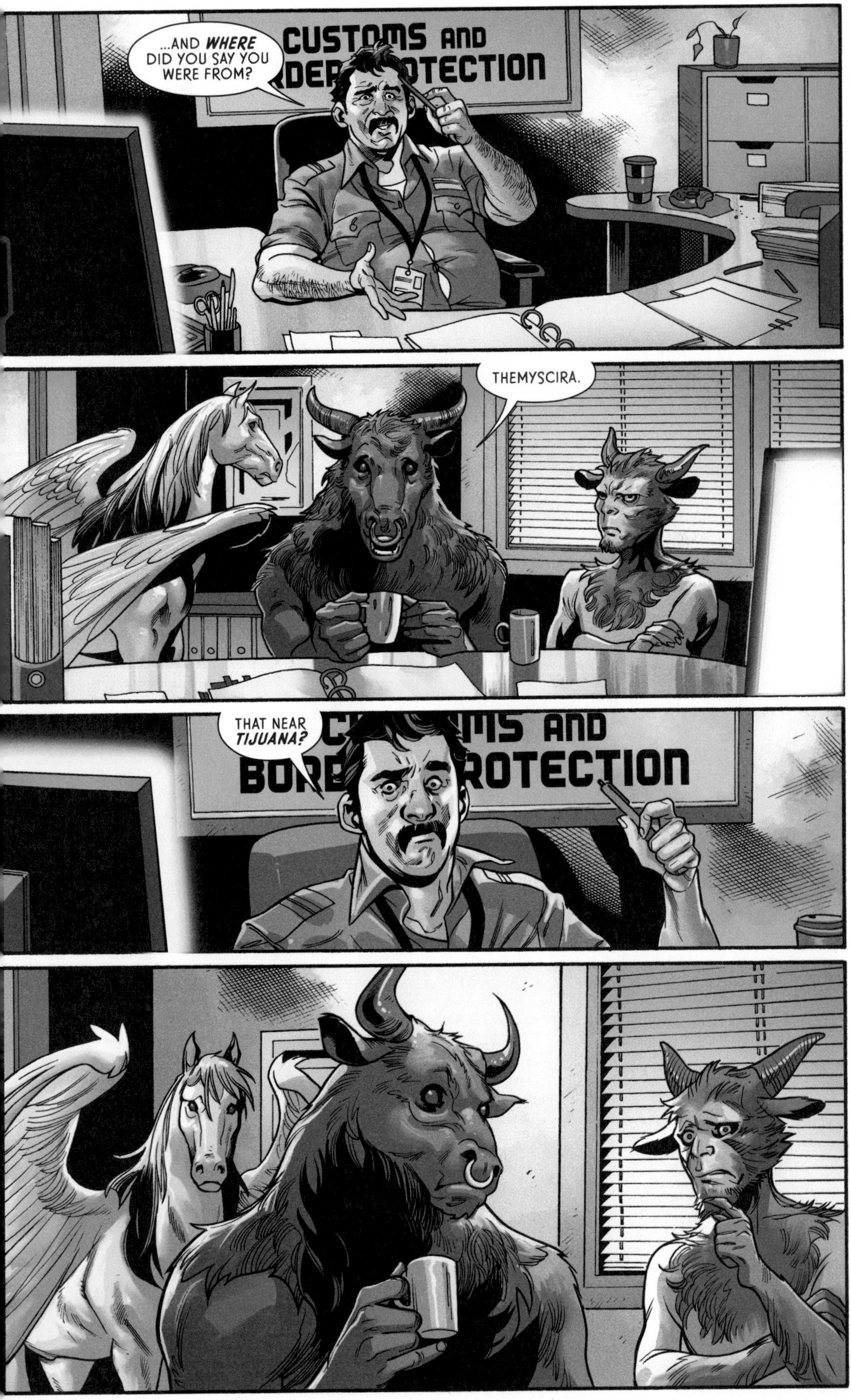

CUSTOMS AND
...AND WHERE DID YOU SAY YOU WERE FROM?
THEMYSCIRA.
THAT NEAR TIJUANA?

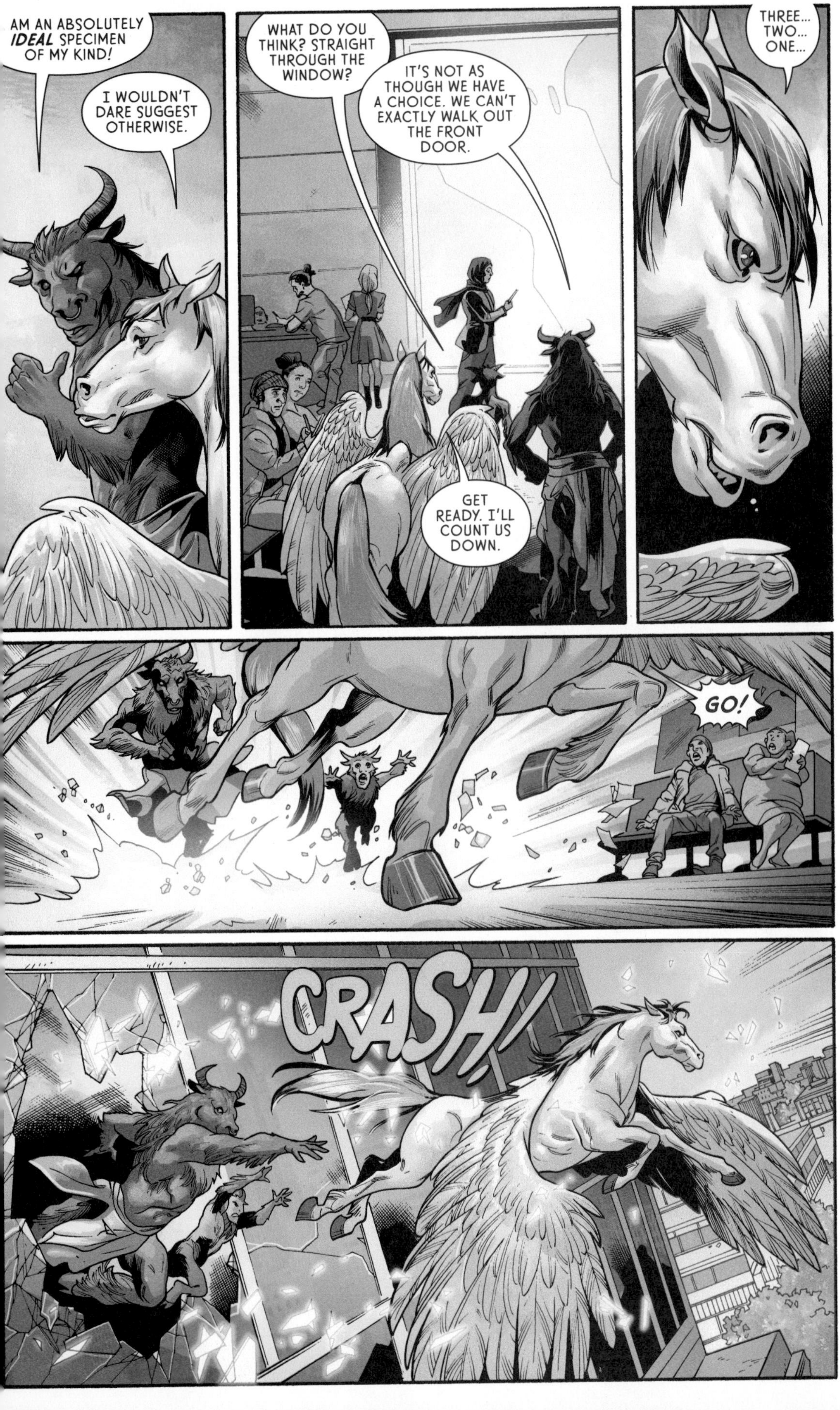
AM AN ABSOLUTELY *IDEAL* SPECIMEN OF MY KIND!
I WOULDN'T DARE SUGGEST OTHERWISE.
WHAT DO YOU THINK? STRAIGHT THROUGH THE WINDOW?
IT'S NOT AS THOUGH WE HAVE A CHOICE. WE CAN'T EXACTLY WALK OUT THE FRONT DOOR.
GET READY. I'LL COUNT US DOWN.
THREE... TWO... ONE...
GO!
CRASH!

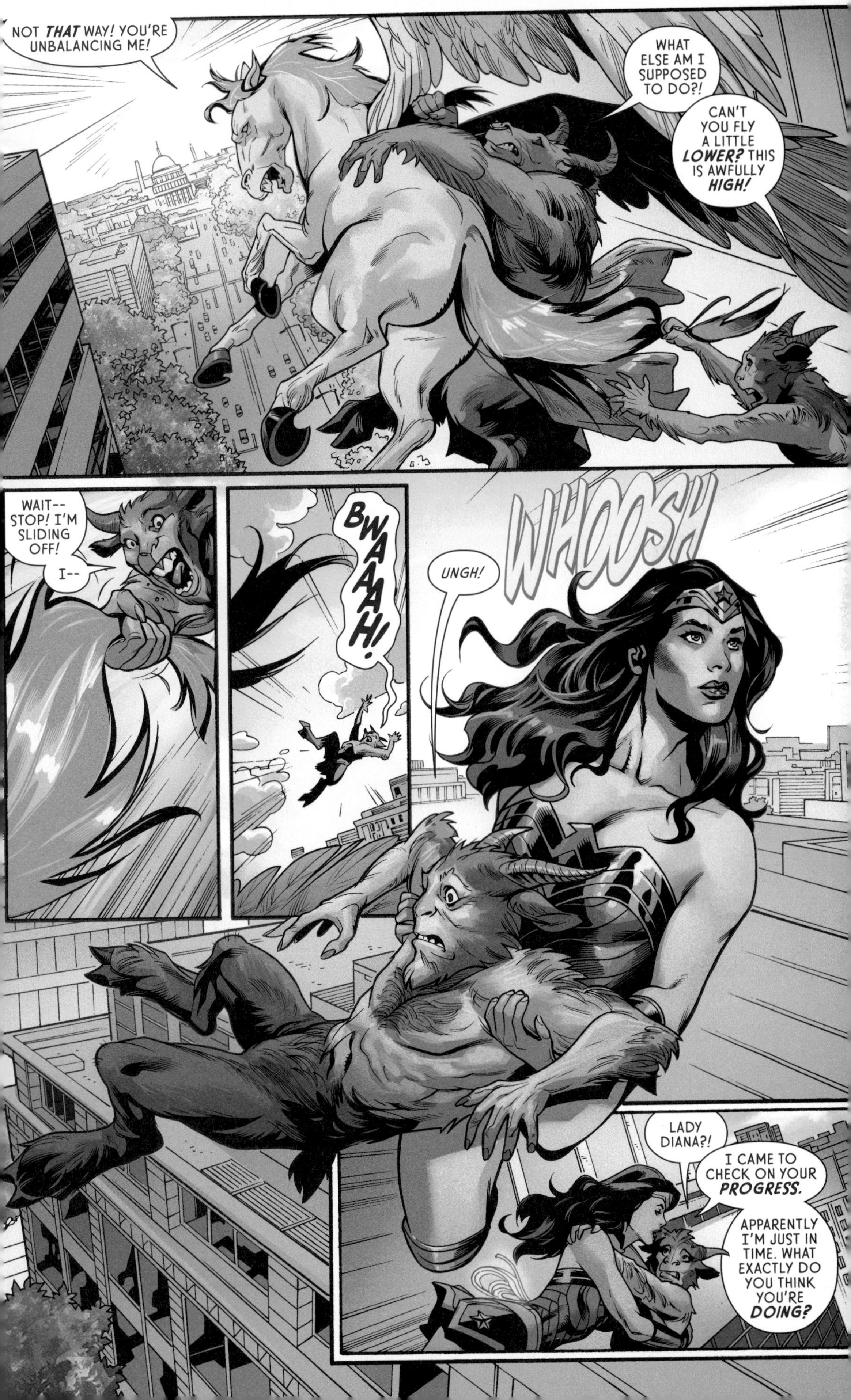

NOT THAT WAY! YOU'RE UNBALANCING ME!
WHAT ELSE AM I SUPPOSED TO DO?!
CAN'T YOU FLY A LITTLE LOWER? THIS IS AWFULLY HIGH!
WAIT-- STOP! I'M SLIDING OFF!
I--
BWAAAAH!
WHOOSH
UNGH!
LADY DIANA?!
I CAME TO CHECK ON YOUR PROGRESS.
APPARENTLY I'M JUST IN TIME. WHAT EXACTLY DO YOU THINK YOU'RE DOING?

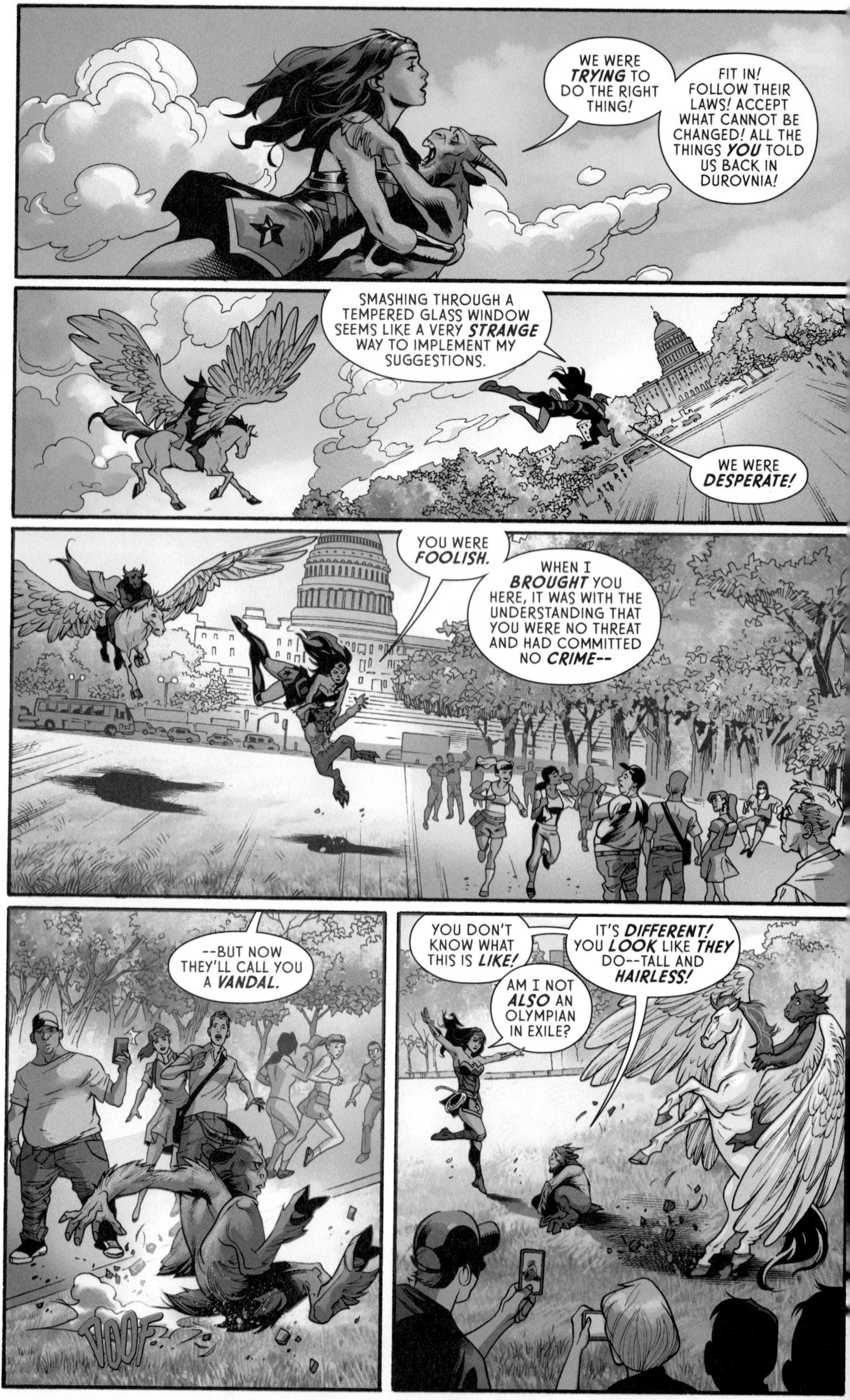

WE WERE TRYING TO DO THE RIGHT THING!
FIT IN! FOLLOW THEIR LAWS! ACCEPT WHAT CANNOT BE CHANGED! ALL THE THINGS YOU TOLD US BACK IN DUROVNIA!
SMASHING THROUGH A TEMPERED GLASS WINDOW SEEMS LIKE A VERY STRANGE WAY TO IMPLEMENT MY SUGGESTIONS.
WE WERE DESPERATE!
YOU WERE FOOLISH.
WHEN I BROUGHT YOU HERE, IT WAS WITH THE UNDERSTANDING THAT YOU WERE NO THREAT AND HAD COMMITTED NO CRIME--
--BUT NOW THEY'LL CALL YOU A VANDAL.
FOOF
YOU DON'T KNOW WHAT THIS IS LIKE!
IT'S DIFFERENT! YOU LOOK LIKE THEY DO--TALL AND HAIRLESS!
AM I NOT ALSO AN OLYMPIAN IN EXILE?

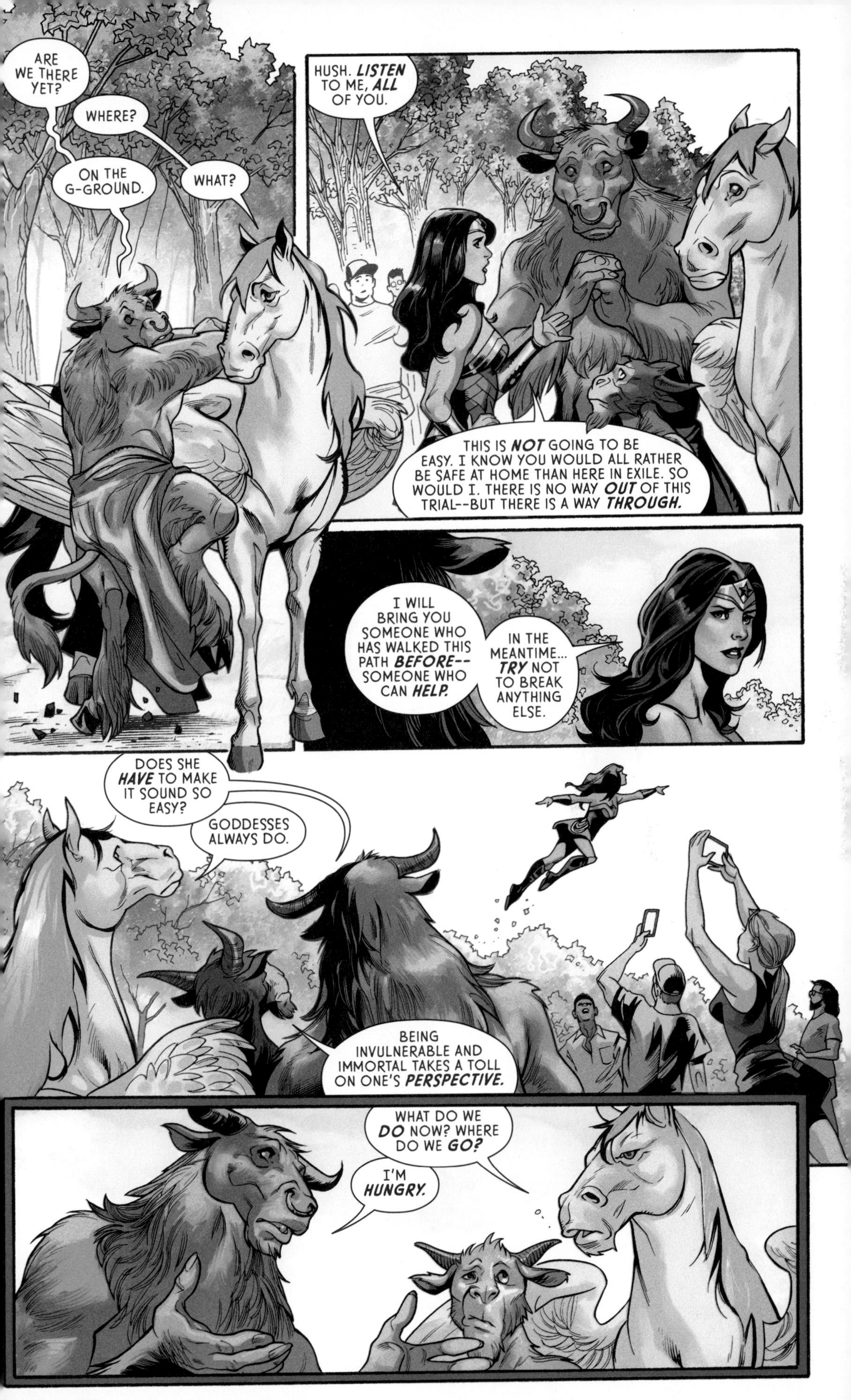

ARE WE THERE YET?
WHERE?
ON THE G-GROUND.
WHAT?
HUSH. **LISTEN** TO ME, **ALL** OF YOU.
THIS IS **NOT** GOING TO BE EASY. I KNOW YOU WOULD ALL RATHER BE SAFE AT HOME THAN HERE IN EXILE. SO WOULD I. THERE IS NO WAY **OUT** OF THIS TRIAL--BUT THERE IS A WAY **THROUGH.**
I WILL BRING YOU SOMEONE WHO HAS WALKED THIS PATH **BEFORE**--SOMEONE WHO CAN **HELP.**
IN THE MEANTIME... **TRY** NOT TO BREAK ANYTHING ELSE.
DOES SHE **HAVE** TO MAKE IT SOUND SO EASY?
GODDESSES ALWAYS DO.
BEING INVULNERABLE AND IMMORTAL TAKES A TOLL ON ONE'S **PERSPECTIVE.**
WHAT DO WE **DO** NOW? WHERE DO WE **GO?**
I'M **HUNGRY.**

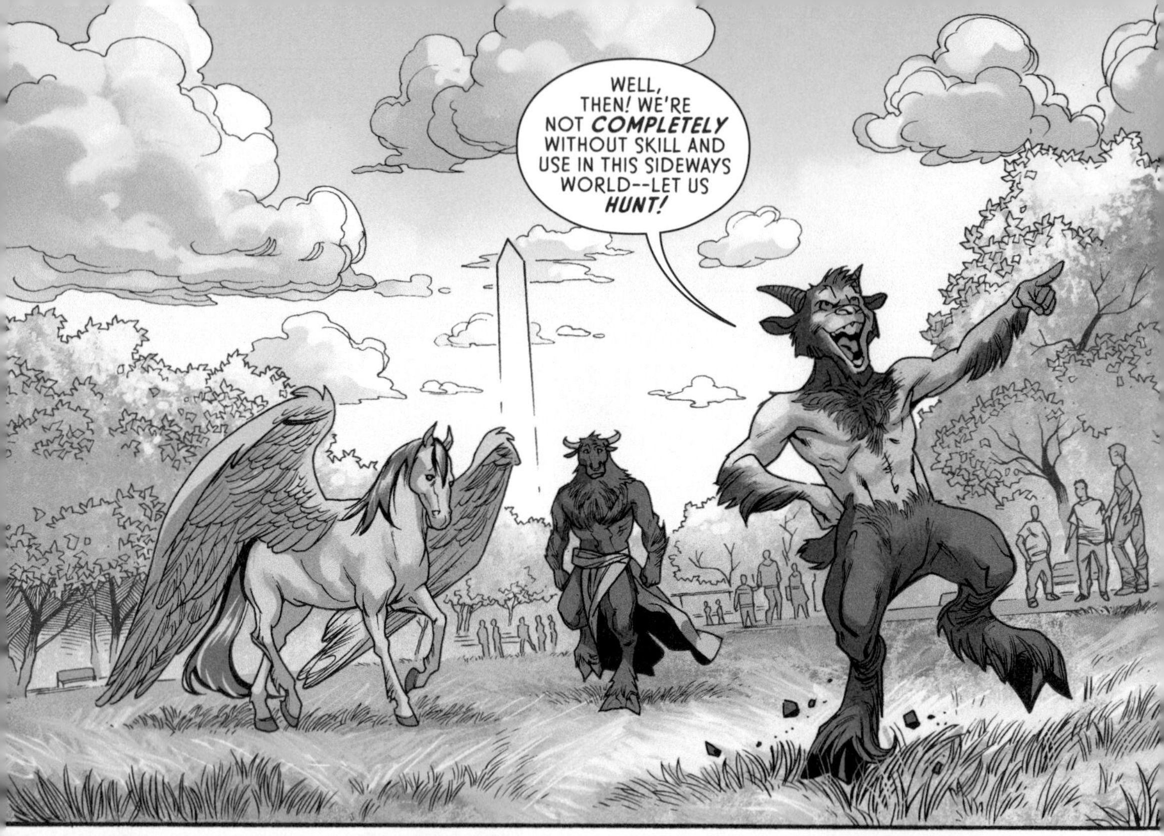
WELL, THEN! WE'RE NOT COMPLETELY WITHOUT SKILL AND USE IN THIS SIDEWAYS WORLD--LET US HUNT!

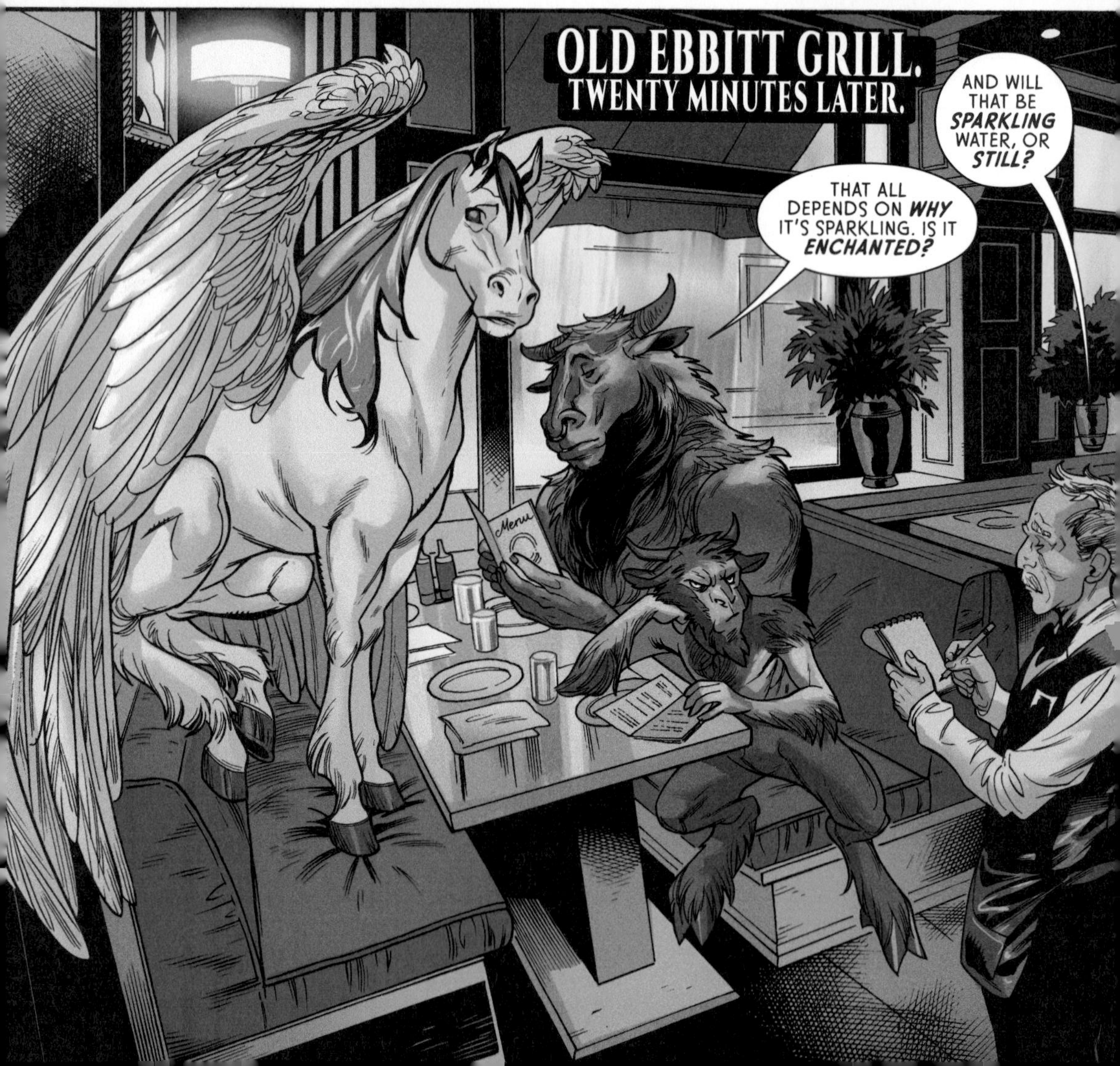
OLD EBBITT GRILL.
TWENTY MINUTES LATER.
AND WILL THAT BE SPARKLING WATER, OR STILL?
THAT ALL DEPENDS ON WHY IT'S SPARKLING. IS IT ENCHANTED?
Menu

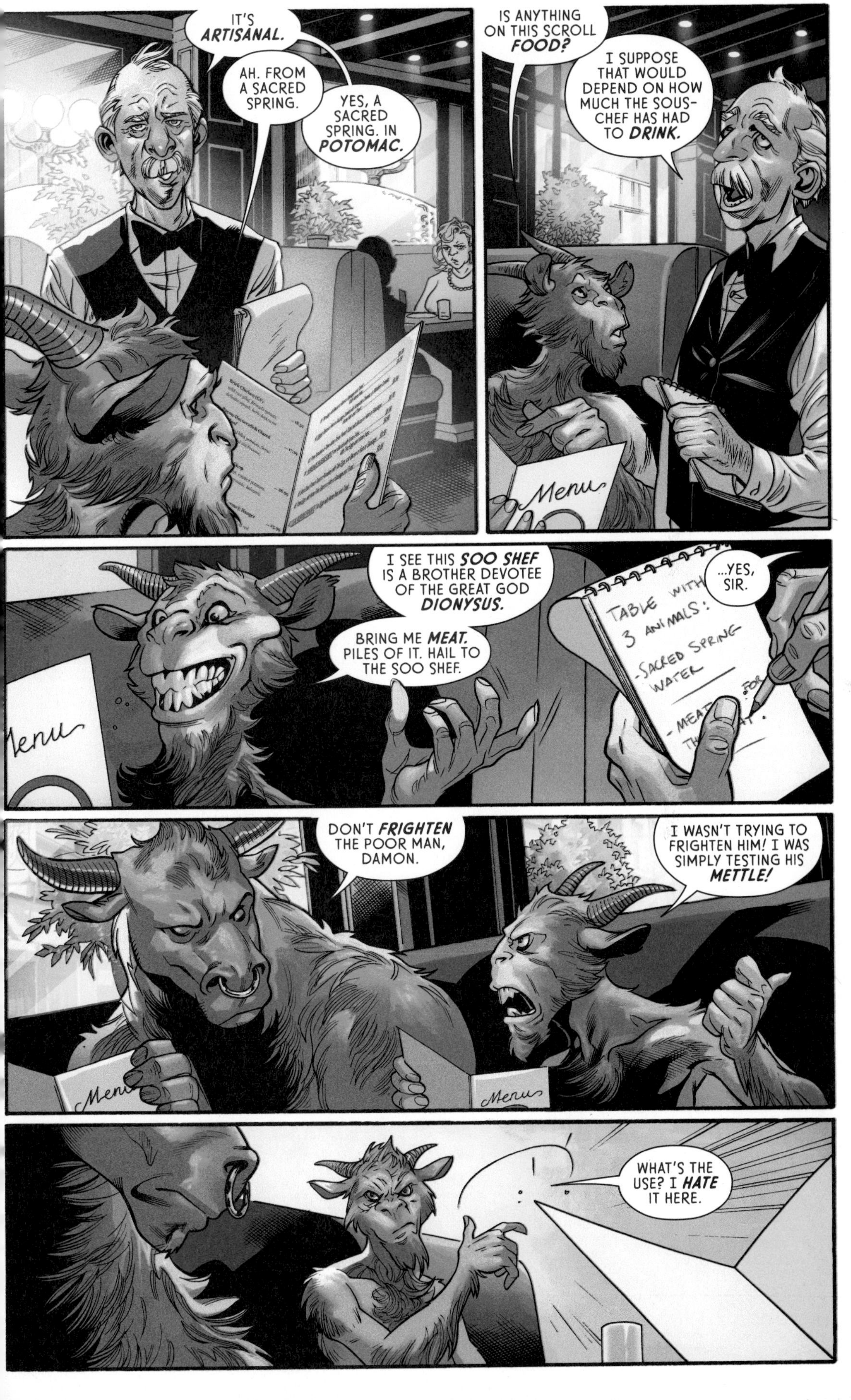
IT'S ARTISANAL.
AH. FROM A SACRED SPRING.
YES, A SACRED SPRING. IN POTOMAC.
IS ANYTHING ON THIS SCROLL FOOD?
I SUPPOSE THAT WOULD DEPEND ON HOW MUCH THE SOUS-CHEF HAS HAD TO DRINK.
Menu
I SEE THIS SOO SHEF IS A BROTHER DEVOTEE OF THE GREAT GOD DIONYSUS.
BRING ME MEAT. PILES OF IT. HAIL TO THE SOO SHEF.
...YES, SIR.
TABLE WITH
3 ANIMALS:
-SACRED SPRING WATER
-MEAT
Menu
DON'T FRIGHTEN THE POOR MAN, DAMON.
I WASN'T TRYING TO FRIGHTEN HIM! I WAS SIMPLY TESTING HIS METTLE!
Menu
Menu
WHAT'S THE USE? I HATE IT HERE.

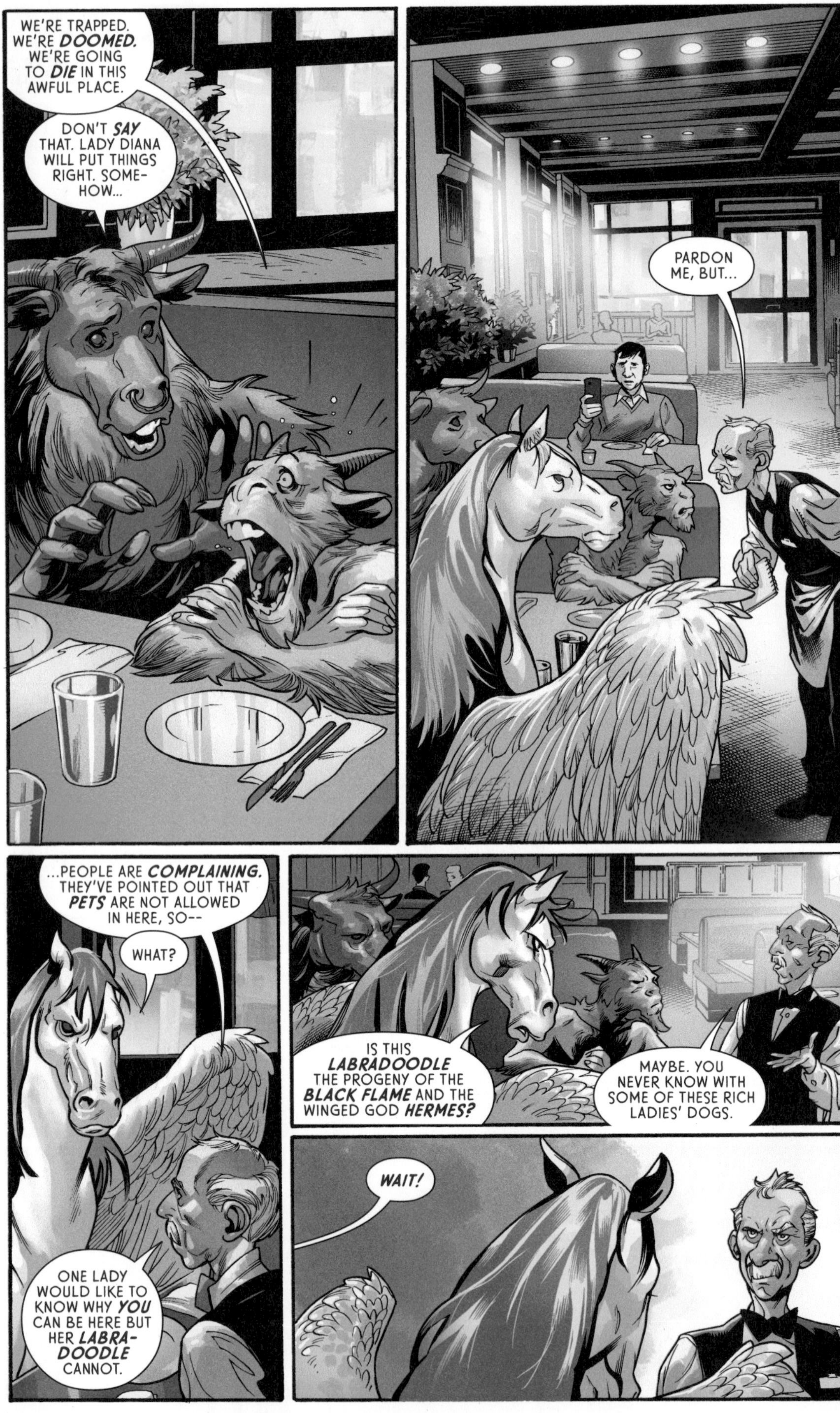
WE'RE TRAPPED. WE'RE DOOMED. WE'RE GOING TO DIE IN THIS AWFUL PLACE.
DON'T SAY THAT. LADY DIANA WILL PUT THINGS RIGHT. SOME-HOW...
PARDON ME, BUT...
...PEOPLE ARE COMPLAINING. THEY'VE POINTED OUT THAT PETS ARE NOT ALLOWED IN HERE, SO--
WHAT?
ONE LADY WOULD LIKE TO KNOW WHY YOU CAN BE HERE BUT HER LABRA-DOODLE CANNOT.
IS THIS LABRADOODLE THE PROGENY OF THE BLACK FLAME AND THE WINGED GOD HERMES?
MAYBE. YOU NEVER KNOW WITH SOME OF THESE RICH LADIES' DOGS.
WAIT!

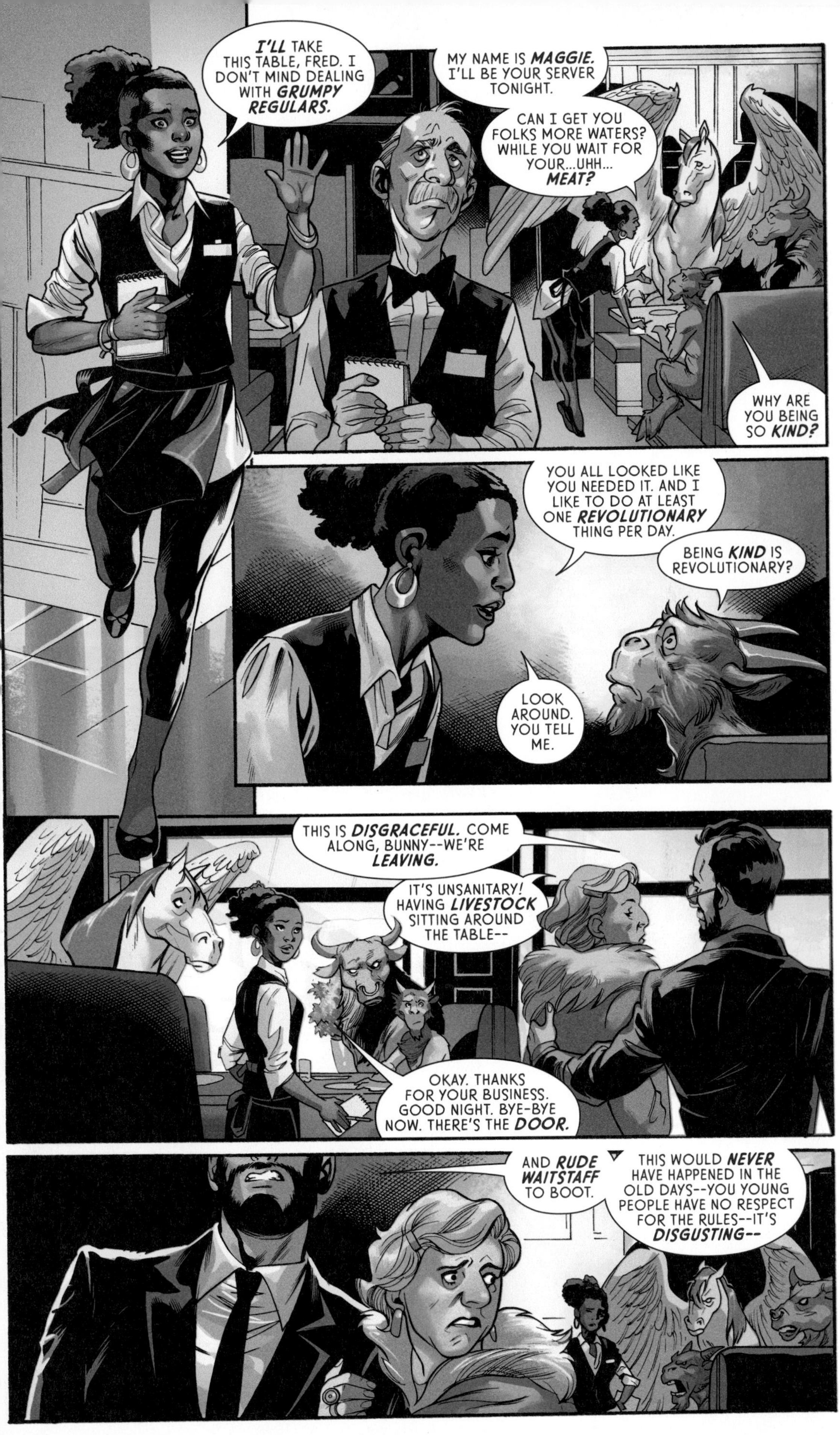
I'LL TAKE THIS TABLE, FRED. I DON'T MIND DEALING WITH GRUMPY REGULARS.
MY NAME IS MAGGIE. I'LL BE YOUR SERVER TONIGHT.
CAN I GET YOU FOLKS MORE WATERS? WHILE YOU WAIT FOR YOUR...UHH... MEAT?
WHY ARE YOU BEING SO KIND?
YOU ALL LOOKED LIKE YOU NEEDED IT. AND I LIKE TO DO AT LEAST ONE REVOLUTIONARY THING PER DAY.
BEING KIND IS REVOLUTIONARY?
LOOK AROUND. YOU TELL ME.
THIS IS DISGRACEFUL. COME ALONG, BUNNY--WE'RE LEAVING.
IT'S UNSANITARY! HAVING LIVESTOCK SITTING AROUND THE TABLE--
OKAY. THANKS FOR YOUR BUSINESS. GOOD NIGHT. BYE-BYE NOW. THERE'S THE DOOR.
AND RUDE WAITSTAFF TO BOOT.
THIS WOULD NEVER HAVE HAPPENED IN THE OLD DAYS--YOU YOUNG PEOPLE HAVE NO RESPECT FOR THE RULES--IT'S DISGUSTING--

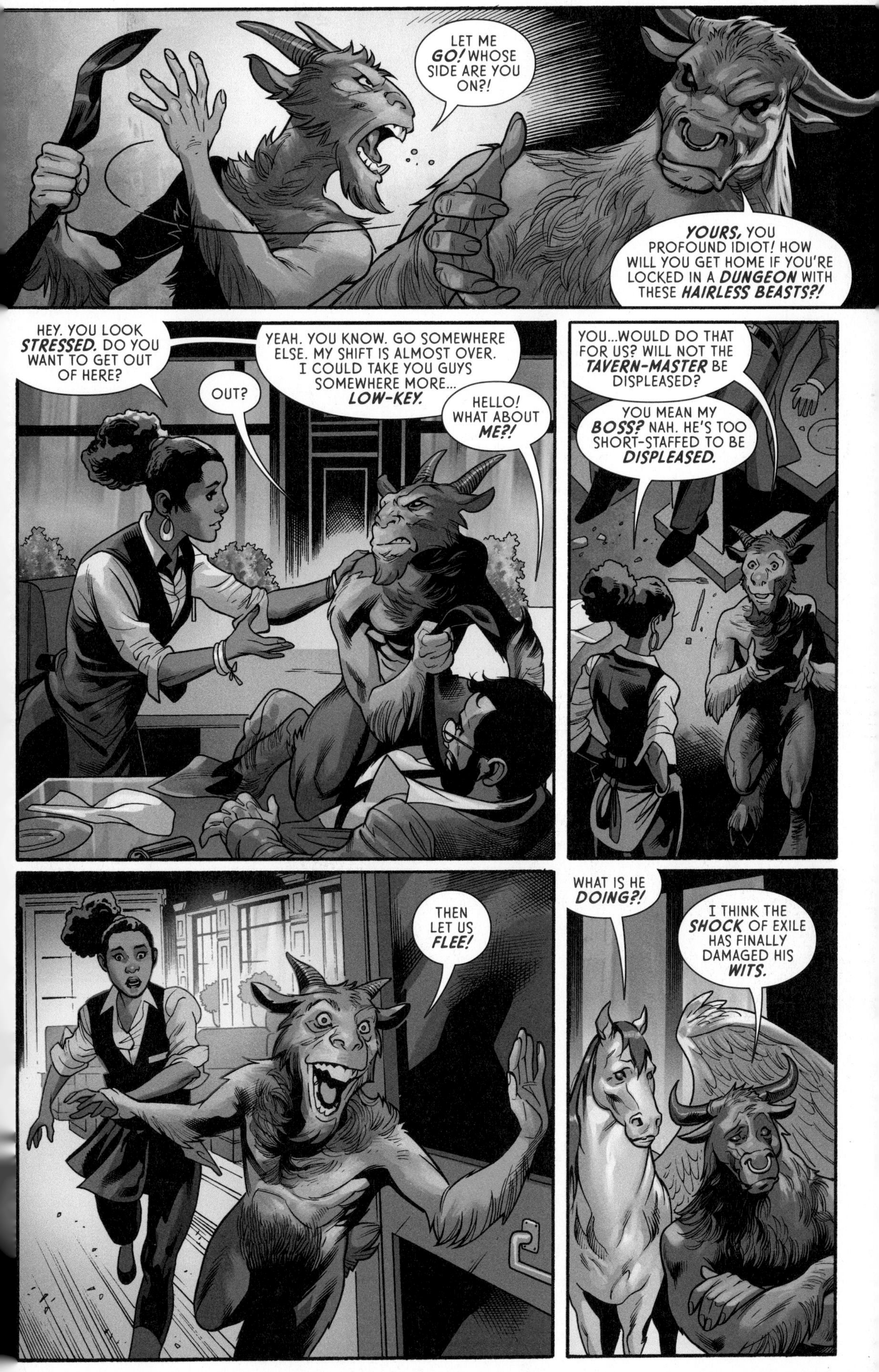
LET ME GO! WHOSE SIDE ARE YOU ON?!
YOURS, YOU PROFOUND IDIOT! HOW WILL YOU GET HOME IF YOU'RE LOCKED IN A DUNGEON WITH THESE HAIRLESS BEASTS?!
HEY. YOU LOOK STRESSED. DO YOU WANT TO GET OUT OF HERE?
OUT?
YEAH. YOU KNOW. GO SOMEWHERE ELSE. MY SHIFT IS ALMOST OVER. I COULD TAKE YOU GUYS SOMEWHERE MORE... LOW-KEY.
HELLO! WHAT ABOUT ME?!
YOU...WOULD DO THAT FOR US? WILL NOT THE TAVERN-MASTER BE DISPLEASED?
YOU MEAN MY BOSS? NAH. HE'S TOO SHORT-STAFFED TO BE DISPLEASED.
THEN LET US FLEE!
WHAT IS HE DOING?!
I THINK THE SHOCK OF EXILE HAS FINALLY DAMAGED HIS WITS.

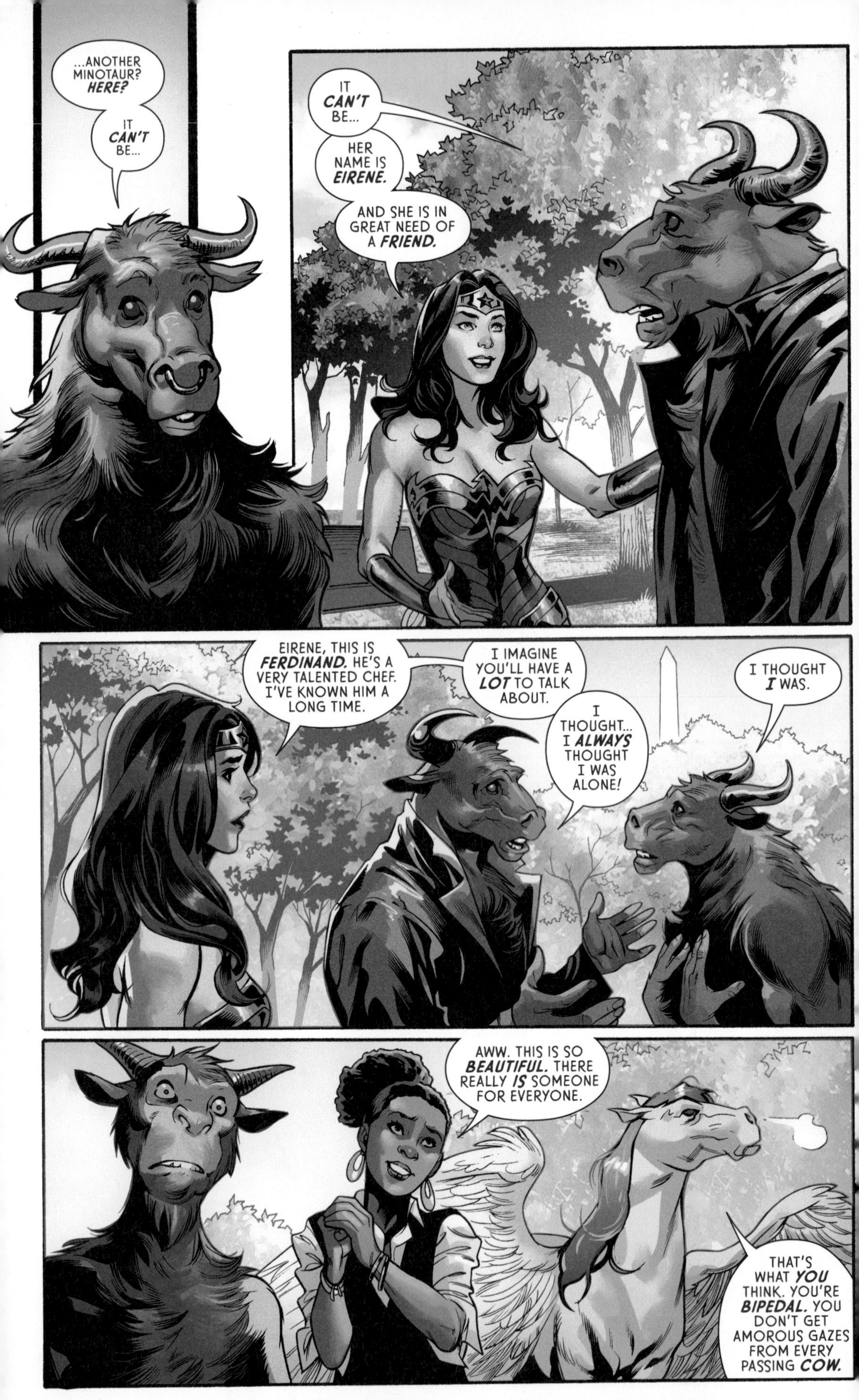
...ANOTHER MINOTAUR? HERE?
IT CAN'T BE...
IT CAN'T BE...
HER NAME IS EIRENE.
AND SHE IS IN GREAT NEED OF A FRIEND.
EIRENE, THIS IS FERDINAND. HE'S A VERY TALENTED CHEF. I'VE KNOWN HIM A LONG TIME.
I IMAGINE YOU'LL HAVE A LOT TO TALK ABOUT.
I THOUGHT... I ALWAYS THOUGHT I WAS ALONE!
I THOUGHT I WAS.
AWW. THIS IS SO BEAUTIFUL. THERE REALLY IS SOMEONE FOR EVERYONE.
THAT'S WHAT YOU THINK. YOU'RE BIPEDAL. YOU DON'T GET AMOROUS GAZES FROM EVERY PASSING COW.

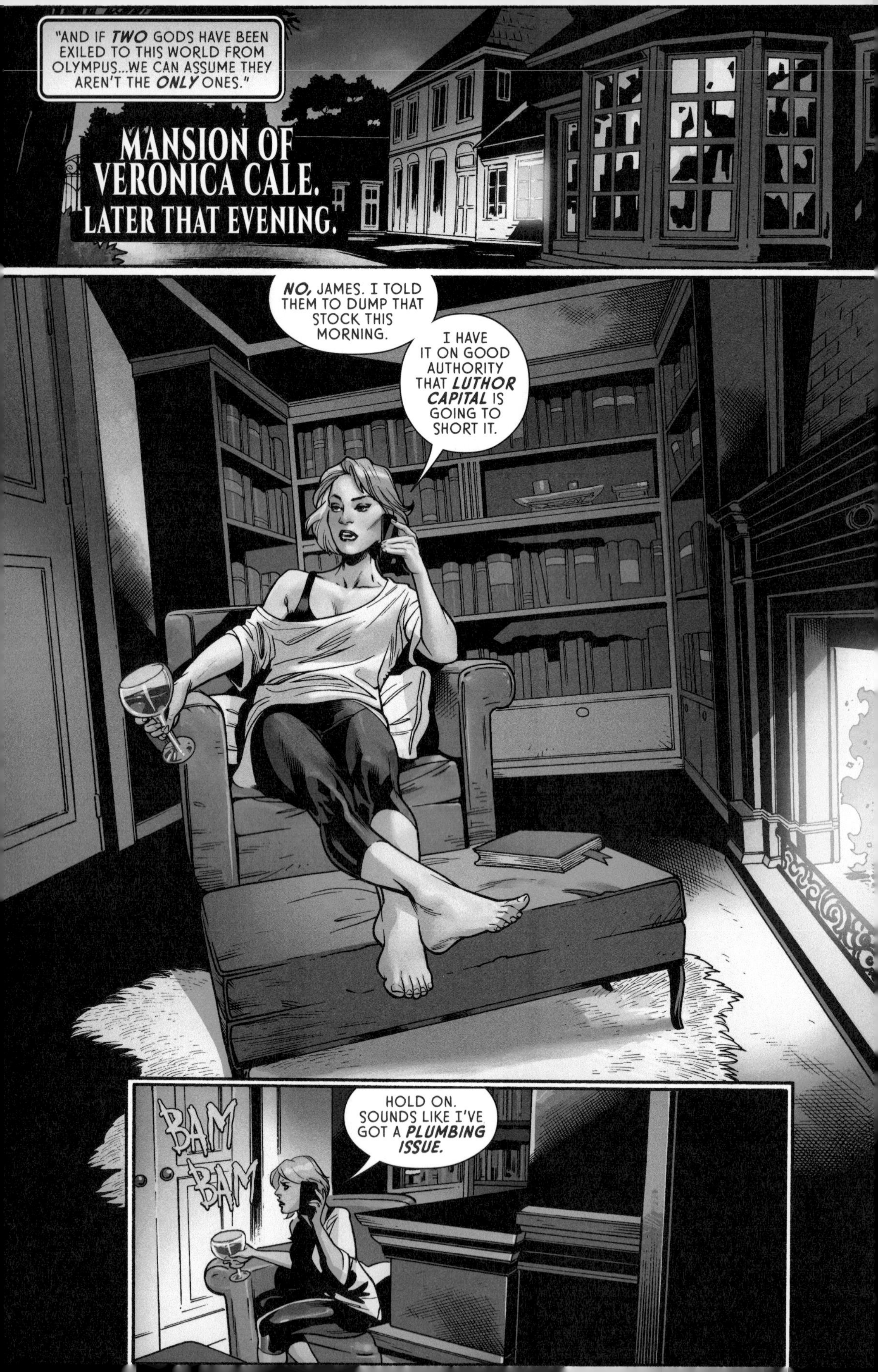
"AND IF TWO GODS HAVE BEEN EXILED TO THIS WORLD FROM OLYMPUS...WE CAN ASSUME THEY AREN'T THE ONLY ONES."
MANSION OF VERONICA CALE. LATER THAT EVENING.
NO, JAMES. I TOLD THEM TO DUMP THAT STOCK THIS MORNING.
I HAVE IT ON GOOD AUTHORITY THAT LUTHOR CAPITAL IS GOING TO SHORT IT.
BAM
BAM
HOLD ON. SOUNDS LIKE I'VE GOT A PLUMBING ISSUE.

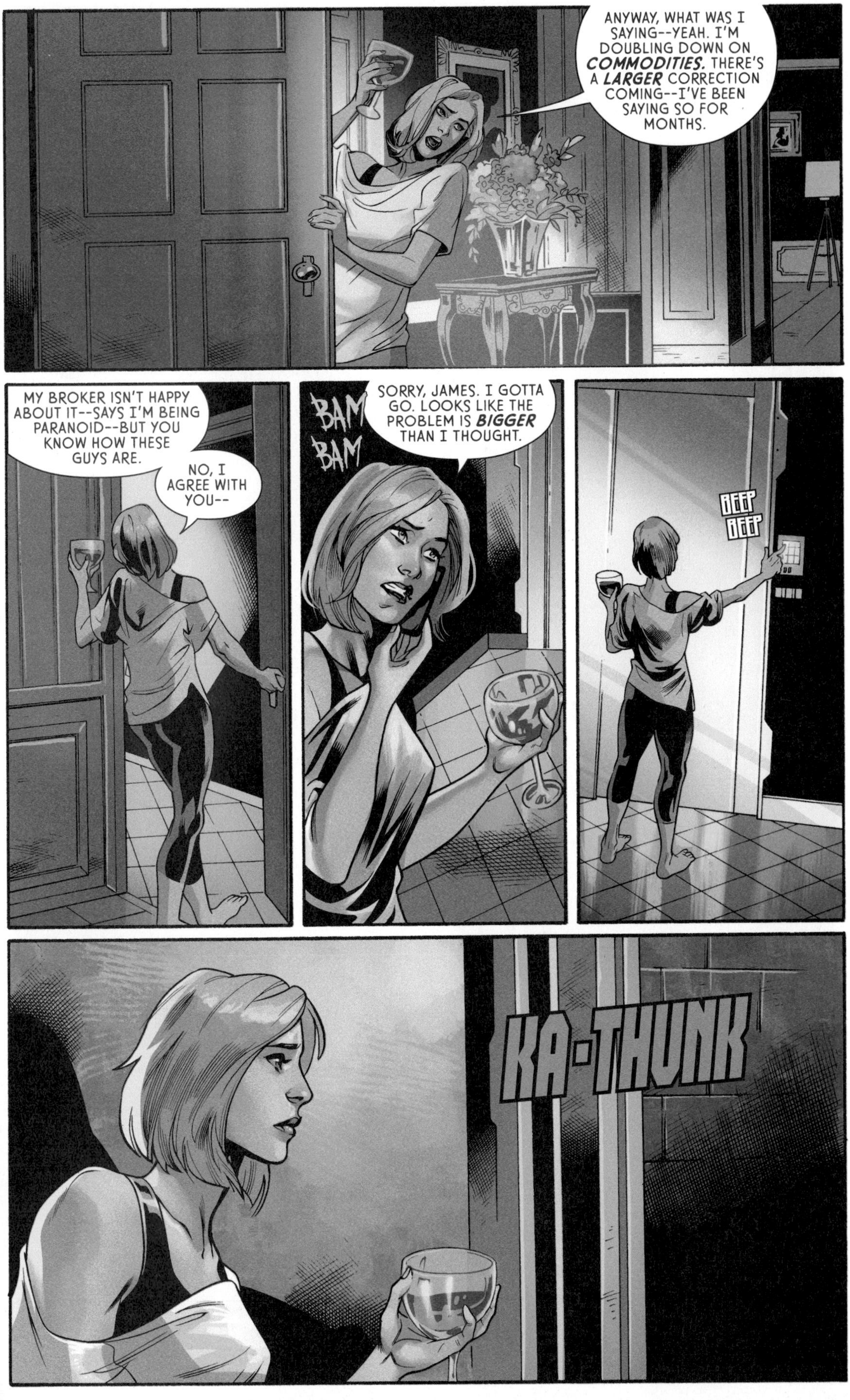
ANYWAY, WHAT WAS I SAYING--YEAH. I'M DOUBLING DOWN ON COMMODITIES. THERE'S A LARGER CORRECTION COMING--I'VE BEEN SAYING SO FOR MONTHS.
MY BROKER ISN'T HAPPY ABOUT IT--SAYS I'M BEING PARANOID--BUT YOU KNOW HOW THESE GUYS ARE.
NO, I AGREE WITH YOU--
BAM
BAM
SORRY, JAMES. I GOTTA GO. LOOKS LIKE THE PROBLEM IS BIGGER THAN I THOUGHT.
BEEP
BEEP
KA-THUNK

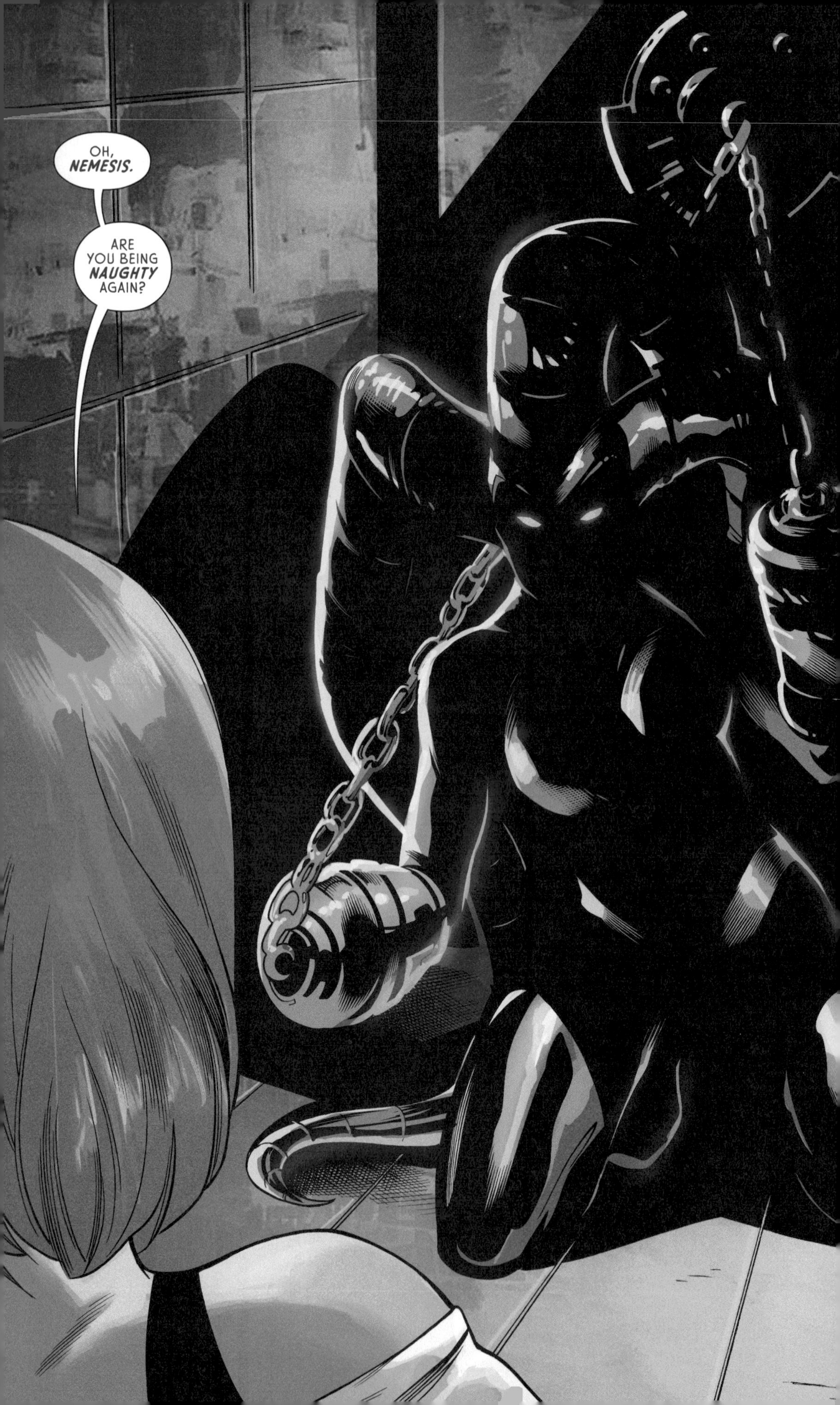
OH, NEMESIS.
ARE YOU BEING NAUGHTY AGAIN?

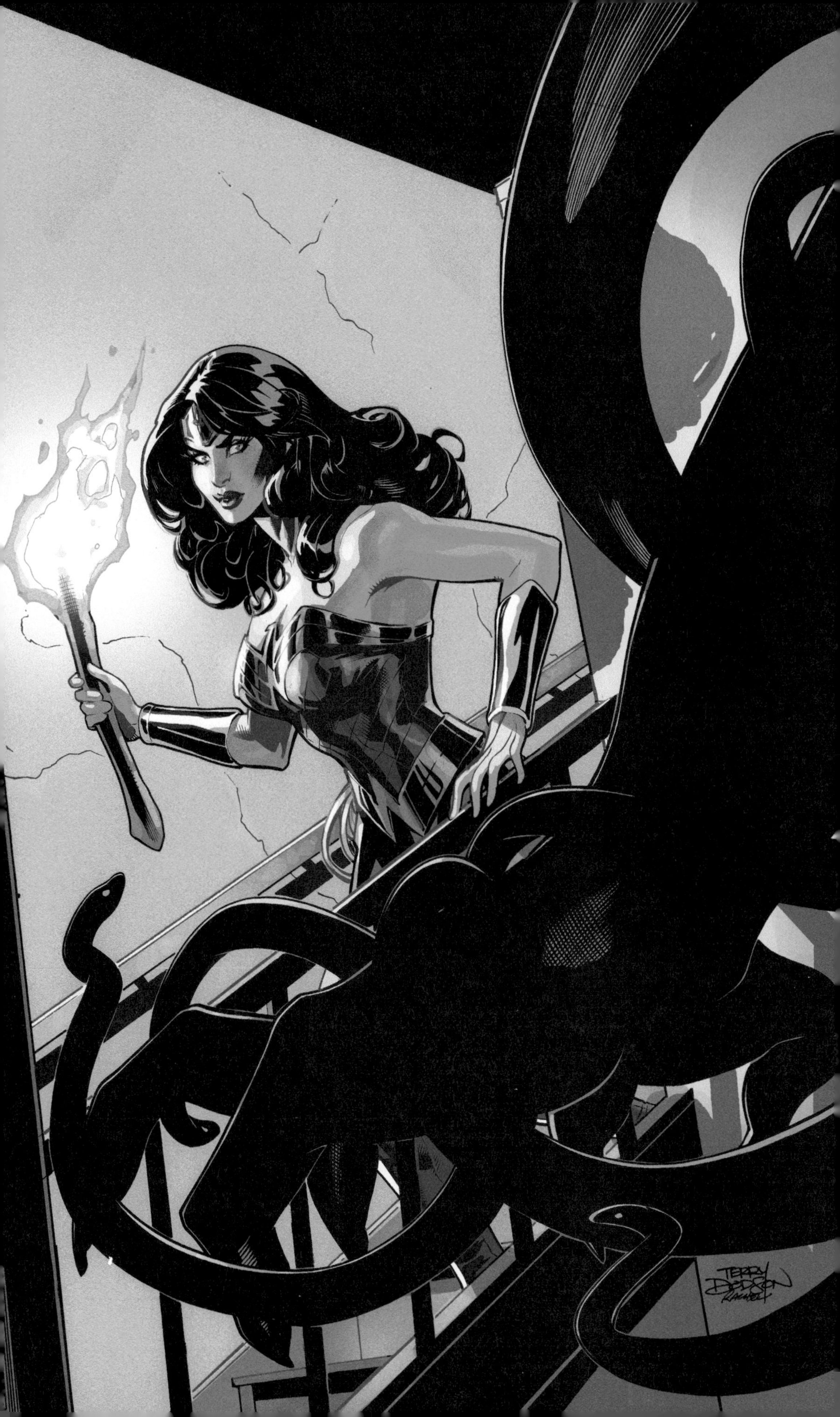
TERRY DODSON
RACHEL

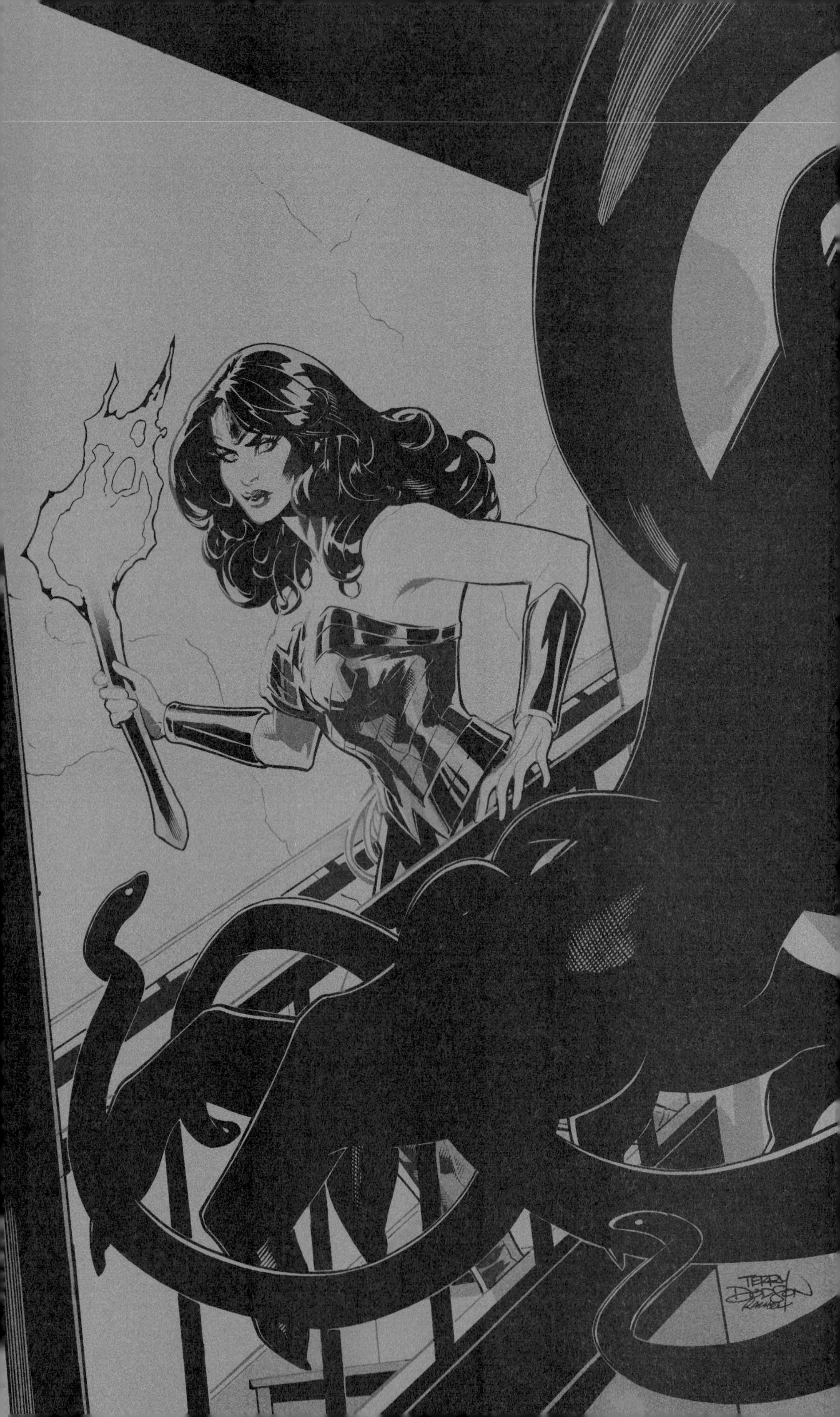
TERRY DODSON

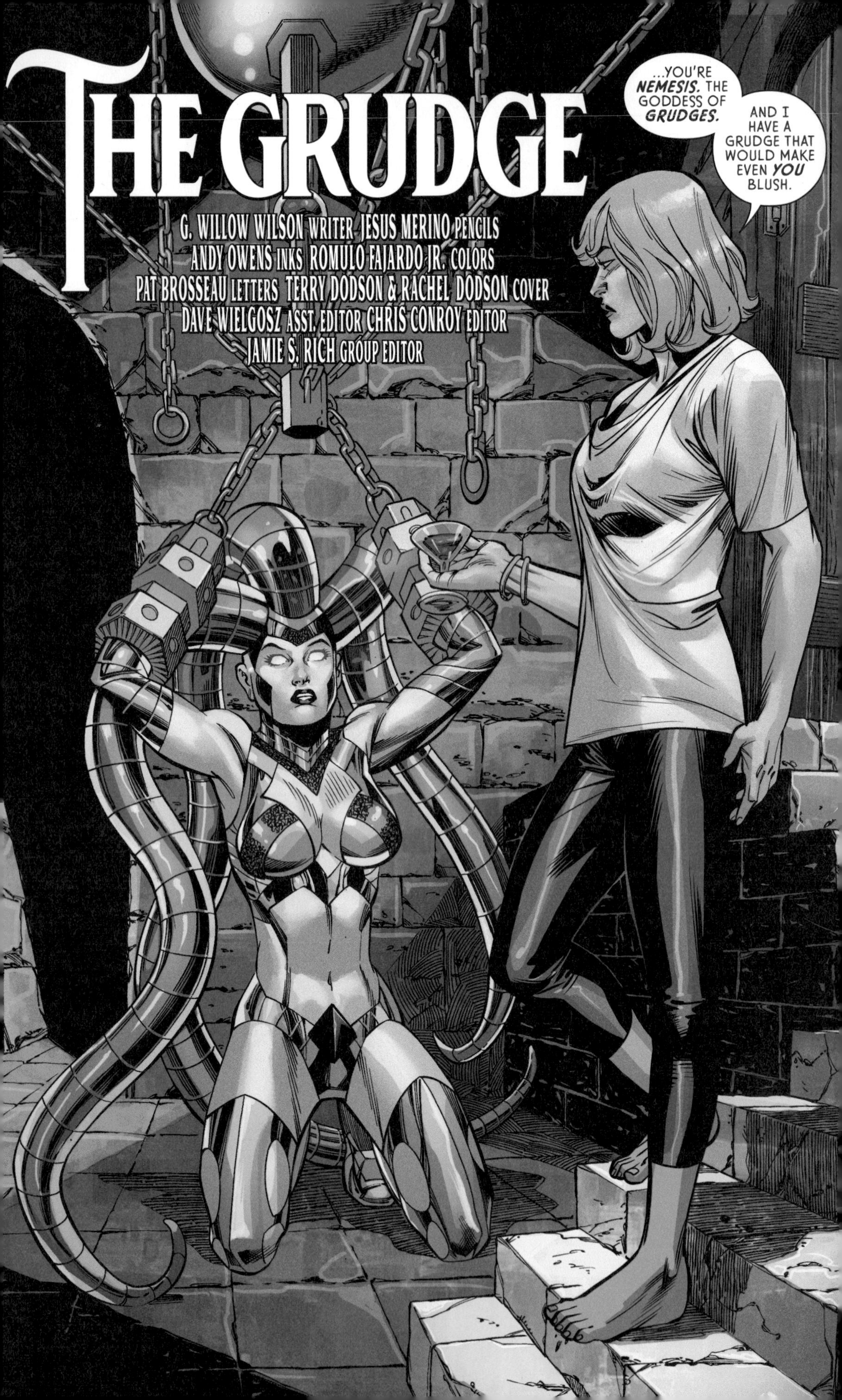
THE GRUDGE
G. WILLOW WILSON WRITER JESUS MERINO PENCILS
ANDY OWENS INKS ROMULO FAJARDO JR. COLORS
PAT BROSSEAU LETTERS TERRY DODSON & RACHEL DODSON COVER
DAVE WIELGOSZ ASST. EDITOR CHRIS CONROY EDITOR
JAMIE S. RICH GROUP EDITOR
...YOU'RE NEMESIS. THE GODDESS OF GRUDGES.
AND I HAVE A GRUDGE THAT WOULD MAKE EVEN YOU BLUSH.

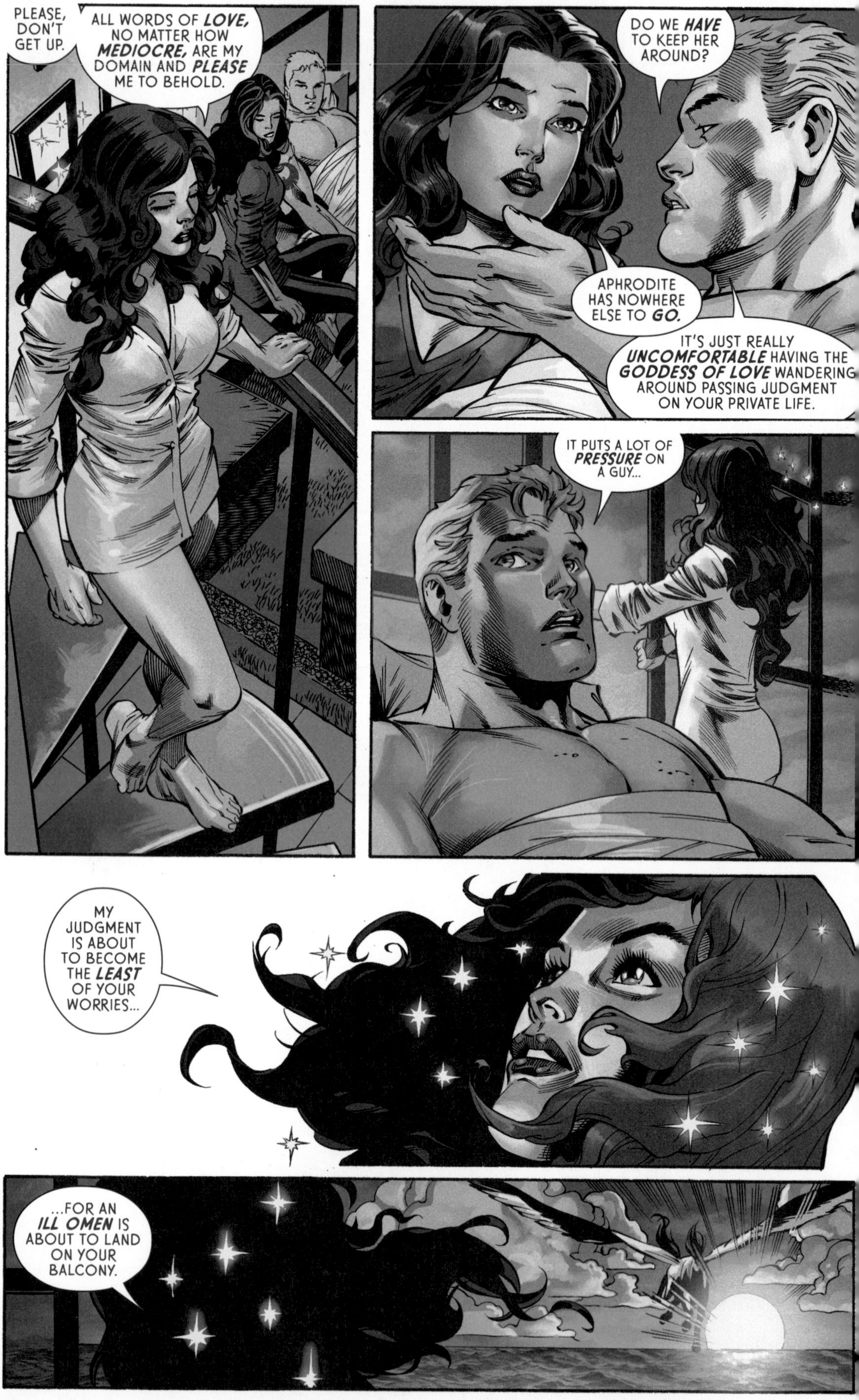
PLEASE, DON'T GET UP.
ALL WORDS OF *LOVE,* NO MATTER HOW *MEDIOCRE,* ARE MY DOMAIN AND *PLEASE* ME TO BEHOLD.
DO WE *HAVE* TO KEEP HER AROUND?
APHRODITE HAS NOWHERE ELSE TO *GO.*
IT'S JUST REALLY *UNCOMFORTABLE* HAVING THE *GODDESS OF LOVE* WANDERING AROUND PASSING JUDGMENT ON YOUR PRIVATE LIFE.
IT PUTS A LOT OF *PRESSURE* ON A GUY...
MY JUDGMENT IS ABOUT TO BECOME THE *LEAST* OF YOUR WORRIES...
...FOR AN *ILL OMEN* IS ABOUT TO LAND ON YOUR BALCONY.

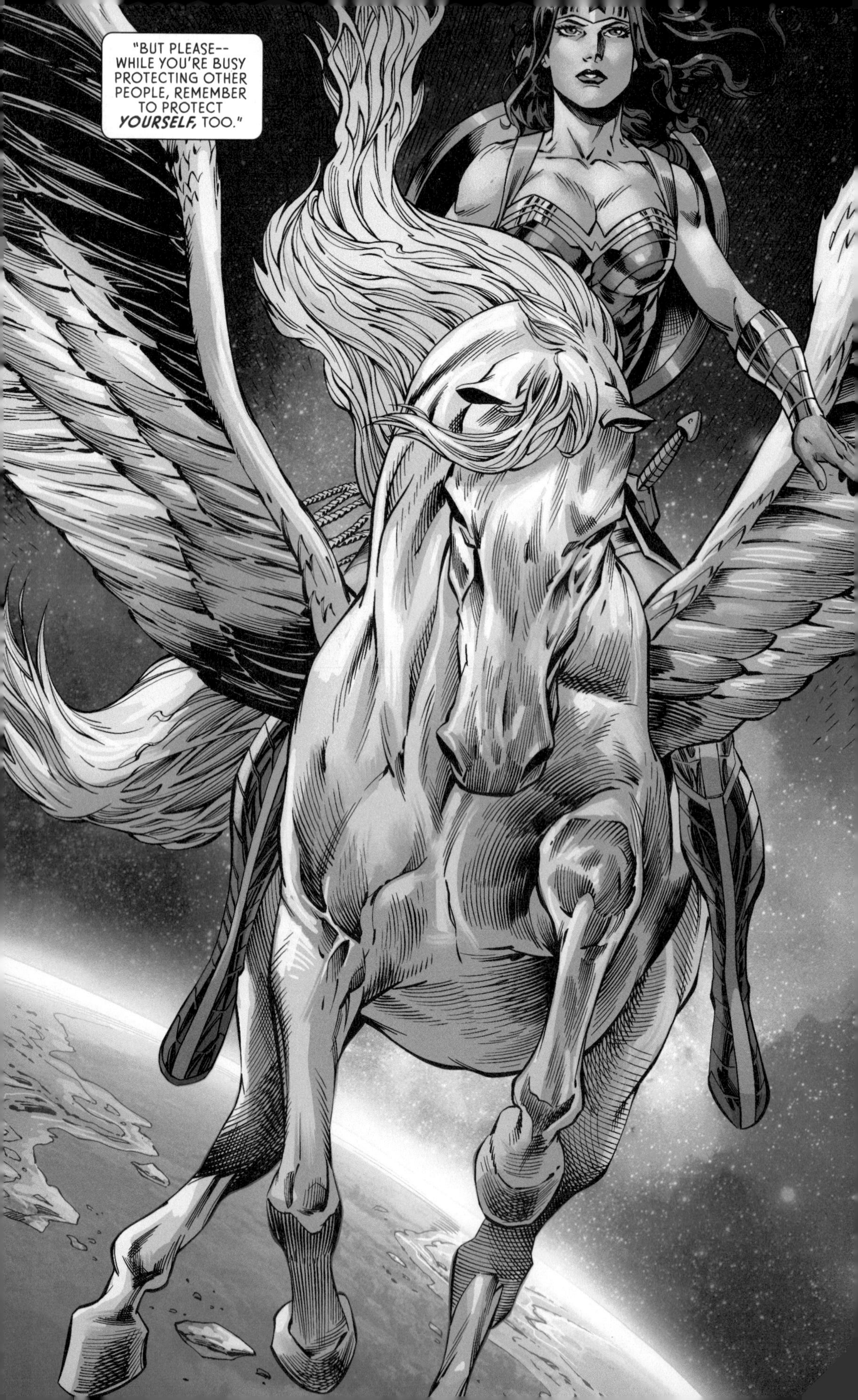
"BUT PLEASE--
WHILE YOU'RE BUSY
PROTECTING OTHER
PEOPLE, REMEMBER
TO PROTECT
YOURSELF, TOO."

TELL ME MORE. WHAT DID YOU SEE? WHAT HAPPENED?

I WAS WALKING WITH EIRENE AND DAMON AND THE GIRL CALLED MAGGIE WHEN THERE WAS A GREAT *FLASH,* AS THOUGH A STAR HAD DESCENDED ON EARTH--

--AND WHEN THE LIGHT FADED, THERE WAS A SMOKING CRATER IN THE GROUND, AND PEOPLE *SCREAMING.*

FOR A MOMENT, I THOUGHT I WAS LOOKING INTO THE REALM OF *HADES* HIMSELF.

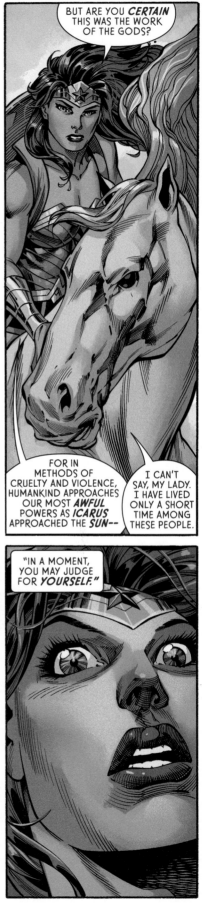

BUT ARE YOU *CERTAIN* THIS WAS THE WORK OF THE GODS?

FOR IN METHODS OF CRUELTY AND VIOLENCE, HUMANKIND APPROACHES OUR MOST *AWFUL* POWERS AS *ICARUS* APPROACHED THE *SUN*--

I CAN'T SAY, MY LADY. I HAVE LIVED ONLY A SHORT TIME AMONG THESE PEOPLE.

"IN A MOMENT, YOU MAY JUDGE FOR *YOURSELF.*"

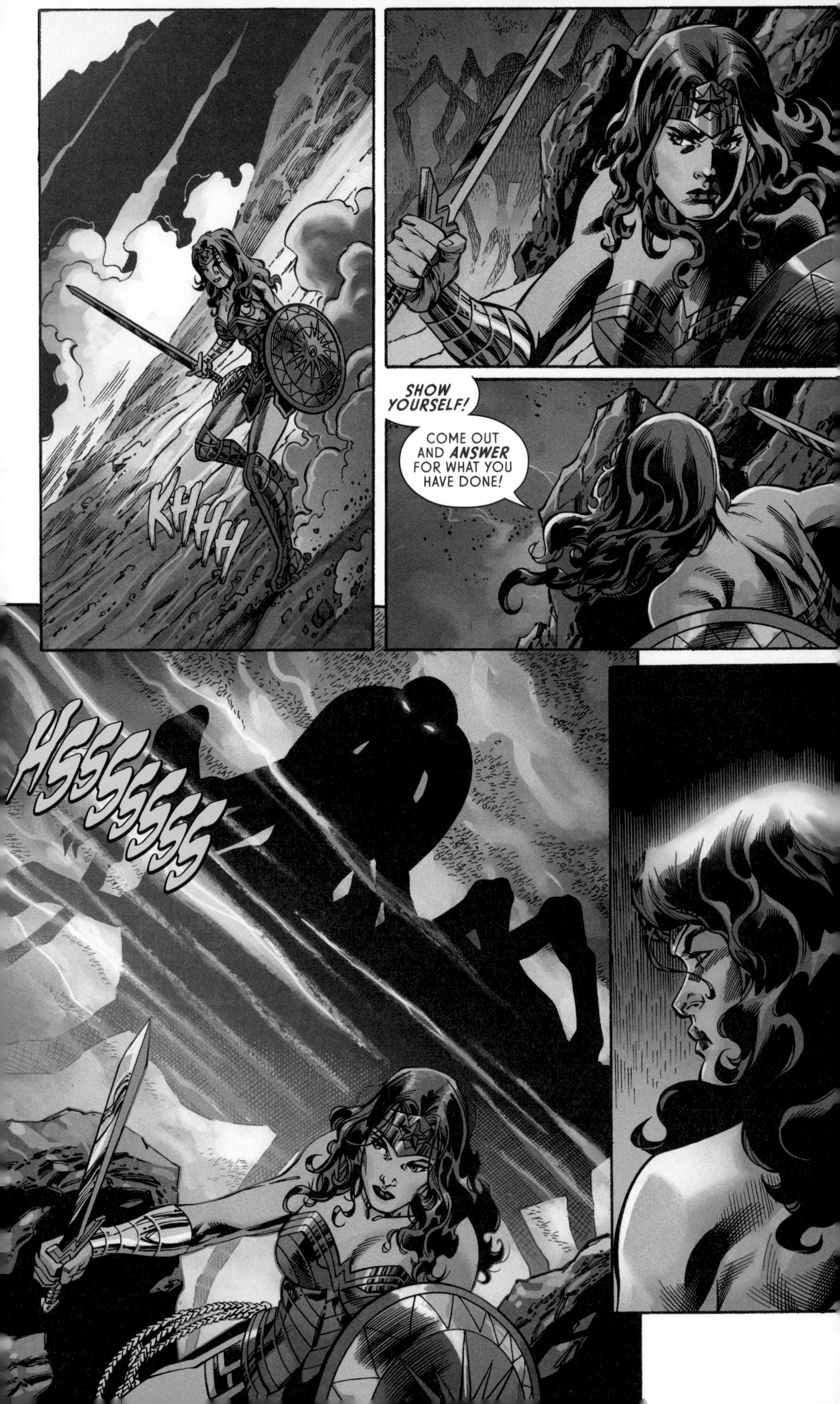
KHHH
SHOW YOURSELF!
COME OUT AND ANSWER FOR WHAT YOU HAVE DONE!
HSSSSSSS

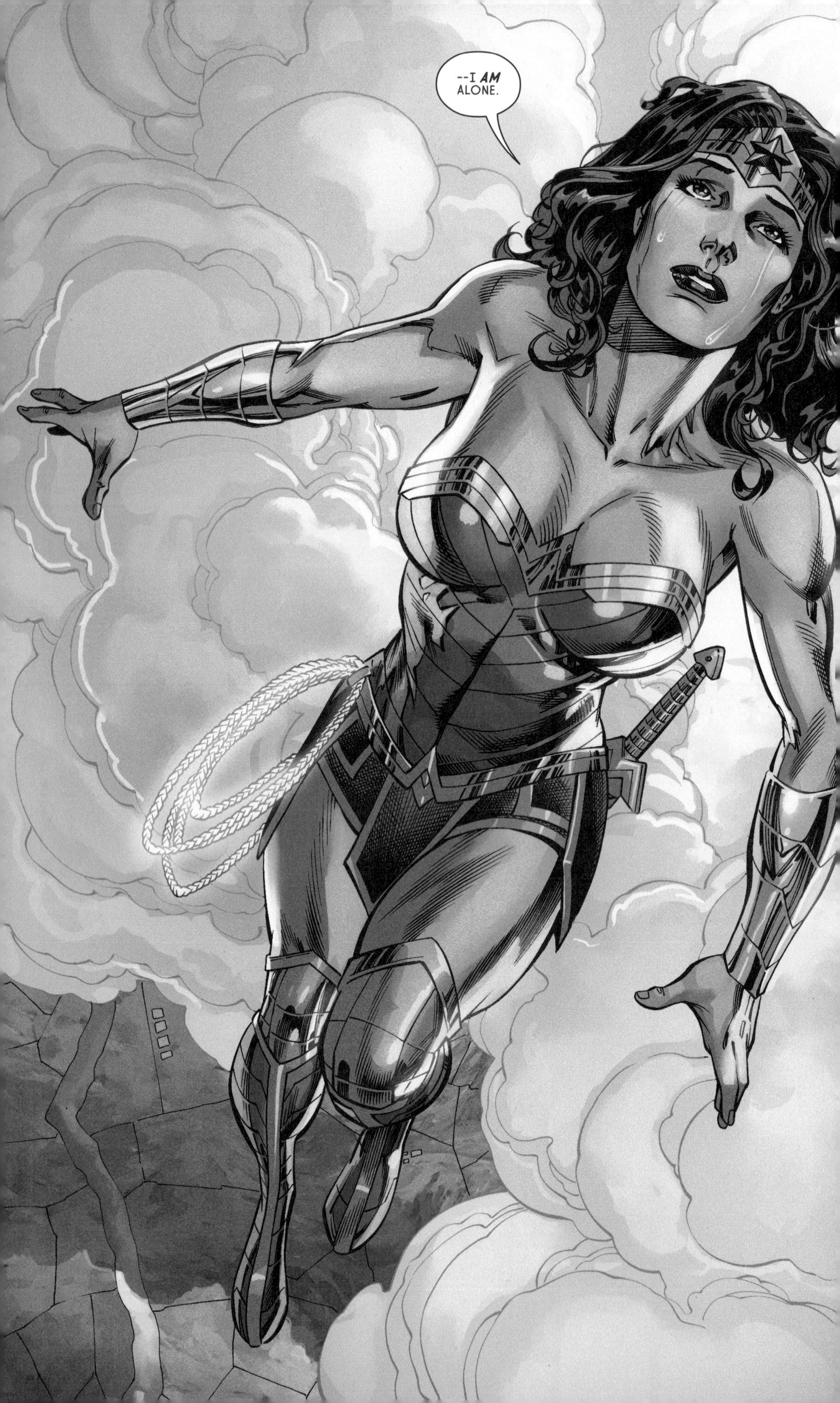
--I *AM* ALONE.

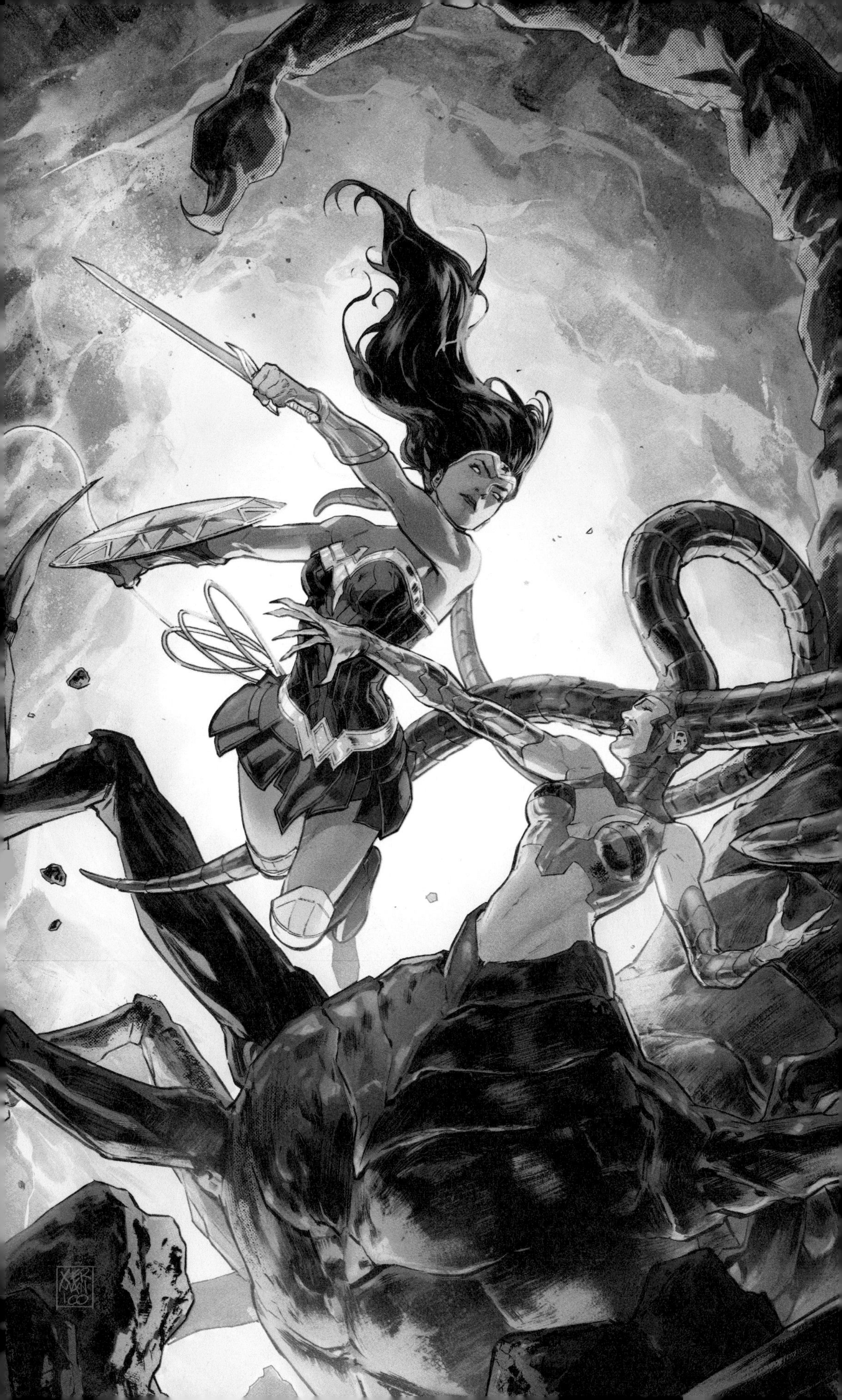

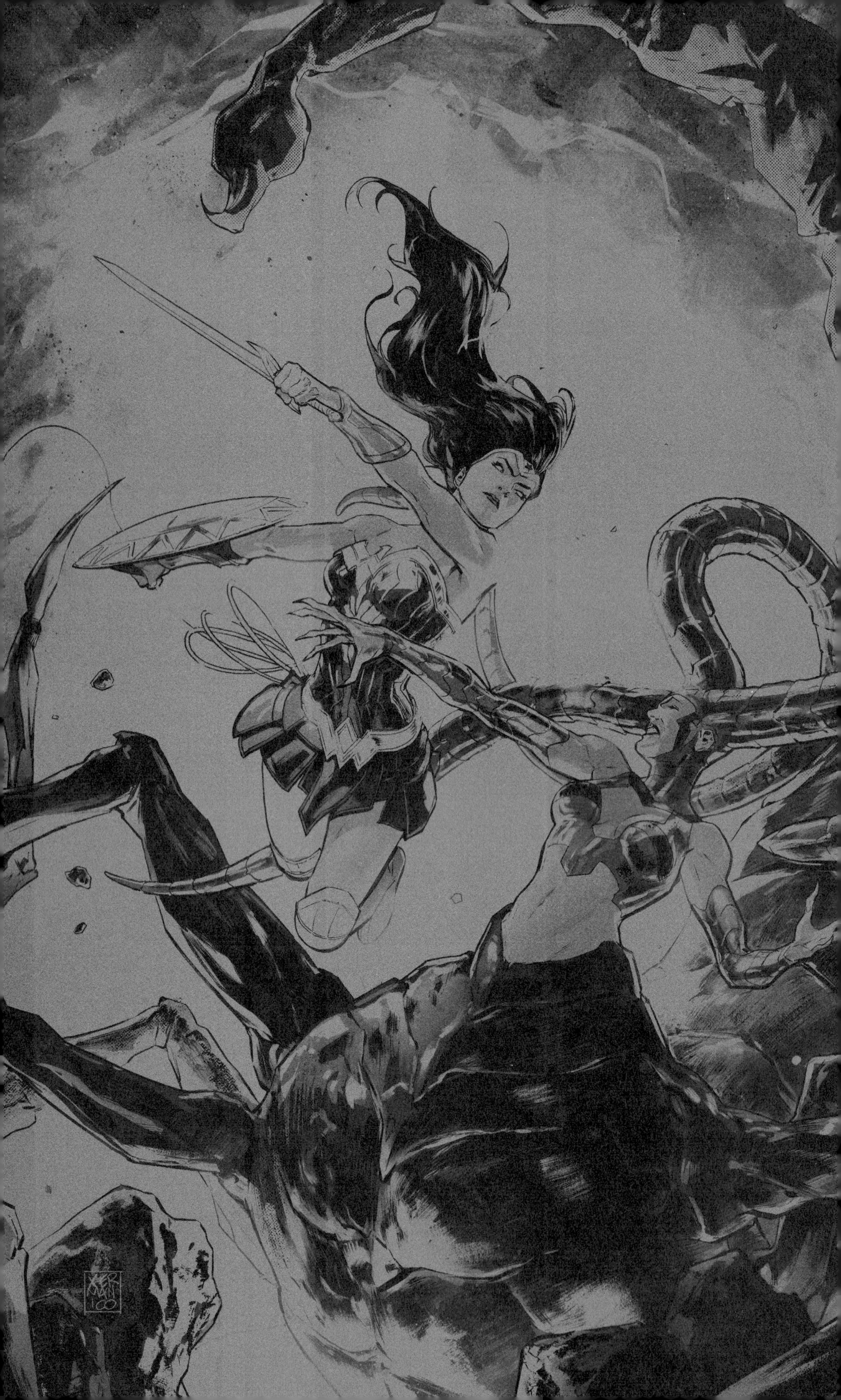

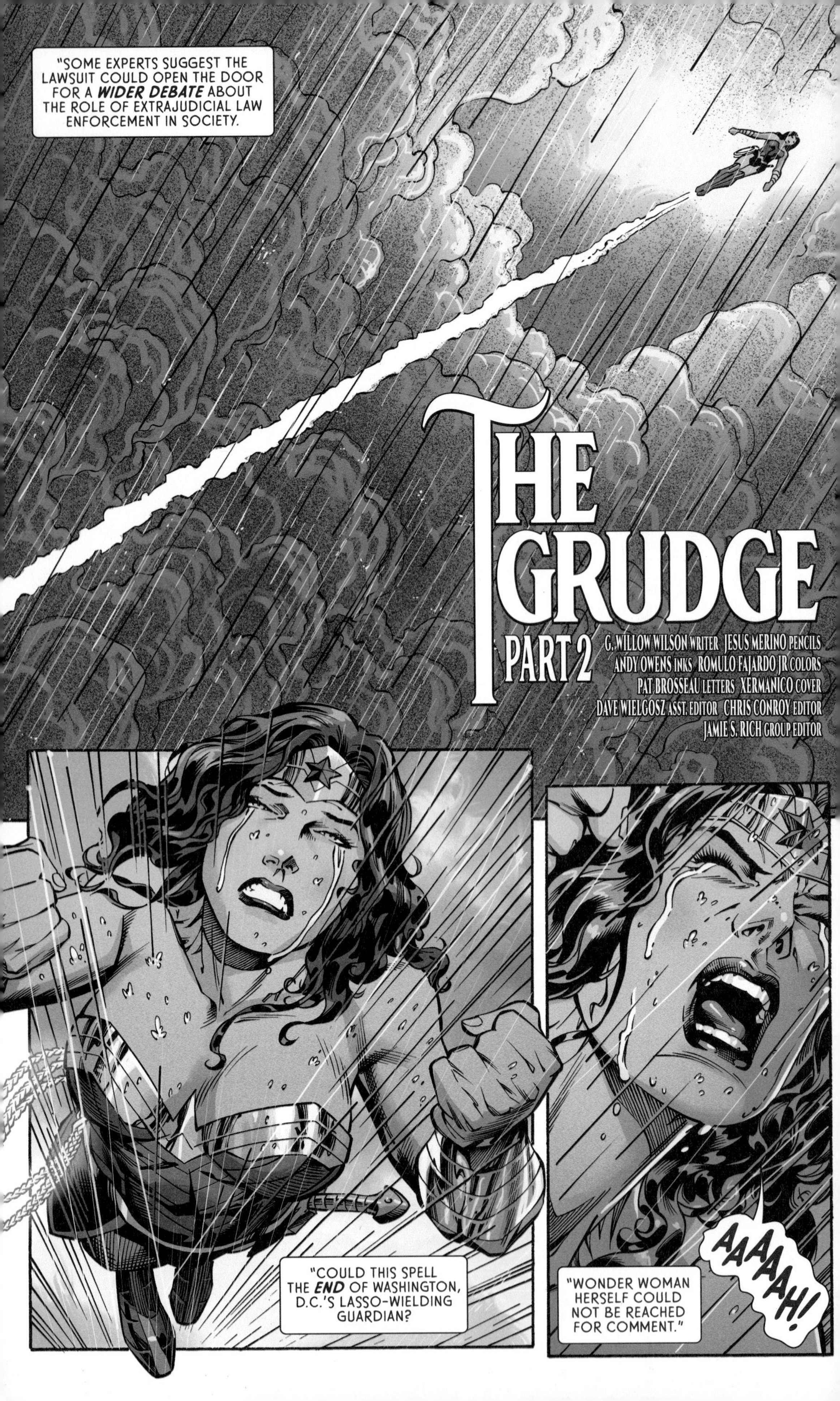
"SOME EXPERTS SUGGEST THE LAWSUIT COULD OPEN THE DOOR FOR A WIDER DEBATE ABOUT THE ROLE OF EXTRAJUDICIAL LAW ENFORCEMENT IN SOCIETY.
THE GRUDGE
PART 2
G. WILLOW WILSON WRITER JESUS MERINO PENCILS
ANDY OWENS INKS ROMULO FAJARDO JR COLORS
PAT BROSSEAU LETTERS XERMANICO COVER
DAVE WIELGOSZ ASST. EDITOR CHRIS CONROY EDITOR
JAMIE S. RICH GROUP EDITOR
"COULD THIS SPELL THE END OF WASHINGTON, D.C.'S LASSO-WIELDING GUARDIAN?
"WONDER WOMAN HERSELF COULD NOT BE REACHED FOR COMMENT."
AAAAAH!

VARIANT COVER GALLERY

WONDER WOMAN #58 variant cover
by **JENNY FRISON**

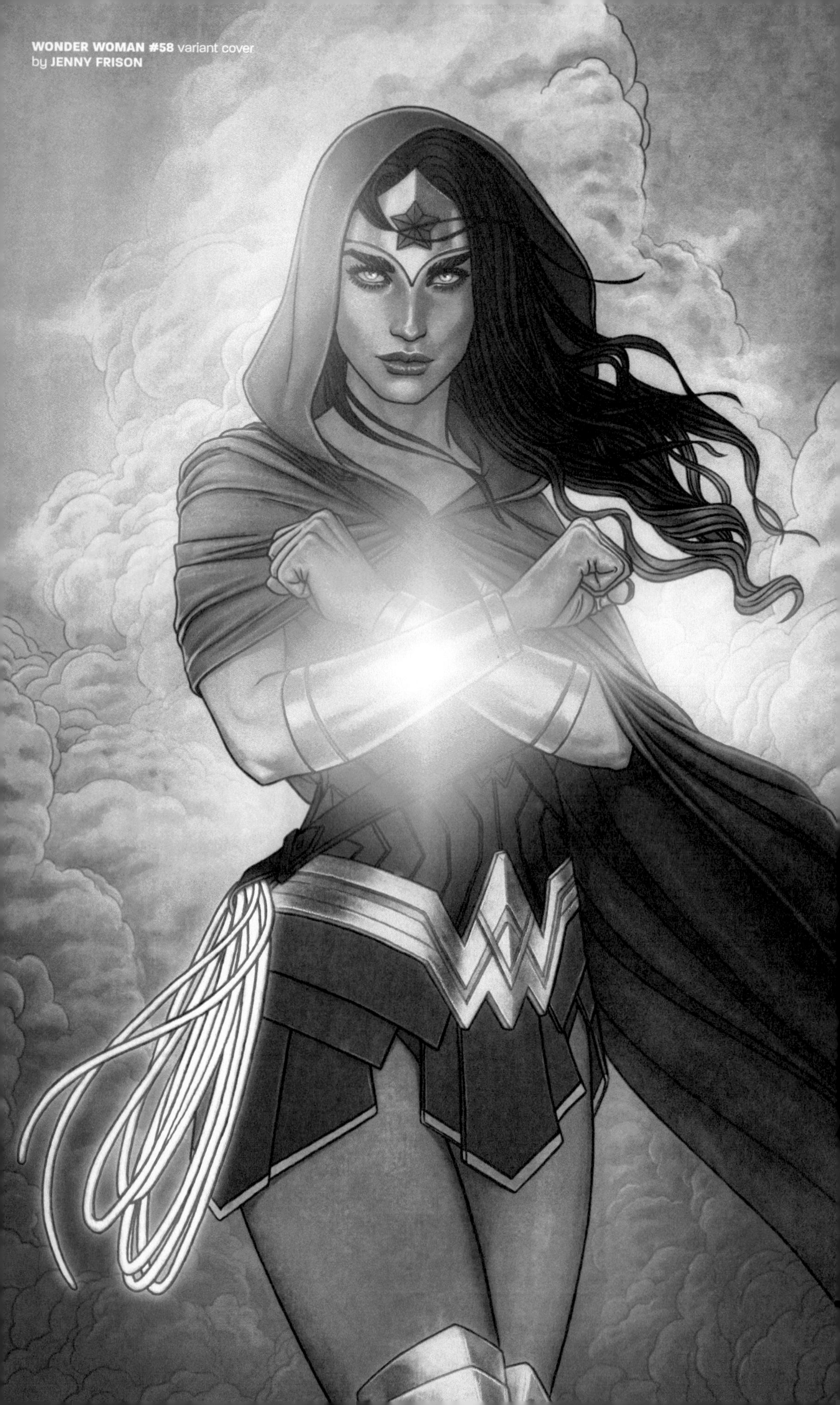

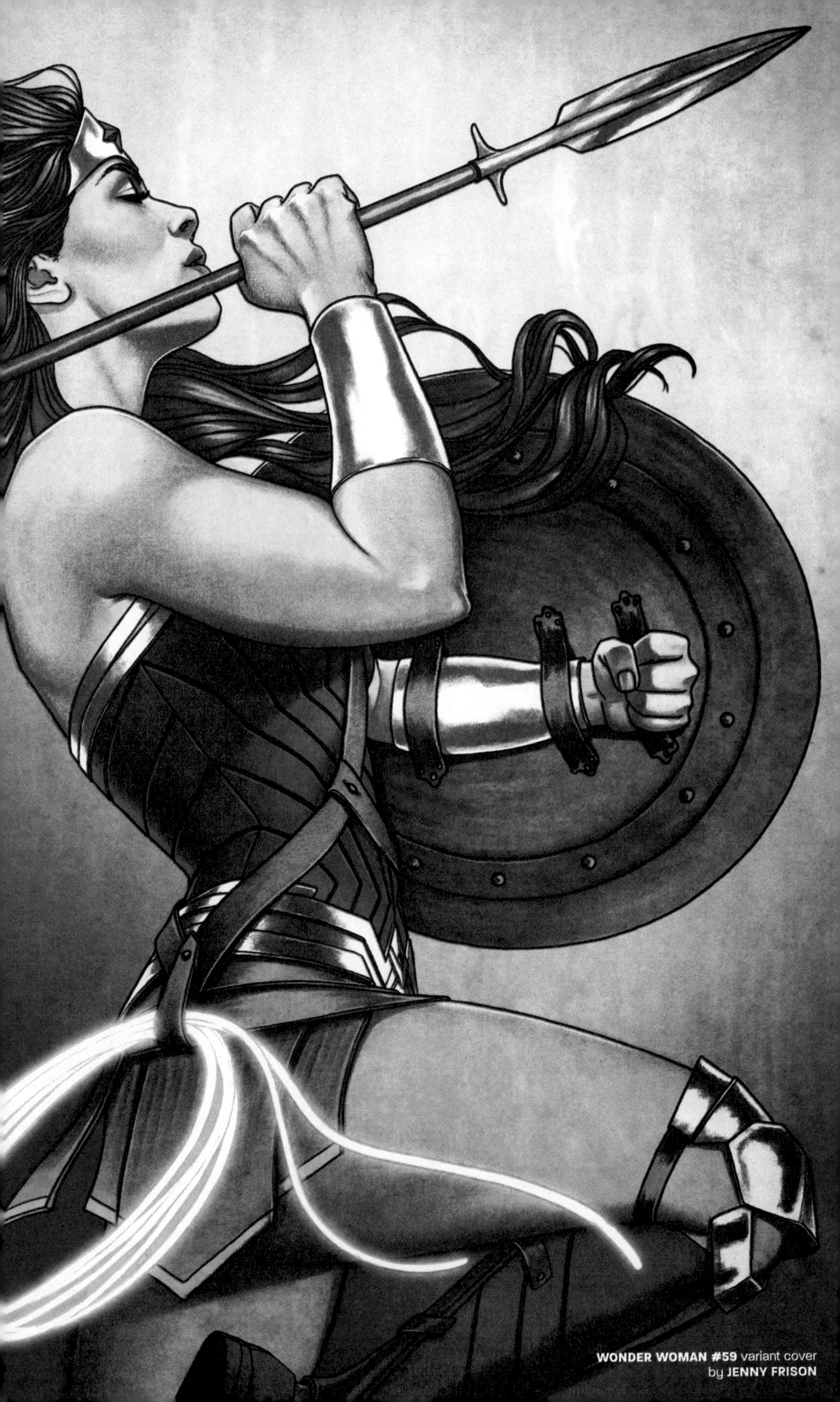

WONDER WOMAN #59 variant cover
by **JENNY FRISON**

WONDER WOMAN #60 variant cover
by **JENNY FRISON**

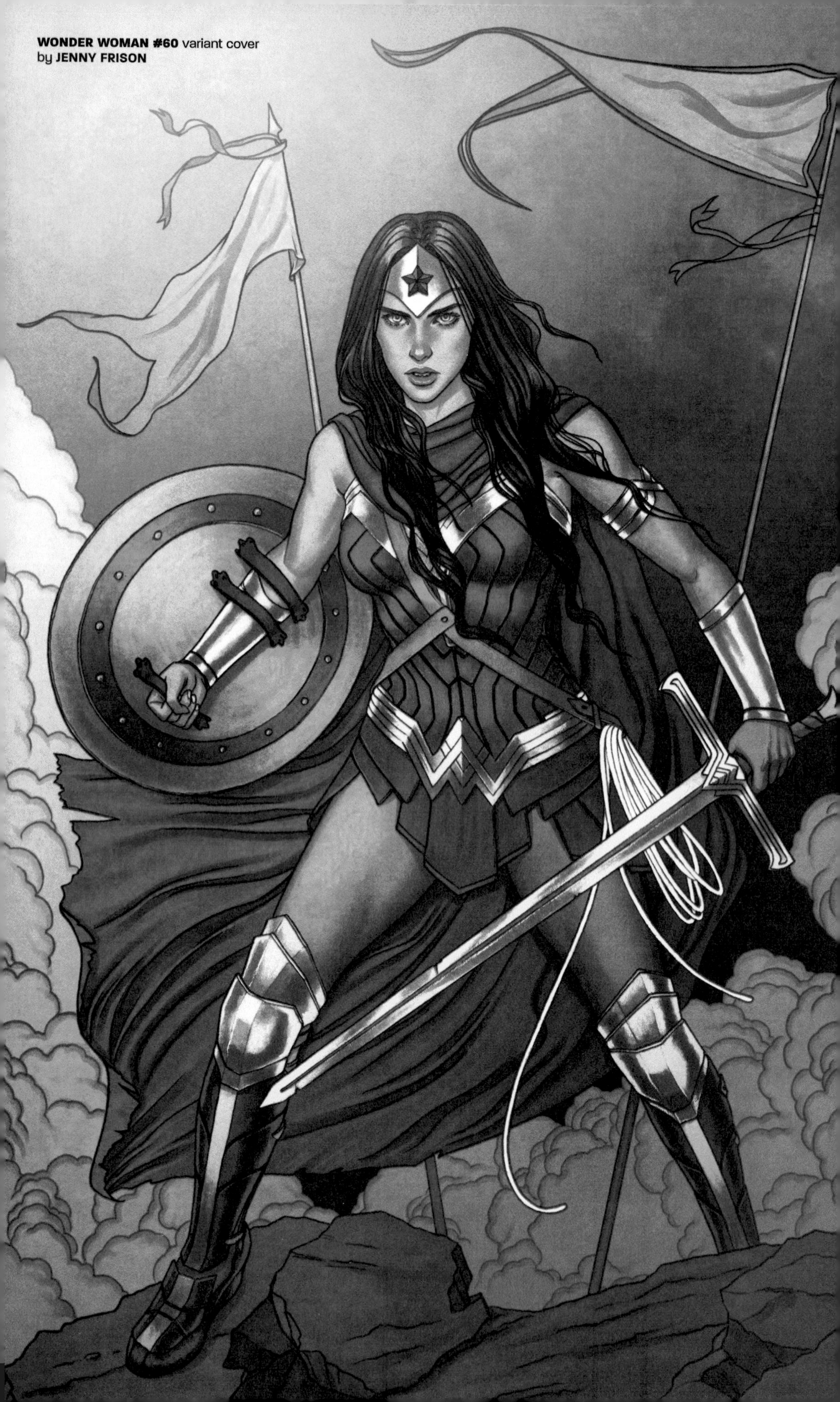

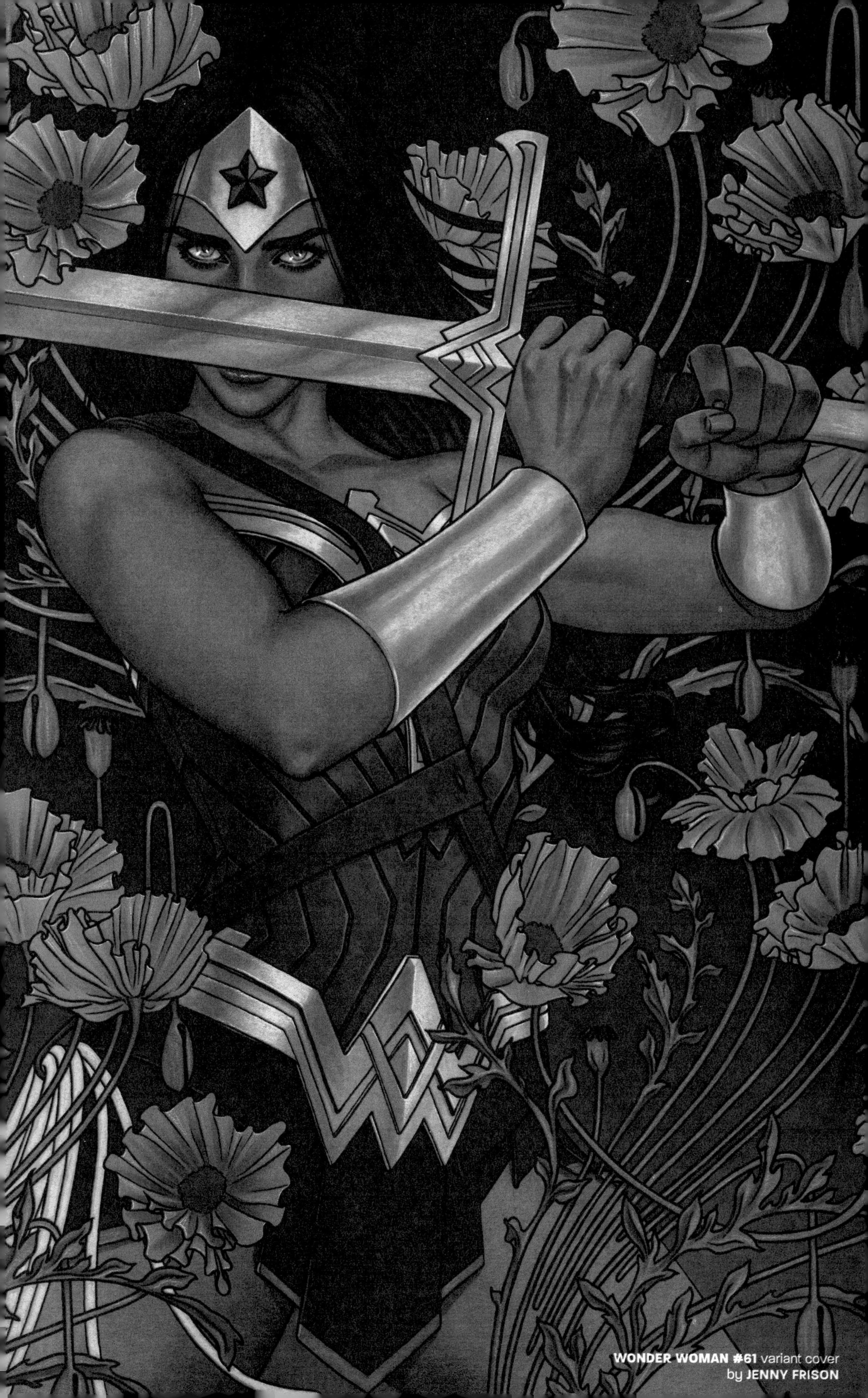

WONDER WOMAN #61 variant cover
by **JENNY FRISON**

by **MATTEO SCALERA**

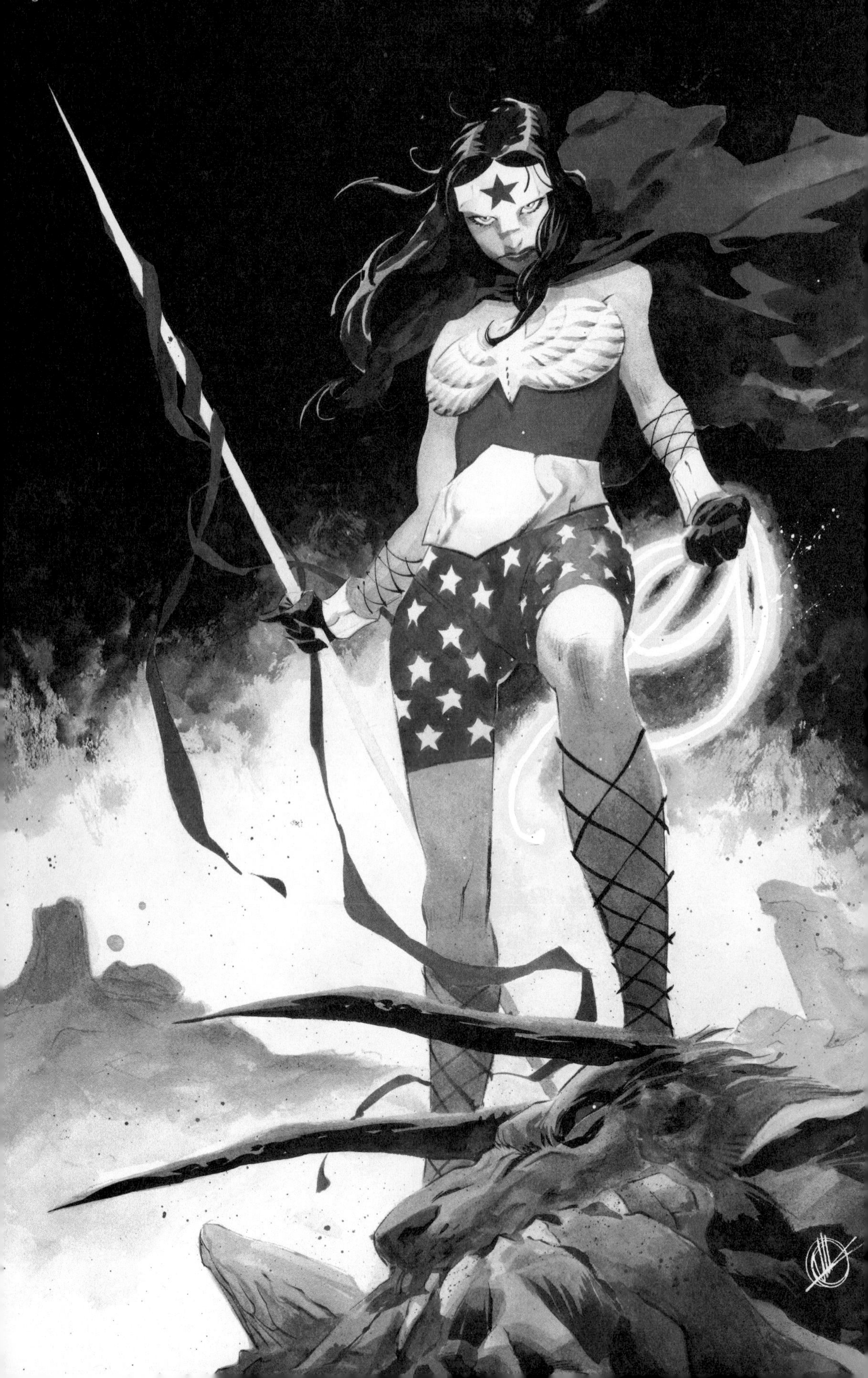

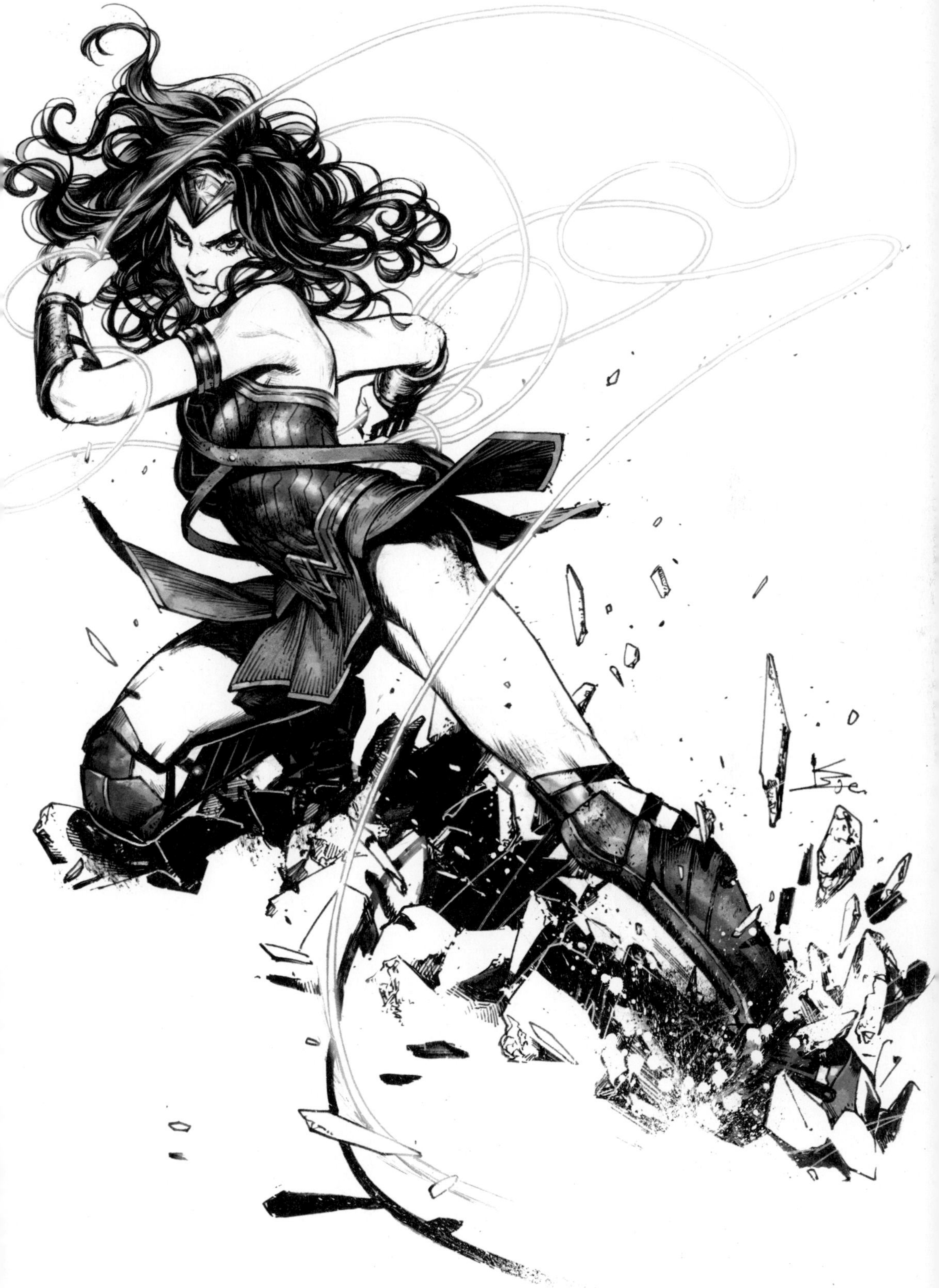

WONDER WOMAN #63 variant cover
by **KAMOME SHIRAHAMA**

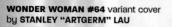

WONDER WOMAN #64 variant cover
by STANLEY "ARTGERM" LAU

WONDER WOMAN #65 variant cover
by **STANLEY "ARTGERM" LAU**

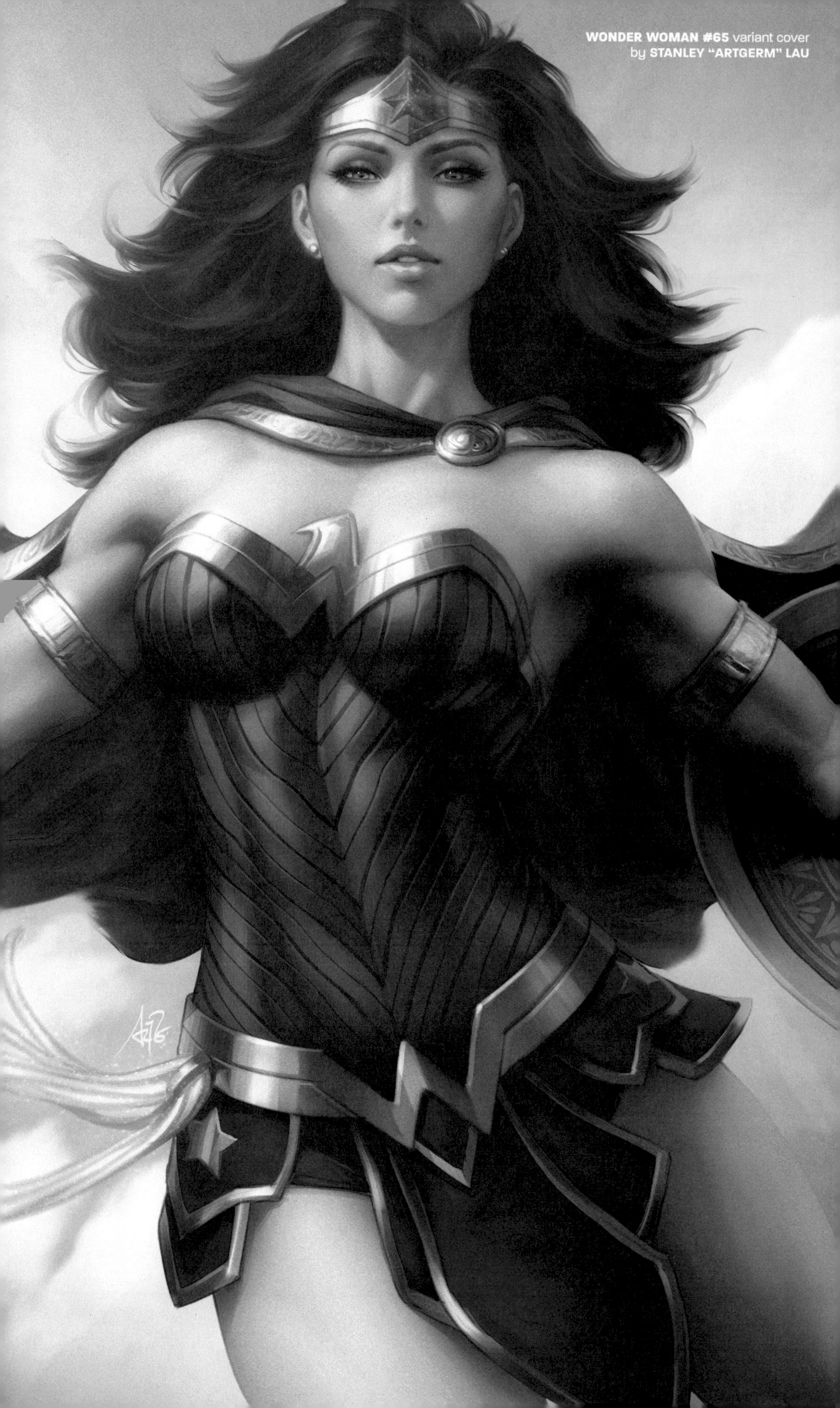

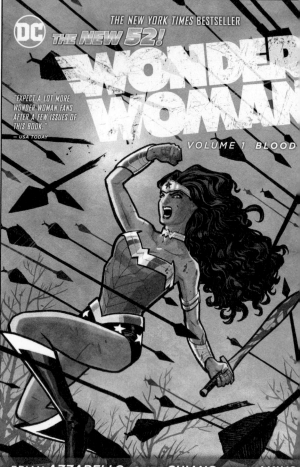

"Greg Rucka and company have created a compelling narrative for fans of the Amazing Amazon."– **NERDIST**

"[A] heartfelt and genuine take on Diana's origin."– **NEWSARAMA**

DC UNIVERSE REBIRTH

WONDER WOMAN

VOL. 1: THE LIES
GREG RUCKA
with LIAM SHARP

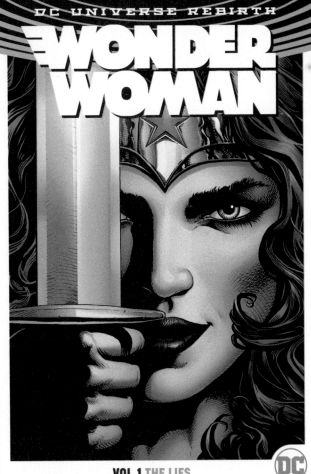

VOL.1 **THE LIES**
GREG RUCKA • LIAM SHARP • LAURA MARTIN

JUSTICE LEAGUE VOL. 1:
THE EXTINCTION MACHINES

SUPERGIRL VOL. 1:
REIGN OF THE SUPERMEN

BATGIRL VOL. 1:
BEYOND BURNSIDE

WONDER WOMAN BY
GREG
RUCKA
with J.G. JONES
& DREW JOHNSON

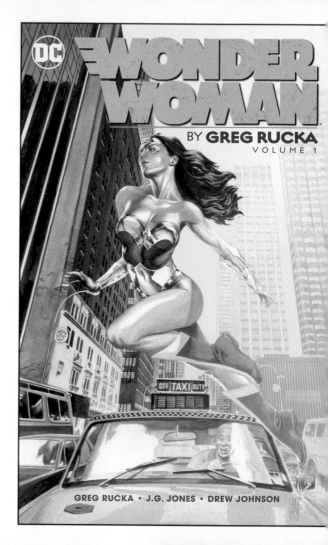

BATWOMAN: ELEGY
with J.H. WILLIAMS III

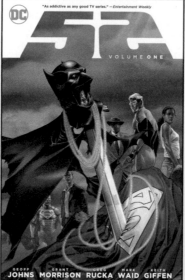

52 VOL. 1
with VARIOUS ARTISTS

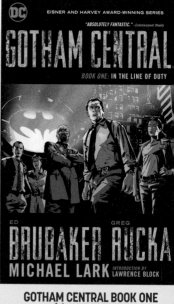

GOTHAM CENTRAL BOOK ONE
with ED BRUBAKER
& MICHAEL LARK